General Sir Frederick Poole

Frederick Poole

General
Sir Frederick Poole

HENRY POOLE

Copyright © 2023 Henry Poole

The moral right of the author has been asserted.

Apart from any fair dealing for the purposes of research or private study, or criticism or review, as permitted under the Copyright, Designs and Patents Act 1988, this publication may only be reproduced, stored or transmitted, in any form or by any means, with the prior permission in writing of the publishers, or in the case of reprographic reproduction in accordance with the terms of licences issued by the Copyright Licensing Agency. Enquiries concerning reproduction outside those terms should be sent to the publishers.

Matador
Unit E2 Airfield Business Park,
Harrison Road, Market Harborough,
Leicestershire. LE16 7UL
Tel: 0116 2792299
Email: books@troubador.co.uk
Web: www.troubador.co.uk/matador
Twitter: @matadorbooks

ISBN 978 1803136 073

British Library Cataloguing in Publication Data.
A catalogue record for this book is available from the British Library.

Printed and bound by CPI Group (UK) Ltd, Croydon, CR0 4YY
Typeset in 11pt Minion Pro by Troubador Publishing Ltd, Leicester, UK

Matador is an imprint of Troubador Publishing Ltd

Contents

	Illustrations	ix
	Introduction	xi
1	Early Life	1
2	Alice	11
3	Peace-Time Soldier	21
4	Promotion	29
5	Loos	47
6	Counter-Battery Pioneer	57
7	Under Fire	69
8	Trench Mortars	77
9	Proceed at Once to Russia	83
10	The Inter-Allied Conference	101
11	The March Revolution	113
12	The Provisional Government	125
13	Petrograd and Moscow	133
14	Coups	145
15	Dealing with the Bolsheviks	161
16	Buying the Russian Banks	171
17	Finland	179
18	North Russia	187
19	Recall	205
20	South Russia	217
21	Cornwall	223
	Bibliography	229
	Index	233

Illustrations

Between Pages 56 and 57

1. Frederick Poole, 1897
2. Poole family wedding, 1897
3. Frederick and Alice Poole with bridesmaids, 1906
4. Alice Poole on her wedding day, 1906
5. Beryl Nicolson
6. Charles and Martha Sabine Hanson outside Fowey Hall
7. Haconby Hall, Lincolnshire
8. Fowey Hall, Fowey, Cornwall, east façade
9. Fowey Hall, south façade
10. Alice Poole, in landau outside Fowey Hall
11. Frederick Poole on the *Diana*
12. Torfrey, Golant
13. Frederick and Alice Poole with Charles Poole
14. Frederick Poole outside Torfrey
15. Alice Poole, in old age
16. Frederick Poole at rest

Between Pages 144 and 145

17. Sir Frederick Lugard
18. Sir Frederick Lugard, *Spy* cartoon
19. The *Corona*
20. The end of the line at Zungeru, Northern Nigeria

21 Frederick, Alice, Charles and Robert Poole, September 1914
22 Frederick Poole in the trenches
23 Percy Notcutt in front of a dug out
24 Percy Notcutt observing from a trench
25 General Sir Henry Wilson, General Poole's patron
26 Frederick Poole
27 General Poole in the Carpathians, January 1917
28 British officers at the Inter-Allied Conference, January 1917
29 General Poole in Moscow, June 1917
30 General Poole in Moscow, June 1917
31 Poole with officers and guns, June 1917
32 Poole with officer and horses, June 1917
33 Abandoned guns, June 1917
34 General Poole at William Cazalet's dacha at Khimki, June 1917
35 The Winter Palace, November 1917
36 At the Finnish border, March 1918
37 General Poole on HMS *Glory*, July 1918
38 General Poole at Archangel, August 1918
39 Parade at Archangel, August 1918
40 Allied troops in Archangel, August 1918
41 General Poole and General Denikin, December 1918
42 Arriving to meet General Krasnov, December 1918
43 General Poole with General Krasnov, December 1918
44 Banquet menu, 29 December 1918

Text Illustrations

Frederick Poole	ii
Nigeria	6
The Western Front in 1915	32
La Bassée	33
Ploegsteert	44
Archangel and Northern Russia	190
Poole for Parliament	225

Introduction

My paternal grandfather was Major General Sir Frederick Poole. As a junior officer, despite showing enterprise and bravery in India, South Africa, Somaliland and Northern Nigeria, he was turned down three times for the Staff College. He left the army in February 1914 rather than accept a posting to Jamaica, a colonial backwater with an unhealthy climate far from his young family, but remained in the Reserve of Officers.

He returned to the army six months later on the outbreak of the First World War. His drive and originality brought him to the attention of senior commanders on the Western Front. This led to his rapid promotion from major to brigadier general, and from commanding a single heavy artillery battery to commanding the artillery of an army corps in June 1916.

My grandfather by this point had been noticed by Sir Henry Wilson, an ambitious general with powerful political connections determined to reach the top of his profession. Wilson unlocked an extraordinary new sphere of action for his protégé. Poole was sent to Russia in December 1916 to report on the state of its artillery. He proceeded to carve out a role for himself whilst Russia was overwhelmed by revolution and descended into chaos and civil war. When the Allies decided to intervene militarily, Poole was chosen as Commander-in-Chief in North Russia in May 1918. He led the Allied capture of Archangel in August 1918 and, subsequently, was sent to south Russia to report on the White forces fighting the Bolsheviks.

Being sent to Russia was a stroke of great good fortune for Poole. The qualities which had worked to his advantage on the Western Front equipped him to interpret a highly unpredictable situation that had become of critical concern. If Russia was defeated by the Germans, the Allies risked losing the war. After gaining control of Russia's huge resources, Germany would be able to circumvent the Allies' naval blockade and concentrate its armies on the Western Front for a decisive blow before America's entry into the war could tip the balance back.

Poole proved himself a good judge of who would survive and who could be trusted. Had his advice to recognise the Bolsheviks when they first seized power been followed, it might just have averted both Russia's descent into civil war and the fruitless Allied intervention. He also recommended a trustworthy intermediary, Poliakov, when the British government decided to purchase the Russian banks, helping secure the best possible deal.

I never knew my grandfather, who died in 1936, but as a child in the 1950s I touched a nerve when I asked my father about him. 'Was he one of the waffling old generals in the First World War?' My father replied, 'He had an original mind beneath a veneer of regularity'. Years later, in my father's house in Cornwall, I discovered an archive of my grandfather's papers, including his diary and many of the letters he wrote to his wife. This archive has allowed me to write this book, telling the story in his own words and from his own perspective.

I would like to thank Helmut Kusdat for organising my research visits to Romania and the Ukraine and those who organised my four visits to Russia. The London Library has proved a wonderful resource in the writing of this book. I am grateful to its staff and to many others for help and encouragement, not least Beth Archer, Rosemary Burch, Andrew Duncan, Bernard Farrant, John Freeman, Peter and Marguerite-Marie Gouldstone, Ros Hedley-Miller, Penny Isaacs, Peter Judd, Jane Myles, Peter Pininski, Geoffrey Poole, Martin Poole, Lucy Sheppard, Martin Sheppard, Kate Stratton, Andrei Tolstoy-Miloslavsky and the late Jonathan Steinberg, my tutor at Trinity Hall, Cambridge, to whom I owe so much.

1

Early Life

Frederick Poole was born on 3 August 1869, when Britain was the greatest power in the world. His father was the Reverend Robert Poole, who had been appointed rector of West Rainton in County Durham in 1859. Robert Poole's parish was being transformed at this time from a quiet backwater by the expansion of the coal mines, which provided the fuel to propel the industrial revolution and the massive wealth it created. He organised the building of the church, the rectory and the school, and threw his energies into pastoral care.

Robert Poole was a warm and kindly man. As a curate he had caught the eye of Elizabeth Longstaff, a young childless widow with modest private means, an optimistic nature and a zest for life.[1] They got married in 1858. By the time they were settled in the rectory, their family had expanded to four boys and two girls. A shadow was cast in 1868 when two of the boys died of fever, a sadly common occurrence in Victorian families. Frederick was their seventh child. He was christened Frederick, a family name, and Cuthbert, after the Anglo-Saxon saint buried in the nearby Durham Cathedral. With the birth of two more boys, 'Little Sutton', the nanny who arrived in 1873, was hard pushed to keep order in this bustling and cheerful household at the centre of the community.

In 1875 Robert Poole died of bronchitis at the age of forty-eight. The family had to leave the rectory and start again. Elizabeth, a widow for the second time and responsible for seven children, had to make the decisions

---

1 Elizabeth Lawrance Longstaff, née Pawlett (1832-1917).

that had previously rested in her husband's hands. She moved the family to Cheltenham into the home of her brother, her only sibling. It was not a comfortable solution, as he was a bachelor in middle age whose life was turned upside down by this sudden invasion. Henry, the eldest boy, went to Oxford, as was expected.[2] When it came to her two daughters, she put her own ideas into practice. Gertrude and Mary went to Cheltenham Ladies College, which provided an excellent education, particularly in mathematics. They both gained an external BA degree from London University whilst at the college, whose headmistress, Miss Beale, later founded St Hilda's College, Oxford.

Elizabeth Poole found it increasingly difficult to cope with Frederick. He was a strong and pugnacious boy who liked teasing and practical jokes, which were endlessly repeated. He would not settle down to work and would not do what he was told. She decided to send him to Durham School, as his brother Henry had been educated there and had returned there as an assistant master after university.

Frederick Poole entered Durham School in August 1882. The memory came back years later when he was a parent watching the struggles of his own children, 'If a boy starts backward when he goes to school it is such a terrific handicap for him – nobody bothers about him and he always drops behind'.[3] Fortunately, Frederick had inherited both his father's capacity to achieve results and his mother's refusal to bow down when times were hard. Encouraged by his brother Henry, who had gained a rowing blue at Oxford, he became a successful oarsman and was made captain of the boat club in 1887.[4] He earned further sporting laurels playing in the rugby team. He also settled down to work, winning a mathematical prize in 1885 and a French prize in 1887. He was made a monitor.

After leaving Durham School in August 1887, Frederick Poole was shocked to discover a change in his mother. Her love of conversation and society had led to her becoming extravagant and being taken in by flattery, which resulted in her becoming reckless in money matters. She was rapidly

---

2   Robert Poole's grandfather had decided that Oxford was the right university and he had sent his sons there and he had even gone so far as to secure the equivalence at Oxford of his Cambridge degree – *ad eundum gradum*.
3   Letter to Alice Poole, 29 October 1915.
4   Rowing on the River Wear had become one of the school's principal sports under the headmastership of the Reverend W. Fearon (1882-84).

squandering the money inherited from her mother and exhausting the generosity of her brother. The breach between Frederick and his mother became permanent, leaving a painful emotional scar.

Frederick's sisters were now in their late twenties. Gertrude was on the teaching staff of Cheltenham Ladies College and Mary was running the household and trying to maintain a social life on slender means. In Mary's circle of friends was Florence Dove, a childless army officer's widow left ill provided for. Gertrude and Mary were strong-willed women, but Florence had a softer touch. Together they provided the civilising influence Frederick needed after the rough world of boarding school, and he learned how tact and charm could smooth his passage in life. They also gave him the motherly direction and assurance absent from his life, becoming, in effect, surrogate mothers.

Since his childhood Frederick had lapped up the stories about the exploits of his paternal uncle, Arthur Poole, as a soldier. Arthur Poole had been commissioned as an ensign in 1859. His gallantry in China in 1862 had won him promotion to lieutenant without purchase, an unusual step up before the 1871 army reforms. His heroism in Afghanistan, holding off a surprise attack on his foraging party against overwhelming odds, despite being severely wounded, caught the public's imagination. Accounts appeared in the local and national press and in books describing the campaign. He was mentioned in despatches and promoted from captain to major in 1881. He received another mention in despatches and further promotion after his service in Burma in 1887.

Frederick Poole decided he wanted to become a soldier. He passed into the Royal Military Academy at Woolwich in February 1888 with Gertrude's help; it was her mathematical coaching that got him into Woolwich. It was teaching, he said, such as he had never had before or after.[5] At Woolwich he discovered that mathematics provided the key to drawing and interpreting the maps used in moving and positioning artillery, and in directing its firepower accurately. There was also plenty of sport. As well as playing cricket and being in the rugby fifteen, he developed a taste for foxhunting. He became good at billiards and used his mathematical skills at bridge to good effect.

Ready for life as an officer, Frederick Poole was commissioned as a

---
5 Unpublished memoir by Dorothy Mattinson, the daughter of Frederick Poole's brother Henry.

second lieutenant in the Royal Garrison Artillery in February 1889. Posted at Gibraltar from 1889, he was promoted to lieutenant in 1892 and sent to serve in British India with No. 2 Mountain Battery at Ambala in the Punjab. He learned Urdu, the lingua franca of the Indian Army, with his certificate for passing the oral examination in it, dated 3 January 1893, marked as 'good'. He felt at ease with the climate, even in the hottest months of the year, and found the colour and diversity of India irresistible after his upbringing in England and the constricting routine of garrison duty at Gibraltar. At Ambala, when off duty, he would wander through the bazaars.[6]

He also fell in love. He was twenty-three, newly arrived and missing the attentions of his sisters and Florence Dove. The object of his affections was Beryl Nicholson, who was five years older than him and a childless officer's widow. She had just returned from England and was feeling lonely and dispirited. Although the attraction was mutual, marriage was out of the question. Beryl had only a life interest in Captain Nicholson's estate, which was conditional on her remaining unmarried. She only had enough money in her own right to live comfortably as a single woman, while Poole was penniless and at the start of his army career.

Beryl returned to England without remarrying. She bought Lane End, a house with stables and paddocks at Dunchurch, which was then a quiet village outside Rugby. She became a keen gardener, kept dogs and rode to hounds regularly. Always on the move, visiting friends and relations, she joined the Sesame Club, a fashionable ladies' club in the West End of London, which served as her base when in town. She and Frederick Poole wrote to each other regularly and the club provided a perfect setting for enjoying each other's company with propriety when he came home on leave.

In 1896, No. 2 Mountain Battery was transferred from Ambala to Quetta, a garrison town in the province of Baluchistan on the route through the Bolan Pass to Afghanistan. The change suited Poole. It was a healthy outdoor life with plenty of sport, albeit of a hazardous nature. The Quetta Hunt had to cope with irrigation ditches, many as deep as twenty feet with rough banks.[7] Quetta was close to the North-West Frontier, an unsettled region in rugged and precipitous yet beautiful surroundings. Its warlike

---

6 He thought of them years later when a visit to the Grand Bazaar in Istanbul left him disappointed.
7 *Baily's Hunting Directory* (1931-32).

tribesmen were known for their combination of bravery and cruelty, as well as the occasional display of chivalry. Expeditions against them presented young officers with a rare opportunity to see action and to impress their superiors.

Frederick Poole went on home leave in 1897 to attend the wedding of his brother Francis. In one of the photographs Francis sits beaming next to his bride flanked by rather serious looking fellow clergymen. Frederick, a stocky figure, standing a little apart at the back, is immaculately groomed and wearing a well-tailored morning coat. With a twinkle in his eye, he comes over as a young man confident in his surroundings. His chief friend at this time was Hartley Graham, who had a cottage in the Lake District. He had met Hartley at a Durham School reunion for old boys. They shared a passion for walking and had long discussions about poetry, philosophy and other topics.

After his leave, Poole saw active service in 1897 in a campaign known as the Tirah Expedition, aimed at reasserting British authority over a number of tribal areas on the North-West Frontier. He set off fortified by a silver hip flask for spirits, gained his first fighting experience, and won his first campaign medal. Promoted captain in June 1899, he subsequently saw action in 1900-1902 in the Boer War in South Africa, where he won a DSO and three mentions in despatches.[8] The Royal Humane Society also awarded him a certificate for saving life in the Vaal River in 1902.

His record of service might well have led at this point to his selection for the Staff College at Camberley, for which he was the right age (he was thirty-three on 3 August 1902). Preference in selection for Staff College at Camberley was, however, given to infantry and cavalry officers, as it was unusual for an artillery officer to progress to high command. Those with influence and connections, often with the added boost of three years spent at Oxford or Cambridge, also had the edge in being allocated the few places available at the Staff College.[9]

Instead of being chosen, Poole was 'selected for special service in Somaliland'.[10] This was a euphemism for being turned down for Staff College but offered an opportunity to join another military campaign.

---

8 He had used his own initiative to secure his posting in South Africa.
9 When the British Expeditionary Force went to France in 1914 it had fewer than a thousand officers who had graduated from Staff College.
10 *Times*, 22 December 1936.

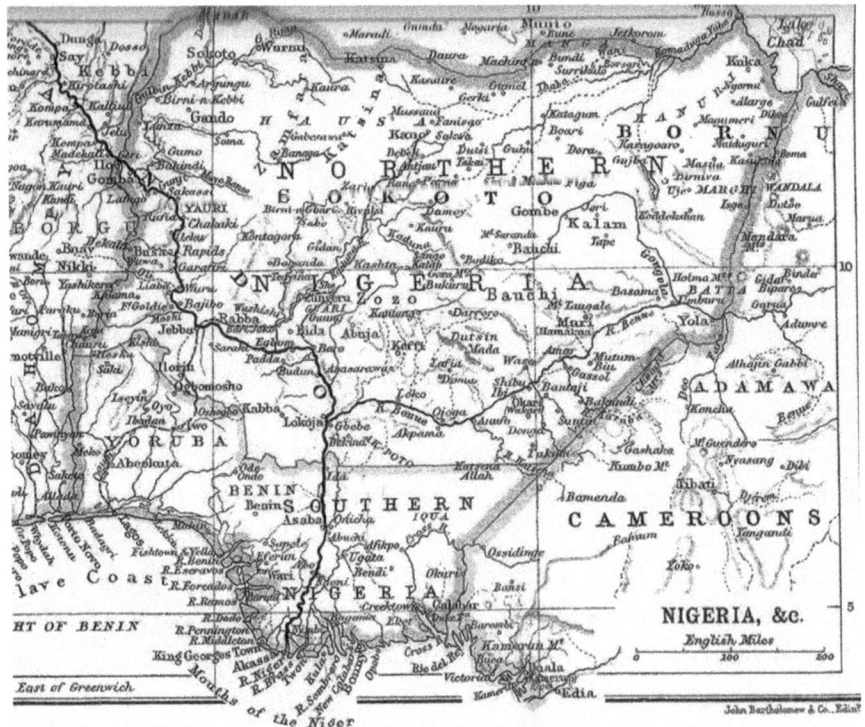

Nigeria

Under the command of an Indian Army officer, Major General Sir Charles Egerton, Poole's earlier service in India stood him in good stead. He joined the supply and transport section of the Somaliland Camel Corps. Knowing little or nothing about camels, in his innocence he gave the camels water every day. The camels grew fatter and he was congratulated on making them look healthy. Poole saw action in Somaliland and was mentioned in despatches.

He then got wind of a new opportunity from Captain Charles Orr. They had been commissioned at the same time, had served together and had become close friends. Orr had moved to Northern Nigeria and had become responsible for a huge province, reporting directly to the High Commissioner, Sir Frederick Lugard. Although service in Northern Nigeria came with a severe health risk, the pay and leave were generous. For Poole, denied entry to the Staff College yet hungry for more responsibility, this was a tempting opportunity.

Lugard appointed Poole as Intelligence Officer. Poole's brief was to keep Lugard well informed. If there was any suggestion of a challenge to British authority, Lugard needed to be forewarned so as to be able to move swiftly and decisively. Lugard also required detailed reports, describing each province and subjects of special interest to him, as well as maps covering the whole of Northern Nigeria.[11]

The Elder Dempster line provided a sea passage from Liverpool to the delta of the River Niger. Conditions on board were primitive – poor food, no ice for drinks and a lack of washing facilities. Now adept at finding a way to ease his passage in life, Poole made friends with the ship's captain, gaining both the freedom to go up on the bridge and a few extra comforts.

On arrival at Forçados, passengers had to climb down the ship's side on a rope ladder before being taken ashore in a small boat, an unpleasant experience at the best of times and alarming if there was a sea running. Poole then faced a tedious journey in a canoe poled by Africans up the Niger, past the confluence with the Benue at Lokoja and into the Kaduna River at Baro. He soon got into the habit of making his own way along the riverbank. The last twenty-two miles from the highest navigable point to Zungeru, the administrative capital of Northern Nigeria, were by narrow-gauge railway. The journey from Liverpool to Zungeru took thirty days.

Zungeru had a few simple wooden bungalows with minimal facilities. Poole, however, was accustomed by army life to making do with few possessions beyond his clothing and a conveniently portable military chest. He took to the routine. He would wake at 5 a.m. to exercise his polo ponies before breakfast. He would work without a break from 8 a.m. to 4 p.m., play polo,[12] and, after supper, enjoy a couple of rubbers of bridge before staggering off to bed by 10.30. Sunday was the only day off, apart from public holidays. He also found time for reading. Judging by his pencil annotations and cross-references, his favourite reading was *The Rubáiyát of Omar Khayyám*, a parting gift from his friend Hartley Graham.

Poole accompanied the High Commissioner on a tour of inspection in his official yacht, the *Corona*. The party went down the Niger to Lokoja and then eastwards along the Benue. It was the rainy season; water levels were

---

11 The two volumes of F.R. Lugard's *The Rise of Our East African Empire* (Edinburgh and London, 1893) are packed with information and analysis, as well as maps and illustrations and gripping accounts of the author's adventures on the way. These include getting lost in impenetrable forests, narrow escapes from death at the hand of wild animals and fighting off unknown tropical diseases.
12 He won a cup inscribed, 'Zungeru Polo Club 1904 Captain Poole's Tin Belly Owner up'.

high and the Benue was navigable almost as far as the border with French Equatorial Africa

Whilst investigating the Ogboni, a powerful secret society with little respect for British authority, Poole found informants and persuaded them to talk despite their well-founded fear of being murdered for doing so. The result was a detailed picture of the inner workings of the Ogboni far beyond what anyone else in Lugard's team had produced. This showed a determined streak in Poole's character, which made him refuse to give up until he had to get to the root of the matter. This worked to his advantage except when, as sometimes happened, his persistence tipped over into obsession, narrowing his focus and hobbling his judgement.

He added colour and context to his reports. His report on the Munshi tribe began with: 'Their arrow poison is the deadliest known in West Africa, a wound from it causing almost instant death; it was principally the fear caused by this that enabled them to hold their own against their neighbours; safe in the dense forest and underwood which covers their country, they defied all comers'. Poole's conclusion, however, sits squarely on the sober territory familiar to his hard-working father, 'It is probable that, with a little patience and tact, we shall soon be able to establish friendly relations with the more influential chiefs; and then, through them, work on to the small "jungle" tribes who are at present the chief malefactors, and get them under proper control'.

Poole's reports were typed out by clerks and submitted to Lugard, who made corrections, tightened up the wording and added the occasional comment. When Lugard produced his annual report for 1904 to the Colonial Office, he demonstrated such a magisterial grasp of Northern Nigeria that no one could doubt that he knew far more than anyone else about the region.[13] In the meantime, Lugard had the means to quell anyone rash enough to probe into his activities.

After completing twelve months of service in Northern Nigeria, Poole arrived back in England on home leave in October 1905 so exhausted that he contemplated resigning. His sister Mary made him welcome in Cornwall. She had decided to make a fresh start and had gone with her mother to live in Cornwall after her elder sister, Gertrude, had got married and moved away from Cheltenham. Mary had taken up hunting foxes and had caught

---

13   Annual Report for 1904 to the Colonial Office (dated 23 October 1905).

Early Life

the eye of John de Cressy Treffry. They were married in 1899.[14] Even as a younger son John Treffry was comfortably off, as the Treffry family had for long been wealthy landowners and their fortune had been multiplied by the Cornish mining boom.

Poole recovered and decided to go back to Northern Nigeria, provided his leave was extended from four to six months. This arrangement was confirmed by Major E.F. Lugard, who served as political adviser to his brother.[15]

---

14 John and Mary Treffry lived at Penarwyn, which stands on the high ground above Par, facing southwards towards the sea. The house, completed in 1894, used to be surrounded by fine hunting country and to have extensive grounds as well as the stables and kennels occupied by the Fowey Harriers. Treffry was the Master from 1883 until 1925, apart from an interval from 1897 to 1900 occasioned by the death of his first wife.

15 The combination of fanatical Mahdi priests stirring up a 'Jehad' (Holy War) and the large, untamed, warlike Munshi tribe on the warpath was an irresistible draw.

2

Alice

Alice Hanson, the daughter of Charles Hanson, who had recently built Fowey Hall a few miles from Penarwyn, had been born and brought up in Canada, first in the countryside and then in Montreal. In 1890, at the age of twenty, Alice was uprooted when her parents moved to England, where she experienced life in three different houses in London and two in Cornwall. She also spent a few months in France with her brother learning French. Her parents were constantly entertaining and there was a stream of visitors. It is unclear where Frederick Poole and Alice Hanson first met but it was probably out hunting in Cornwall. In the early days of their romance Alice was self-assured and Frederick was nervous. He addressed her as 'Nan', telling her it was the local word for goddess, a salutation which ceased after his final return from Northern Nigeria.

Charles Hanson was a remarkable man. Born in Fowey in 1846, he had gone to Canada when he was twenty-two years old to make a fresh start. He had thought of becoming a Wesleyan minister but discovered a natural gift for making money. Having prospered by trading in timber close to the American border in the province of Quebec, he established the stockbroking business of Hanson Brothers in Montreal. After returning to England, he became a partner in Coates, Son and Company, a stockbroking firm based at 99 Gresham Street in the City. He created a lucrative connection, whereby Hanson Brothers – now run by his brother Edwin – used Coates, Son and Company to tap the London capital market at a time when the Canadian economy was expanding rapidly. Charles Hanson also entered the insurance world and became Chairman of the Gresham Life Assurance Society. As the

Gresham had branches in the Austro-Hungarian Empire, Hanson travelled to Vienna and Budapest and received a Knight's Cross in the Order of Franz Joseph in 1908.

Sailing was in the blood of the Hanson family and was the inspiration for the building of Fowey Hall. Charles Hanson's father had spent his life on trading vessels and had died at sea. Even before his father's death, Charles Hanson had sailed the Atlantic, running the blockade of the Confederacy during the American Civil War of 1861-65 and meeting Martha Sabina Applelbe, whom he married in Canada in 1869. When they settled in England, Hanson introduced his wife to his birthplace, arriving on a sailing vessel. Martha Sabina was overcome by the beauty of Fowey's natural situation at the end of a steep wooded valley with a large, sheltered, deep-water anchorage and the protection of high cliffs. She decided it was the place to build their home.

Charles Hanson therefore acquired a substantial area of land, which provided a commanding situation overlooking the harbour and its approach by sea. Fowey Hall was completed in 1899. The house was cleverly positioned so that it caught any sunshine. It provided an almost Mediterranean feel of light and warmth even in winter. The fitments, fireplaces, flooring, plasterwork and panelling gave an immediate sense of quiet comfort and secure living. Hanson employed Italian craftsmen and builders, believing they were the best, with marble imported from Italy.

Alice had not grown soft in the comforts of Fowey Hall. She could keep up on long country walks and rode well to hounds, winning the approval of Mary's husband, John Treffry. She did not flinch when her mischievous brother took her out sailing in rough weather. As well as being a good sport, Alice was a sympathetic and patient listener, untroubled by the cold as she and Frederick Poole sat together in the wooden summer house among the trees on the edge of the secluded lawn at Penarwyn.

Alice and her parents entertained Frederick Poole in the final days of his leave from Northern Nigeria. The couple had long and intimate conversations in Hyde Park. Frederick realised that Alice understood him and his emotional needs. Love turned into commitment and at last, on the eve of his departure, they became engaged. Alice received a flood of congratulatory letters and put together a celebratory book of humorous verses, which included one from Mary Treffry, relieved at the thought of shifting her brother's belongings:

> That you will now take charge,
> Of all the socks and ties and hats
> And coats and boots and cricket bats,
> And many other things,
> That fill my house from floor to floor,
> In every cupboard, every drawer,
> When he goes forth abroad.

At this point Alice had never met anyone from Frederick Poole's family other than his sister Mary. Her parents were determined, however, to celebrate Alice's engagement in great style with a ball at Fowey Hall, even though her fiancé would be far away and she could only communicate with him by a mail service which took a month to arrive. As the unhealthy climate of Northern Nigeria carried a risk of his dying, Alice had indeed to accept a separation which might prove permanent. On 17 May 1906, in the last stages of his journey back to Zungeru, Poole wrote a farewell letter with the words on the envelope, 'In case of my death, this letter is to be sent as soon as possible to Miss Hanson, Fowey Hall, Fowey, Cornwall'.

It was natural for Poole to expect Alice to be on close terms with his sister Mary, but more of a stretch to ask her to become friends with Florence Dove, his old acquaintance from Cheltenham days, and with Beryl Nicholson, two widows she had never met but who knew her future husband well. Just in case she forgot, Poole's expectations were laid out in his unsent letter of farewell, 'Go to Mary dear if you feel bad at first – she will comfort you and also dear old Florence, who was always my pal and who understood me better than anyone. Also, there is always Mrs Nicholson – you know what her friendship has been in my life; she will always help you when you feel it hard'.

Alice got straight to the point in the first of her letters to Frederick in Northern Nigeria, 'Always remember, darling, that you are the only man in the world for me. You do know it; but moments of depression will come and I believe that thought will help you'. She then touched on Beryl Nicholson:

> I had such a nice letter from Mrs Nicholson and I am sending it to you as I know she will not mind and I hope she will like my reply. You know it is not very easy for me to say much; but I told her I agreed with her about you and I thanked her for her sympathy in the separation from you. I also said that I very much wanted to be

friends with so old and tried a friend of yours; and I thought we had made a start as I had heard of her from you and that, with her kind letter, made me, too, feel that I already knew her a little. I also said that if she should be in Town while we were there, I hoped she would let me know and would come and see me. I know all this will interest you, dear.[1]

She then thanked him for giving her a copy of *A Tropical Dependency*, a book written by Lugard's wife Flora on the history of Northern Nigeria.[2] She told him of her visit to Penarwyn: 'The drive and the garden and the house were all filled with thoughts of you, dearest, and all that sunshiny afternoon and the other times we have had there came back so vividly'.[3] She described the softer side of Mary's character and then added, 'Yesterday Mary gave me some photographs of you, taken at various periods of your life. I do like them, especially the two of you as a boy. What a jolly boy you must have been. That you were a pickle you have confessed!'[4] The letter ended, 'Goodnight, my dear one, I like to feel that you pray for me every night. Always your Nan'.[5]

Alice had by now met her future mother-in-law and had navigated her way through sensitive territory:

Mary took me to see your mother this morning and she gave me a very kind welcome. We talked somewhat of you and she seemed relieved at the thought that you did not expect to be long in so bad a climate as that of Northern Nigeria and she wanted to know if I had heard from you since you started. We were not there very long. I have promised to go to see her again; but, though I shall try, I may not be able to get over this time. Mary told me the other day of your troubles with her, dearest.[6]

---

1   Alice Hanson to Frederick Poole, 22 April 1906.
2   Frederick Poole to Alice Hanson, 19 April 1906. It was heavy reading for a bride-to-be and a reminder of the competing claims of Northern Nigeria, 'The map at the end of it is the best one published and it will have a special attraction for you as it was compiled by my clerk under my supervision!'
3   Alice Hanson to Frederick Poole, continued 23 April 1906.
4   Alice Hanson to Frederick Poole, continued 24 April 1906.
5   Alice Hanson to Frederick Poole, ended Wednesday 25 April 1906.
6   Alice Hanson to Frederick Poole, 26 April 1906.

Alice

Frederick felt relieved about Alice's meeting with his mother, 'I'm glad you went over to see my mother, dear, and that she wrote to you nicely. Poor old thing, she has wrecked her life, which might have been happy and comfortable, and I am most awfully sorry for her'.[7]

His thoughts were on Beryl Nicholson in a letter posted when his ship called in at Sierra Leone, 'It was most awfully nice to see B.N. in Town before I sailed – she is a real good woman, the salt of the earth. I want you to like her very much, dear. I hope she wrote a nice letter to you and that you liked it'.[8] Alice responded, 'I wrote you about B.N's letter – it was such a nice one as you have already seen. I'm glad she saw you in Town. I want very much to like her and, as there are three of us wanting two of us to like each other, we ought to accomplish it'.[9]

Alice concluded after meeting Florence Dove, 'What a dear she is; but what a lonely life, Freddy. It is hard lines'.[10] Florence was now on her own in a small flat in London. She had gallantly laid on a supper party, one of the guests being Major Lawrence of the 14th Hussars who had known Mary well in the now distant Cheltenham days.

Writing to Alice in June 1906, Frederick was all too conscious of entering territory beyond his previous experience:

> But you see, dear, all my interests before you have been in the wilds … Are you looking at the moon tonight, dear? I am sitting writing in the moonlight – she is lovely tonight nearly full and a clear bright sky with my old friend the Southern Cross showing up brightly. I have watched him and lived with him and got to know him in South Africa, Somaliland and here – and many a night steered my course by him.[11]

Despite Alice's calmness, reassurance and steadfastness, Frederick succumbed to yet another attack of nerves, fearful of giving up the hard-won financial security won by serving in Northern Nigeria,

---

7   Frederick Poole to Alice Hanson, 3 June 1906.
8   Frederick Poole to Alice Hanson, 15 April 1906.
9   Alice Hanson to Frederick Poole, 11 May 1906.
10 Alice Hanson to Frederick Poole, 27 May 1906.
11 Frederick Poole to Alice Hanson, 6 June 1906.

My sweet old Nan, you are very plucky, you say you are not afraid of being poor, but I am, most awfully, principally for your sake, but also for both our sakes, because I have seen so much misery and wasted lives wrecked by it in my eighteen years soldiering. It's all very well in theory, darling, to say 'love will make up for everything' but my experience tells me that it doesn't work in practice – poverty at any time is awful, but real poverty as a soldier is damnation; it cripples your enterprise and initiative and spells ruin and misery. I am putting it all very strongly before you, dear, because I don't want you to go into it all with your eyes shut for fear you should be 'disillusioned' after.

You see, darling, I have been 'through the mill' and I speak feelingly. I was crippled and hampered for lack of means and I came to the conclusion that I must make an effort to get out of the ruck, so I gave a great shove and a flounder and got into a land where a man gets proper work and proper responsibility and a 'living wage'. So, if you think, dear, that I am cowardly when I tell you that I personally dread poverty worse than anything in the world, you will know it is on the principle of the burnt child dreading the fire. Well, well, darling, this is a very strong tirade, but there is a good deal of sense in it as you will realise when you think it over practically. Of course, sweetheart, I know as well as you do that when we think it over so to speak in conjunction with each other it doesn't seem so difficult. So, love is a big factor after all you see! Well so much for that, darling, let it stop at that, it's no use writing about it all now; we must put our heads together and fix up something.[12]

Finally, Frederick Poole made up his mind to leave Africa. Swift and decisive action had by now dealt with the threat to British authority in Northern Nigeria, Sir Frederick Lugard had resigned as High Commissioner and the pace of government business had settled down to a quiet and even tempo. Poole was not inclined towards a life in the Colonial Service, unlike his friend Charles Orr. He disliked the administration and paperwork required to deal with law and taxation issues, as well as the wide range of routine issues which demanded time and patience. Having squared the position

---

12 Frederick Poole to Alice Hanson, 15 July 1906.

Alice

with the incoming High Commissioner, Sir William Wallace, and with his replacement arranged, Frederick returned to England to marry Alice.[13]

After his return Frederick tried again to get into Staff College. Sir Frederick Lugard provided a reference:

Abinger Common, Surrey, 9 September 1906

Sir, Captain Poole, RA, DSO, who has recently resigned his appointment as Intelligence Officer, Northern Nigeria, is desirous of being noted for employment on the Army Staff. I have the honour to request that the War Office may be informed – if the Secretary of State concurs – that I consider Captain Poole well fitted for such employment. He is an officer of much ability, precise and careful in his work, and an unusually hard worker. He is good at cartography, and I have found him most valuable as an Intelligence Officer. I have the honour to be your obedient humble servant, Frederick Dealtry Lugard.

The recommendation was not accepted. Lugard's unorthodox career jarred with the normal workings of the establishment. He was an outsider without private means, who had neither been to one of the great public schools nor to Staff College. Yet he had risen meteorically from the humble rank of captain to becoming High Commissioner of Northern Nigeria in 1900, holding the acting local rank of brigadier general and having almost no limit to his authority until his resignation six years later. The only immediate benefit of Lugard's goodwill was an introduction to Sir Savile Crossley, who commanded the Norfolk Militia and was looking for a new adjutant.

Sir Frederick Lugard was too busy writing his final report on Northern Nigeria to attend Poole's wedding. His letter of refusal promised that he and his wife would drink Poole's health on the day. Later at least Poole had the satisfaction of seeing in print some official recognition of his services.

Political and Intelligence sections have been created in the High

---

13 His friend Hartley Graham had already taken the plunge and in one of his many instructions Poole had asked Alice to organise a generous wedding present.

Commissioner's office, which, under the able control of Major Lugard, DSO, and of Captain Poole, DSO, have very greatly increased efficiency in these branches, and enabled the High Commissioner to cope with work which was becoming too heavy to be dealt with without decentralization. The whole-hearted devotion with which the staff has worked is beyond any praise of mine, and I do not believe that there is a more capable and devoted set of public servants in any of His Majesty's possessions, temperate or tropical.[14]

Lugard's report has an Olympian tone, but it was justified given the extent of his success in establishing a well-organised administration that could provide justice and stability without being a financial burden on Britain in a region long plagued by the slave trade, religious fanaticism and anarchy. He gave little hint of the terrifying risks he had run with the minimal forces at his disposal when tact and diplomacy failed.

Poole knew the inside story and had spelled this out for Alice's benefit after his return to Nigeria from home leave:

it must have been a particularly anxious time for the Chief, as he insisted on taking it on against the orders of the Colonial Office. As it turned out a success, it's all right; but if there had been any hitch and we had suffered a reverse, he would have been disowned and disgraced by the Home Government. That is one of the great points about him, and one reason why they are all so afraid of him in the Colonial Office. He will not be stopped by them from doing what he knows to be essential for the good of the country, and he is always prepared to take on all responsibility for his actions.[15]

Poole never forgot what Lugard had taught him about leadership.

Charles Orr could not be at Poole's wedding as his leave had expired and he had had to return to North Nigeria. His letter of congratulation informs us, however, that his sister had formed golden opinions of Frederick:

---

14   Lugard, Report to the Colonial Office for 1905-6.
15   Frederick Poole to Alice Hanson, 27 May 1906.

Alice

2 Bennett Street, St James's, SW, Thursday night, 29 November

My dear Old Poodle, I didn't send you a wire this morning since you were probably drenched with them, but before I go to bed I must drop you a line to wish you all success and happiness in your married life. Even the little I saw of the lady who is by now Mrs Poole was enough to show me that you were a lucky man, though, taking into consideration the fact that you have been my close friend, for over eighteen years, it is hardly likely that I should consider the luck as all on your side.

I have been dining with my sister, a farewell dinner, and she particularly asked me to send her best wishes to you. I leave for Liverpool tomorrow night and hope to return to this country the spring after next. It is nearly 2 a.m. (as I have been finishing up packing), so I won't try to add more except once more my best wishes to you and Mrs Poole. Always yours sincerely, C.W. Orr.

Frederick Poole and Alice Hanson were married at the church of St Fimbarrus in Fowey on 28 November 1906. It was a grand affair, but the gift that touched Poole came from his aged nanny, now in an old people's home. She had dipped into her meagre savings to buy an inkwell with a silver top.

A thirty-seven-year-old army captain just back from the colonies may not have been a glittering match for the daughter of a very wealthy and successful man; but, at the age of thirty-six, Alice was married. In turn, Frederick Poole's fear and earlier experience of poverty was never likely again to be a reality. More to the point, they were in love. It proved to be a very happy marriage.

3

Peace-Time Soldier

After winning the general election of 1906 with a huge majority, the Liberal Government focused on social reform, which led to the introduction of the old age pension in Lloyd George's People's Budget of 1909. The priority in British defence spending became the expansion of the Navy to deal with the perceived threat from Germany, caused by its fast-rising economic power, its interest in acquiring colonies and the expansion of its naval power. Military expenditure had no champion and suffered accordingly, leaving few career opportunities for an ambitious officer like Poole, who had to content himself with the adjutancy of the Norfolk Militia.[1]

Captain Poole launched himself into every aspect of the Norfolk Militia's affairs and became well liked in the tight circle of old-established, rich, well-connected families with large properties in the area and with plenty of shooting to offer. Major Edward Evans Lombe, who belonged to this circle, wrote, after retiring on health grounds, 'Dear Poole, I do most awfully appreciate your exceedingly nice letter. If you had been with me in the regiment the whole twenty-five years, you could not have written me a more charming letter, and I value it very much'.[2]

Poole's interest in the Norfolk Militia, however, dwindled rapidly. Although Crossley was wealthy and well connected, he was a supporter of

---

1 Sir Savile Crossley passed over as a keepsake the letter approving his appointment. 'My dear Crossley, The King thinks that Captain Poole's record is an excellent one, and he quite approves of him for the adjutancy of the Norfolk artillery. Yours sincerely, Knollys.' Lord Knollys, Private Secretary to Edward VII, to Sir Savile Crossley, 17 November 1906.
2 Evans Lombe to Frederick Poole, 13 February 1908.

the Conservative Party and so had little or no chance of bringing official influence to bear in Poole's favour during a Liberal Government. Even after a third rejection for Staff College, Poole parted on good terms with Crossley, whose letter suggests that Poole was tempted by a life in the colonies.

12 Carlton House Terrace, 25 January 1908

My dear Poole, Well, I am not surprised though of course I do not want to lose you having taken so long to find you. But I can't for a moment stand in your way though it will put me in the cart – for I can't think any sane gunner would take on the adjutant's job under the existing circumstances of the muddling of the War Office. You were quite right to wire as you did. I think you will get the job – you are certainly fit for it. If you do, will you at once turn a quarter of your mind on invalid gunners fit for the job of taking us on? … Whatever the result of this NZ business you have been properly straight with me and I shall wish you the success you deserve in your career. But if you take it or not I don't think you will be able to retire at forty – you will be called on for other work and will be too keen to retire to a quiet country bovine life at that age and, if you do, the call of the wild or the call of life will pull you out again, Yours ever, Crossley.

Still only a captain after twenty years of service, Poole now joined No. 31 Heavy Battery stationed at the Citadel in Plymouth. The posting did nothing to satisfy his professional ambitions but there were compensations, including hunting. As he wrote to Alice:

Dearest, I have just got back here and changed and am waiting for dinner. I think I shall go to the theatre tonight I feel so bucked up!
    We had a very pleasant day as far as the weather went, but a poor day as hunting is concerned. We went over much the same ground as you and I rode over that day and found several foxes in those rocky tors, but there wasn't an atom of scent, so we did very little hunting. I got back to Liskeard about five and gave Surprise some gruel and then boxed him and left him with a bunch of hay to eat, so I hope he will have got home all right. Ask Rowe if he got his

bridle all right. I took it off him to let him eat his hay and left it in the compartment where the groom sits. Don't forget this, it's important – as we might lose it.

There were many enquiries for you, darling, and I did miss you so much – it isn't half so much fun without you. I enclose two letters – you'd better answer the Myers *at once* as it may throw them out if they don't hear soon – it's very good of them to ask us, but we have the answer ready as we are hunting the next day at Fowey. I do hope you are all right, darling, and that Ma's cold is better. Goodbye sweetheart, I miss you all the time – come on Thursday if you can. Your own Fred.[3]

He again contemplated leaving the army and in 1909 applied for the post of Chief Officer of the London Fire Brigade. He used every contact at his disposal to substantiate his credentials but was not successful; the post was filled internally.

Promotion in 1909 to major in command of 31 Heavy Battery in 2nd Heavy Brigade rekindled Poole's interest in soldiering. Alice was told, 'The Colonel has been inspecting us and was most awfully pleased with the battery – "far in a way the best turned out of all his batteries", so we are in high favour just now'.[4] Subsequently, at the summer camp in Devon, 'We did a topping good shoot yesterday – everything went right and much honour and glory accrued to No. 31. So far, we are top of all the six batteries as results go, and as all the three batteries of the 1st Brigade did rottenly today in their last shoot, we ought anyhow to beat them easily'.[5]

Poole's request to be considered for a lecturing post for which he was well qualified through his practical map-making experience in Northern Nigeria met with a frosty response:

Inspector General of the Forces, Horse Guards, Whitehall, SW
14 February 1912

Dear Major Poole, I am directed by General Sir John French to acknowledge receipt of your letter to him of the 5th Inst. and to inform

---

[3] Frederick Poole to Alice Poole, 3 November 1908.
[4] Frederick Poole to Alice Poole, 12 April 1911.
[5] Frederick Poole to Alice Poole, 20 July 1911.

you that he has made enquiries about the post of Chief Instructor in Military Topography at the Royal Military Academy vacant next August. Sir John finds that the appointment of a successor to the present holder will be considered in May next, but that preference will be given to applicants who have passed the Staff College.

Yours very truly A.F. Watt – Major. Private Secretary to Inspector General of the Forces.

31 Heavy Battery took part in the British army exercises of 1912. Lieutenant General Sir James Grierson commanding 'Blue Force' gained a clear victory over Lieutenant General Sir Douglas Haig's 'Red Force' by using spotter planes, having better communications and by encouraging his officers to think quickly and use their initiative. Major General Thomas Snow, who commanded the Fourth Division of Eastern Command, took note:

Government House, Woolwich, 22 September 1912

Dear Poole, I hope you will let your battery know how much I appreciate the good work they did during the night move from Royston on 17 September and during the difficult move through Saffron Walden on the evening of the same day. I am quite aware of the special difficulties you have to meet in moving your heavy guns along narrow roads at night. Your march discipline can only be described as excellent. Yours very truly, T.D'O. Snow.

Poole was wise enough to take Snow's praise humbly:

Woolwich, 24 September 1912

Dear General Snow, May I, on behalf of my battery, venture to thank you for the extremely kind letter you sent me regarding our work on manoeuvres. It is a very great pleasure to all of us that you were satisfied with our work; and it will be our endeavour in future to give you no cause to alter your opinion as to the efficiency of the battery. Yours very truly, F.C. Poole.[6]

---

6   Frederick Poole to Major General Snow, 24 September 1912.

When Poole was put to the test in the summer camp on Salisbury Plain in 1913, his stoicism impressed his friend Major Herbert Brake, who commanded another battery in 2nd Heavy Brigade,

> Fargo Camp, Salisbury Plain, 6 May 1913
>
> Dearest, I am better again today and have been about all the time. We had a fearful wet morning but now the wind has gone to the north west and it is fine and very cold. I was quite a hero today! Brake wants me to go away on leave till this beastly weather is over, but I said 'no' fiercely. I really am quite well and it wouldn't be playing the game to go away unless one was really bad. I have strong hopes now that I *shall* be able to get away this weekend and stay till Monday, which is to be a holiday, so in that case I can get home. Won't it be nice?[7]

Despite professional disappointment, Poole's life was pleasant enough. He had comfortable quarters at Woolwich, where 31 Heavy Battery was stationed, and was now a member of the Naval and Military Club. There was enough money, thanks to the generosity of his parents-in-law, to run a leased property at Horbling in Lincolnshire with a nanny to look after his two young sons (Charles, born in 1907, and Robert, born in 1909). There were dogs, horses, pigs, turkeys, ducks and hens. The establishment was run by a married couple, supported by their son, a housemaid and a gardener. There was even a modest car given to them by Alice's brother when he himself traded up to a Cadillac complete with chauffeur. Frederick Poole's sister Gertrude lived nearby at Haconby. Poole improved his golf, went bicycling with Alice and enjoyed shooting, albeit in the challenging conditions of the cold and mud of the Fens. Soon enough shooting of a different kind would decimate many of the neighbouring families accustomed to secure and assured lives.

Even so, life in the Lincolnshire Fens might have seemed a trifle dull compared with London, where Poole's father-in-law had taken the lease of 9 Wilton Crescent, a large house close to Belgrave Square. Wilton, as Poole called it, provided him with an agreeable stopping point with his

---

[7] Frederick Poole to Alice Poole, 6 May 1913.

General Sir Frederick Poole

own bedroom and, at a stretch, accommodation for his entire family. The hospitality extended to glamorous evenings at the Savoy and the indulgence of eating a whole lobster when his father-in-law took him out for the day to the south coast. Poole could also slip round to Dover Street, a short walk away, for a quiet chat with Beryl Nicholson at the Sesame Club.

On summer holidays at Fowey Hall, sailing grew into one of Frederick Poole's passions, so much so that he was presented by its owner with the *Maydie*, a Falmouth Quay Punt twenty-two feet long with beautiful lines, on the condition that he would never sell her, 'Take her out to sea and scuttle her when the time comes'.

Hanson's financial success lured Poole into dangerous territory in which he had little experience. 'I wonder what Ben Smith's investment was – he might have put us on to it. Yesterday was a beastly day, raining all the time. I went into the City first to see Anthony Thornhill, who is starting a tin mine in Cornwall and wants me to show the prospectus to Pa. I don't think the latter will have any truck with it.'[8] Making money from Nigerian tin mines became almost an obsession:

> I saw Sir William and Lady Wallace for a few minutes this morning when I was out riding. I am going to lunch there on Saturday. W.W. says tin is doing badly, no public will come in and so there is no money available to develop it. He seemed to think Harry Kemble's show was doing badly. He, W.W., has got some areas of his own he tells me. I shall hear about it on Sunday.[9]

Inevitably Poole lost money and had to be bailed out tactfully by his father-in-law. This was terrain quite unfamiliar to his strait-laced brother Arthur. In a letter of thanks to Alice for her hospitality when on leave from his regiment in India, Arthur suggested a rather different category of reading to dubious City prospectuses, 'If you haven't read a book called *The Right Stuff* by Ian Hay, do so at once. I read it on board ship'.[10]

After returning in 1913 from summer holidays at Fowey Hall, Frederick Poole learned what the army had in store for him. He was to exchange

---

8 Frederick Poole to Alice Poole, 1 March 1911.
9 Frederick Poole to Alice Poole, 17 August 1911.
10 Frederick Poole to Alice Poole, 1 March 1912; Ian Hay *The Right Stuff: Some Episodes in the Career of a North Briton* (London 1908).

command of the battery in which he had worked so hard, and his comfortable life in England, for banishment to the garrison in Jamaica, which had little strategic significance and an unhealthy climate. As he explained in a letter to Alice:

> Naval and Military Club, 94 Piccadilly, W, 14 August 1913
>
> Dearest, I didn't have to go to Gravesend today, so I came up here and went to the War Office instead to learn the worst! It is Jamaica about November or December – no hope of getting out of it – but if I say I want to retire on 15 February they will arrange that for me and I needn't go out. I don't think that there is any question that it is the best thing to do – the other job leads to nothing and means a lot of discomfort and separation. What do you think about it? I'm too sick about the whole thing to speak. They give one no warning and absolutely treat one without consideration. Hunter Blair was very pleasant but said he was powerless. I do hope neither of the boys will ever want to go into the army. I shall never encourage them to.[11]

In disgust, Poole resigned from the army and embarked on a new life in Cornwall, taking the lease of Cotswold House opposite the main entrance to Fowey Hall. He remained, however, in the Reserve of Officers in case his services might be again be needed.

---

11 Frederick Poole to Alice Poole, 14 August 1913. Hunter Blair was the Assistant Adjutant General.

4

Promotion

Although retired, Frederick Poole was in touch with the War Office so that he could be sure of immediate employment in the army even before war was declared on 4 August 1914. The day afterwards he left home in Cornwall to report for duty at Dover Castle. He found a scene of utter confusion when arriving by train from London at 8 a.m. on 6 August. There was no transport of any kind available at the station and he had to walk up the long and steep hill to the castle and to sleep the night on the floor in a bedroom shared with a brother officer.

Dover was the main port of embarkation for the British Expeditionary Force on its way to stop the Germans, who were advancing in huge force on Paris. Sir John French, the commander of the BEF, and his staff crossed the Channel from Dover on 14 August and Poole's brother Arthur, now a major in the Royal Warwickshire Regiment, the following week. Tight security was imposed to ensure that the enemy would receive no word of British troop movements. Poole was responsible for rounding up alleged German spies and censoring the local press. 'I have several correspondents coming to see me twice a day – we smile at each other and I say, "no news" and that is all.'[1]

His time at Dover was short lived. A War Office order dated 8 September instructed him to report at Woolwich 'for duty with Heavy Batteries'. He was put in command of 114 Heavy Battery, which was raised from scratch on 17 September and, with scant opportunity for training, dispatched across the Channel from Southampton on 3 October.

---

[1] Frederick Poole to Alice Poole, 9 August 1914.

Before leaving for France, Poole met Beryl Nicholson at her club and asked her to watch out for Alice and the two boys in case he was killed in action. Partings before going into danger brought out the usually repressed emotional side of Poole's character, previously expressed in his letter of farewell on the Kaduna River in Nigeria. Beryl Nicholson saw Poole off on his train from Charing Cross station back to Woolwich.

After returning home Beryl wrote to him about Alice, 'It's good she is down in Cornwall with her people and can be at your own home and yet with them, and good for the boys'. She predicted that Poole's chance to make his mark had come at last, 'Be thankful you are at the real thing. I am in spite of everything, for it's your life's work and a noble one, and I know you'll make a job of it. That has been my creed for twenty-two years … Absolute bedrock belief in you … "Inferno" hour – the old "war horse" breathing new air and will be content'.[2]

The military camp at Madrillet was a cheerless spot outside Le Havre. Winter was approaching and pink eye rife among the horses.[3] Poole made his presence felt in the town, checking that Captain Pierson was organising the officers' mess efficiently and seeing that Sergeant Major Gilbert was keeping a watchful eye on both his men and the battery's horses. Poole's French learned at school came back to him, as did his brief experience of diplomacy in Northern Nigeria with the neighbouring French Colonial Empire. 'I find I am beginning to talk French quite volubly and understandably. I have long talks with all sorts of people. They all understand me. I am going to lunch today with the mayor of the town, who is quite a big pot. He is the father of my interpreter.'[4] Being in the warm, comfortable home of the mayor was quite a translation from his first meal on French soil two Sundays before when he had consumed the remains of the picnic basket Alice had thoughtfully provided for him on the cold, comfortless dockside.

On 20 October, 114 Heavy Battery entrained for St-Omer, just twenty-two miles from the Belgian frontier, 'We really had rather fun on the journey – great crowds at all the stations who cheered vigorously and gave all sorts of things to the men. We were about thirty odd hours in the train and then disembarked here.'[5] The French welcome continued as the battery marched

---

2   Beryl Nicholson to Frederick Poole, 29 September 1914.
3   Yves Buffeteau, *Rouen Le Havre, 1914-1918* (Ysec, 2008).
4   Frederick Poole to Alice Poole, 18 October 1914.
5   Frederick Poole to Alice Poole, 22 October 1914.

towards the Front Line. 'Last night Mac and I were billeted in a wine shop.[6] We made great friends with the man and his wife who entertained us royally. When we went to our room there was only one bed and Mac's kit was laid out on the floor. The Frenchman was most distressed and for ten minutes he tried hard to persuade Mac to sleep with him!! "Nous serons très confortables"!'[7]

This idyll ended abruptly at 4.00 a.m. on Monday 26 October when Poole was roused by a staff officer and his battery was ordered to join II Corps. The British Expeditionary Force, which at this stage defended only some twenty miles, or about five per cent, of the Front Line on the Western Front, was engaged in a desperate struggle to secure the approach to the Channel ports on which its communications and supplies depended.

Poole reported at Beuvry, the first village on the road between Béthune and La Bassée, to Brigadier General Headlam, who commanded the artillery of the 5th Division of II Corps. His battery took up position on a farm with its guns concealed in an apple orchard. The following day (27 October), 114 Heavy Battery went into action just as the Battle of La Bassée (10 October to 2 November) was reaching a climax.

Poole had to find and silence the enemy batteries six miles away in the village of Salomé behind La Bassée. They were concealed on the reverse slope of the ridge, which meant that he could not see them whilst they had a clear view of the battlefield on the flat ground below. On his first day in action, he had to rely on bearings taken from a map; but on the second he produced results by working in collaboration with a spotter aircraft. In the back of his 1914 diary is a primitive signalling code for communication between plane and battery. 'Batteries at Salomé very troublesome to infantry. Airman reported our range and direction correct so we proceeded to search. Silenced the battery and set the town on fire. There was a crowd of transport reported there which I hope we scattered. Fired seventy-three rounds lyddite.'[8]

Following this, 114 Heavy Battery was attached to the Meerut Division of the Indian Corps, which held a two-mile section of the front line running from the village of Givenchy, on the northern side of the La Bassée Canal, almost as far as Neuve Chapelle. On 2 November, the Germans finally got their range and fired eighty shells. Being well dug in, the guns escaped

---

[6] Captain K.I. MacIver.
[7] Frederick Poole to Alice Poole, 24 October 1914.
[8] Poole, Diary, 28 October 1914.

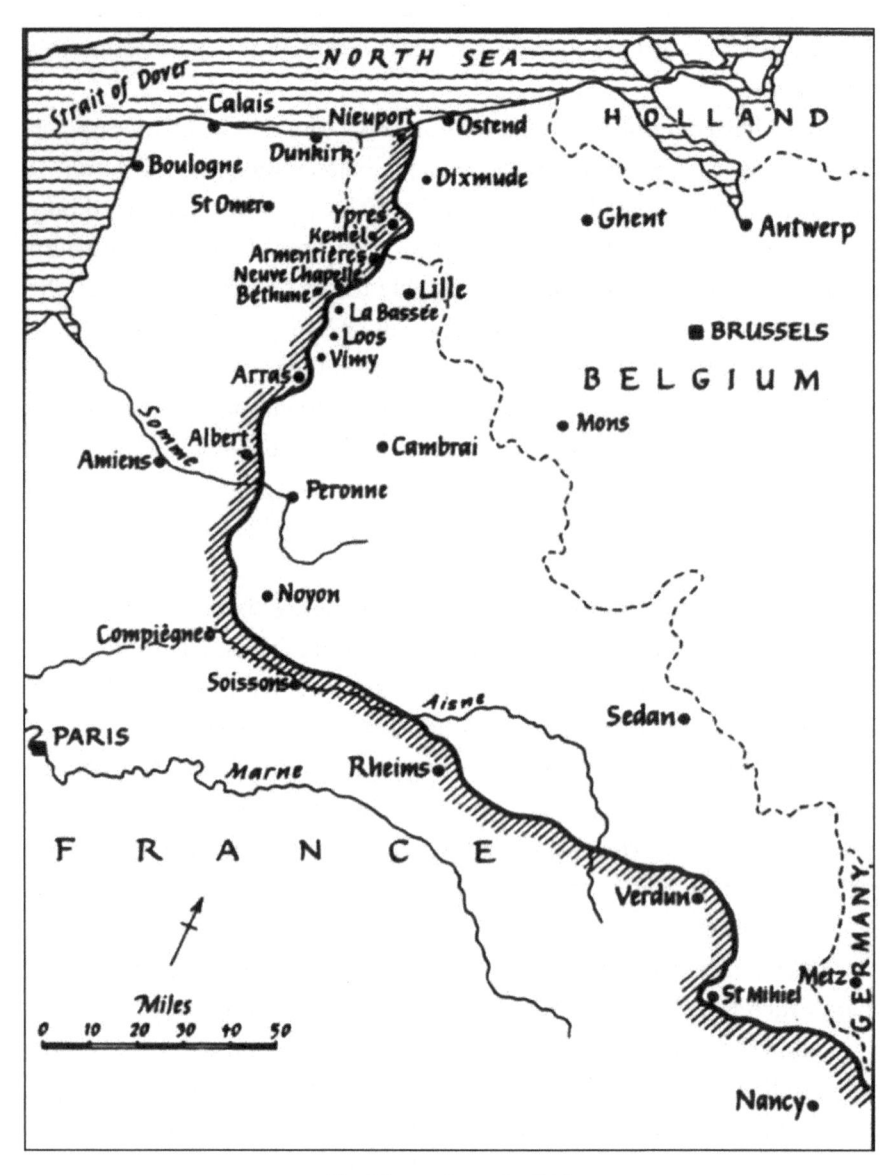

The Western Front in 1915

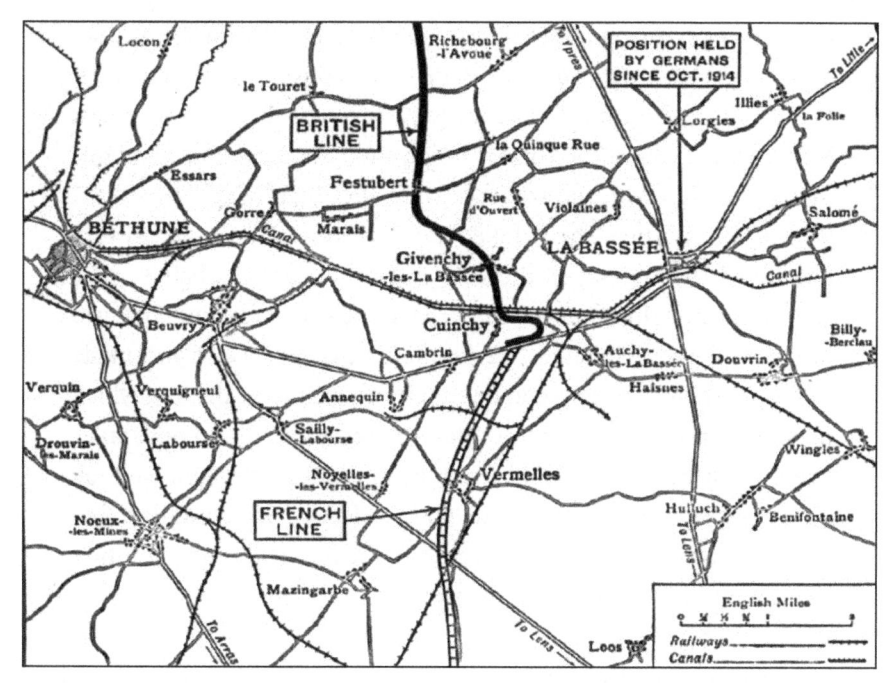

La Bassée

unscathed but both Captain Pierson and Sergeant Major Gilbert were killed. They were buried that night before the battery was moved to a new position. Poole immediately wrote to Mrs Gilbert and Mrs Pierson. Gilbert's experience had been one of the decisive ingredients in transforming 114 Heavy Battery so quickly into a fighting unit. On the grounds of age, Gilbert could with honour have been excused going into battle, but he had insisted on coming. Poole's concern about how his widow and two young children would manage financially became a recurring theme in future letters until his generous father-in-law eventually stepped in to help. Pierson's father, a retired colonel in his seventies, acknowledged the condolences for his son in a manly letter, typical of that generation.

Poole's battery survived a terrifying encounter with a German eleven-inch howitzer, known as a 'Black Maria' because of the smoke released by its high-explosive shells on landing and because of the resulting rock, earth and debris thrown into the air creating huge craters:

At 11.00 a.m. was ordered to engage Ligny le Petit batteries (behind Lorgies). This provoked a reply from a German battery who searched for us in vain, firing about thirty rounds at 12.30 with the airman observing. We engaged a new battery reported near Violanes. While engaged on this target we were severely shelled by a 'Black Maria' which found the correct range and caused us some anxious moments. However, the trenches were successful and we suffered no casualties. Their shells killed three men and wounded twelve and killed four horses in the field just over from the battery. The airman located this battery in an orchard near La Hue and observed for us while we retaliated. We found his place all right and made things pretty hot for him and he shut up shooting for the day, which must have been a relief to our infantry. As he had found our range, I thought it healthier to shift our position and so by night we took up the position recently evacuated by 110 Heavy Battery and shifted back the horses and first-line wagons to the line of the Ammunition Column at Le Hamel. Fired 101 rounds.[9]

It rained incessantly. The ground became saturated and water spilled over from the rivers, canals, sluices and dikes, turning the whole of the flat low-lying region into a sodden, muddy morass. The weather also became exceptionally cold and bitter winds added to the discomfort. Snow was on its way.

Poole found he could cope with the grim rhythm of warfare in which sudden, frenetic periods of action and danger were interspersed with monotony and even tranquillity. Long hours spent shooting in Norfolk and the Fens of Lincolnshire, deep in mud and stoically bearing the cold and wet, had prepared him for the rigours of a harsh winter in northern France. When sailing out of Fowey Harbour in the *Maydie* he had acquired a good sailor's nose for danger and knew how to recognise the early signs of change in the air before calm waters suddenly become turbulent. He had also learned to wear oilskins to keep dry.

Even in the darkest moments, Poole managed to stay calm. 'The roar of the Fourth Division batteries is terrific. The wind is against us but sitting down in my funk pit to write this I feel the ground vibrating with the guns. I do hope Babe will be all right.[10] I see there were a lot of Warwick casualties

---

9 Poole, Diary, 5 November 1914.
10 Babe was the nickname in the family for Poole's brother Arthur, engaged in desperate fighting further north in the First Battle of Ypres.

in a paper I saw yesterday. Well, we are in God's hands as that's all there is to say.'[11]

When the Germans again got in range and 114 Heavy Battery had to be relocated, each gun needed to be pulled by a team of fourteen horses because the axles sank deeply into the mud. Yet the guns were in their new position and ready for action early the following morning. An exhausted Poole still had time to think about the Christmas presents for the 213 men under his command:

> You had better keep on sending things over for the men as you collect them – matches, notepaper, candles, also my 'gum boots'. This mud underfoot is awful. I was done up yesterday for the first time. The day before, I had been working solid from 3 a.m. to midnight. I don't think I had rested more than one hour during that time. Luckily yesterday was a quiet day so I had a good sleep and am very fit again today. Things seem pretty well.[12]

On 23 November the Germans mounted a raid east of Festubert in which the Indian Corps lost and then regained in a counter-attack eight hundred yards of trench, a fifth of their two-mile section of the Front Line. Poole's battery was not involved, as it had just been through a tumultuous experience:

> We are being pulled back today to have a week's rest – rather a nuisance. I don't want to go. Poor Robert Lorraine our ... airman was shot through the lungs yesterday when observing for us. They were pushing shells all around him and one was alas effective. I fear he is pretty bad. I'm sorry, he was such a fine fellow, but I hope he will recover all right. Everybody is well. Croydon is doing capitally as sergeant major – see his wife or write to his wife.[13]

George Croydon had taken over from Gilbert. As his home was in Plymouth, it was a relatively easy journey for Alice to call upon her. Alice's

---

11 Frederick Poole to Alice Poole, 11 November 1914.
12 Frederick Poole to Alice Poole, 18 November 1914.
13 Frederick Poole to Alice Poole, 23 November 1914. Lorraine survived the war and won both the DSO and MC.

address book is full of people who served under Poole and whom she was asked to visit, to invite to stay or otherwise to care for.

It took several months before glimmerings of the real story seeped out:

> I see Sir John French's despatches are out and I get a mention in it for the show at the end of November. I am glad, darling, because I know you will be pleased. What pleases me is that I am the one and only person in Corps Artillery that has got it. As a rule, nobody does get it in these cases as there is no one to urge their claims, so it really is a great compliment. I am awfully sick that Simmy and Mac aren't mentioned – they thoroughly deserve it.[14]

Croydon was promoted, 'The most exciting news I have for you today is that Croydon has got a commission as second lieutenant. I recommended him very strongly as he has done so well and he was in orders last night. It's a great nuisance as I shall probably lose him too and he is very valuable to me, but one mustn't stand in his light. You must write to Mrs Croydon and congratulate her'.[15] In those days it was rare to rise from the ranks and become an officer.[16]

The battery enjoyed a little taste of Christmas in billets away from the Front Line. Cleansed of mud and with clean kit, the men relaxed in a 'smoking concert', and 'asked that the ladies should all be thanked for the things they very kindly sent and gave three cheers for Mrs Poole and also the "little" Pooles'.[17] Poole left for home leave in Cornwall on 9 December, lucky to get away as two days later all leave was stopped. He returned on 18 December, and, being a seasoned yachtsman, managed to sleep peacefully through a rough Channel crossing.

As Christmas approached, Poole had an unexpected encounter with an unhappy young man, twenty years old and in uniform but forbidden to take part in the fighting. He was being chaperoned on a visit to the Front Line and had chanced upon 114 Heavy Battery:

---

14 Frederick Poole to Alice Poole, 20 February 1915. Simmy was Captain Apeltre and Mac was Captain MacIver.
15 Frederick Poole to Alice Poole, 4 March 1915.
16 Croydon remained in the army after the war, reaching the acting rank of major and gaining the OBE.
17 Frederick Poole to Alice Poole, 3 December 1914.

Today it was snowing hard, so I put on my oilskins and a dirty sou'wester and ploughed out through the mud to my battery. When I got there, I saw a staff officer and another standing by a gun. I didn't take much notice but nodded carelessly. The staff officer then came to me and said the Prince of Wales is here and wants to meet you, so up I went and was formally presented to him!! Poor little boy he looked cold and miserable but was very pleasant. I asked him to come in and have a drink, but he wouldn't![18]

Christmas Day came. It was the first Christmas of the war and the sixth Poole had spent on service. He would not have another Christmas with his family until 1919, a year after the war had ended. Poole was comfortable in his oilskins whilst the wretched Indian Corps suffered in their sheepskin coats – a well-meant gesture from the Home Front – now infested by lice.

We are having great changes here. The Indian Corps is done up – the wet exposure in the trenches and very heavy losses have tucked them up badly, so they are being sent away to rest and are being relieved by I Corps – First and Second Divisions. We are going to stay on with them I fancy. I'm glad, as I don't want to rest. They have been pushing at us rather hard for the last few days and gained a little, but we shall soon square it up now I fancy and perhaps do a bit of a push at them. It froze hard last night – a good thing as it will dry this awful wet. We haven't fired a round today it has been so thick a regular fog. No more news. Goodbye sweetheart, Fred.[19]

The conflict had not yet escalated into total war, with conscription, aerial bombing of civilian targets, unrestricted sinking of shipping by submarines and food rationing. The optimism expressed in the 1914-15 edition of *Baily's Hunting Directory*, 'To the men in the field, "Good luck, a successful run, and a safe return home!"', had not been quenched by the slaughter in the battles about to come. Poole still managed to see the war in human terms and had barely begun to refer to the Germans as 'the Huns', rather than the softer term 'the Allemandes' or simply 'the Germans'. He, his brother

---

[18] Frederick Poole to Alice Poole, 23 December 1914.
[19] Frederick Poole to Alice Poole, 25 December 1914.

General Sir Frederick Poole

Arthur, Alice's brother and three of her cousins from Canada and friends and relations were in the Front Line; on the Home Front their families were all working hard in support of the war effort. Frederick Poole had an upbeat New Year message, 'Well, here we are at the end of the year – it has been hard, a lot of ups and downs for us, darling, but it has been a good year to live all the same and I'm glad to have been alive in it. It has taught us all a lot – the country and you and me – and all been for good hasn't it though'.[20]

His steadfastness was mocked on the first day of 1915:

> I had a sad letter from B.N. today. She is staying with her sister Mrs Crum-Ewing and they heard on Xmas Day that the boy Alec was missing. He is with the Camerons and it must have been the first time he was under fire, as they heard from him on the 19th and he was then resting somewhere near here. It is a great blow – he is probably dead, poor boy – the only son and just pulled away from Eton for the war. I'm awfully sorry for them. I expect it was in retaking some trenches that the Lahore Division lost on our right.[21]

Beryl Nicholson's nephew, barely past his school days, had been killed leading his men into attack on an enemy trench.

Poole volunteered for a hazardous assignment at Cuinchy, where the remains of a large distillery was still partially standing despite constant enemy shelling. It adjoined Pont Fixe, a steel girder bridge crossing the La Bassée Canal on the road from Cuinchy to Givenchy. The brewery was the only position that provided a clear view across enemy lines to the triangle formed by two spurs off the railway line that ran parallel with the La Bassée Canal, converging further south. Poole and Captain MacIver were to observe from the distillery. Corporal Bailey would then report their findings by telephone to the artillery batteries pounding the German position before the First Division went into action.

Poole held back nothing from Alice before his ordeal began:

> We are getting more lively now and I am just off for a very nasty job. We have to see a place in the enemy's lines that can only be

---

20 Frederick Poole to Alice Poole, 31 December 1914.
21 Frederick Poole to Alice Poole, 1 January 1915. Alec or Alick Crum-Ewing.

seen from the top of a brewery; and, as they have knocked it to bits with their shell fire and shell it regularly, it's not a very healthy job. However, I hope they will not put us in the bag. It has been raining regularly. The whole thing is now getting very serious – everything is getting washed out and if this goes on all the trenches will soon be under water – these low-lying countries are no place to fight in in the winter.[22]

The three of them were still alive at the end of the day, 'It was a most unhealthy place – the old brewery was being shelled. We took shelter in an inner room for the worst of it but while we were observing they continued to shell it. Corporal Bailey while telephoning had a shell through the wall about a foot from his head but continued to work very coolly'.[23] Their ordeal continued the following day until the attack began.

Poole's battery had a narrow escape from German retaliation, 'One of their batteries had a good try for us this morning. It shelled vigorously the last three places we had been in but we were comfortably watching from a quarter of a mile away – they have had no airman over lately, so they aren't up to date'.[24] Enemy fire intensified and he had no time to write up his diary on 11 January, or on the 13th to 15th, an unusual gap. There was some press coverage, '*Daily Telegraph* has an account of the "Triangle" attack which is absolute rot. It is a shame to gull the General Public in that way'.[25] On 25 January, the Germans counter-attacked, and 114 Heavy Battery fired eighty-nine rounds, 'I see in today's (26 January) "eyewitness" in the paper 114 is mentioned!! We were the battery who got three direct hits on the observing station. We got two houses today which were their infantry billets, so we really have been doing some execution lately'.[26]

The Meerut Division returned to the Front Line after its well-earned period of rest and Poole's battery was reattached to it:

We have had our first day under the Meerut Division today and

---

22   Frederick Poole to Alice Poole, 9 January 1915.
23   Poole, Diary, 9 January 1915. Bailey received the DCM. Poole and Captain MacIver were mentioned in despatches.
24   Frederick Poole to Alice Poole, 11 January 1915.
25   Poole, Diary, 17 January 1915.
26   Frederick Poole to Alice Poole, 27 January 1915.

really done a gallery shoot. There is a road near here – all semi-detached villas about 150 yards apart – occupied by Germans – about a thousand yards back from their trenches. MacIver was out observing from a house just over our trenches and told us about them. We fired on them and put lyddite shell into eight separate houses absolutely blowing them endways. What pleased us most was four hits on different houses in four consecutive shots – at each shot the telephone reported 'house blown up go on to the next'. It was most thrilling.[27]

114 Heavy Battery's winning streak continued, 'We have fairly got the bulge here over the "Allemandes" in guns and aeroplanes. If one of their batteries makes a nuisance of itself, we can always smother it and our aeroplanes also always go in at them when they appear and drive them away'.[28]

A distant relative in Lincolnshire, the Reverend R.G. Barlow Poole, passed the word back much later:

I heard about Fred Poole a little time ago from a man in this village home on leave from the Front. He is with the heavy artillery and said that their casualties had been slight owing to the fact that their company had the best commanding officer in the army, and then he said that this officer had the same name as I and made one clear it must be Fred Poole to whom he was referring. I am sure I went up in his estimation tenfold: such is the value of famous relatives! I think the whole family here regarded me as a person of some importance ever since! The same man told me that Fred had been mentioned in despatches, and I am so glad to hear it. I missed the fact in the paper.[29]

It could not always be an idyll of brave and grateful men under a humane commander doing their best for their country. Drink was a temptation hard to resist and was the downfall of a useful man, 'You will be sorry to hear Pepper is in trouble – he was run in yesterday for being drunk and I shall

---

27 Frederick Poole to Alice Poole, 3 February 1915.
28 Frederick Poole to Alice Poole, 7 February 1915.
29 R.G. Barlow Poole to C. Griffith, husband of Frederick Poole's sister Gertrude, 9 November 1915.

have to see him tomorrow. I'm sorry for his wife's sake – also for his own, as I thought he was much too good a man to be such a fool'.[30]

Second Lieutenant Leslie Notcutt joined the battery, 'a boy about twenty-one just qualified as a civil engineer and will do well – a fine figure of a man with faithful brown eyes like a spaniel. I know the type well – the sort of man who will stick it out if we get into a tight corner'.[31] Just four days later, Poole concluded, 'Notcutt is A1 – a really brilliant man. I am most awfully lucky to have got him'.[32] He had begun to suspect that Notcutt, whom he called Percy rather than Leslie, might help discover new methods which could make 114 Heavy Battery even more effective.

Poole's time with the Meerut Division ended abruptly: 'found orders had been issued for us to march tomorrow and come into action. Went on to see Franks under whose command we now come. Found he had a 2nd Heavy Brigade staff, so quite among old friends. Very glad indeed at the change'.[33] Poole's old friend Brake, now a lieutenant colonel, was there.

Poole's battery was to be part of a massive concentration of siege and heavy batteries assembled in great secrecy for a surprise attack. The concentrated fire of 450 heavy guns would destroy the barbed wire entanglements and fortifications protecting the German trenches at Neuve Chapelle in a short and ferocious bombardment. Before the Germans had any chance of recovering, the infantry would advance and seize the high ground of Aubers Ridge. That 'supposedly' would open the way to Lille and the Belgian frontier.

Although he was only a major, Poole would report directly to Brigadier General George Franks, who commanded No. 1 Heavy Artillery Reserve Group:

> We have been living in such a rush lately I have never had a chance to write. We are now back in action – a little further north than last time and leading a very strenuous life getting in touch with all the new conditions. We are now – all the Siege and Heavy – grouped into two groups under brigadier generals; and our own general I am glad to say is Franks who succeeded me at 31. It is tremendous

---

30 Frederick Poole to Alice Poole, 19 January 1915.
31 Frederick Poole to Alice Poole, 13 February 1915.
32 Frederick Poole to Alice Poole, 17 February 1915.
33 Poole, Diary, 4 March 1915.

luck – he is a great pal of mine and is doing me a treat. All the other batteries are put under lieutenant colonels, but he has declined to put me under one and I remain independent. It's all excellent for us, now we have someone to fight our battles for us and look after us in every way.[34]

Franks could hardly be described as a 'great pal'. He had met Poole only briefly, when taking over the latter battery and comfortable quarters at Woolwich on his retirement from the army in February 1914. What counted in Poole's favour was his record in peacetime at 31 Heavy Battery, endorsed by the likes of Brake; his achievements at 114; and the fact that 114's guns, worn out after intensive use, had just been replaced.

On the day, Poole's battery fired 303 rounds, far eclipsing the 108 fired in the ferocious encounter on 22 November:

I have no time to write. We began a big attack at daybreak this morning and so far all has gone well. We have gained a mile or two and have put the fear of God into the 'Allemandes'. I am all right – the house we were in wasn't hit all day, nothing nearer than fifty yards. We shall be on now for a week or two I expect. We may move on any time. No more time darling – all well – all well. Goodbye sweetheart, Fred.[35]

Failure to press home the initial success allowed the Germans to recover and counter-attack, so the battle of Neuve Chapelle ended in a stalemate. There was praise for Poole, 'Franks came to see me and said he was running me to get command of a brigade'.[36] Franks did his best, but he was still comparatively junior and his efforts did not bear fruit. He got a little irritated when Poole became too effusive in his gratitude, 'I thanked Franks. He said, "I didn't do it for you, but because I thought it was for the good of the show".'[37]

Poole went on home leave to Cornwall. Despite falling ill during his leave, he insisted on returning, 'Stayed in all day – up to Town night

---

34 Frederick Poole to Alice Poole, 7 March 1915.
35 Frederick Poole to Alice Poole, 10 March 1915.
36 Poole, Diary, 16 March 1915.
37 Frederick Poole to Alice Poole, 14 April 1915.

train. Alice came with me as I was very seedy'.[38] They breakfasted at his father-in-law's London house. Then he crossed the Channel to France but collapsed on arrival at his battery, 'Doctor came to see me in morning and ordered me straight off to hospital – arrived Béthune about 12.00 and put straight to bed. Cold very troublesome and some temperature'.[39] Only a deeply ingrained sense of duty could have persuaded a seriously ill man to exchange a comfortable bed in a warm room – not least in his father-in-law's luxurious London home – for a horrendous journey by rail, sea and road to the rigours of the Front Line in the depths of a harsh winter.

On 28 April 114 Heavy Battery joined a group of batteries stationed about ten miles north of Neuve Chapelle. Poole now reported to Colonel Arthur Currie in III Corps, which was commanded by Major General Sir William Pulteney. Poole had the good luck to take over the comfortable house near Armentières vacated by his peacetime command, 31 Heavy Battery, when it went further north to join in the Second Battle of Ypres. 'Was called for to see GOC III Corps at Bailleul, but the whole thing was a washout as they changed their plans.'[40]

In the event, 114 took up position behind Hill 63 in the vicinity of Ploegsteert Wood:

> We annoyed the Huns considerably yesterday – we shelled a big house with some success and I think it must have belonged to a general as they at once tried reprisals and made an effort to knock us out. However, they never got the range to us, so no harm was done. There is a big avenue of trees about four hundred yards in front of us where we have put down a battery of dummy guns for their aeroplanes to find, so that always catches the shells meant for us. I hope they will continue to bombard it.[41]

The battery made its presence felt. 'In the afternoon had an aeroplane which put us on to a battery south of Frelinghien. We routed it in fine style getting a direct hit on a gun second round and two more, later, also one bang into funk pit.'[42]

---

38 Poole, Diary, 29 March 1915.
39 Poole, Diary, 31 March 1915.
40 Poole, Diary, 2 May 1915.
41 Frederick Poole to Alice Poole, 5 May 1915.
42 Poole, Diary, 12 May 1915.

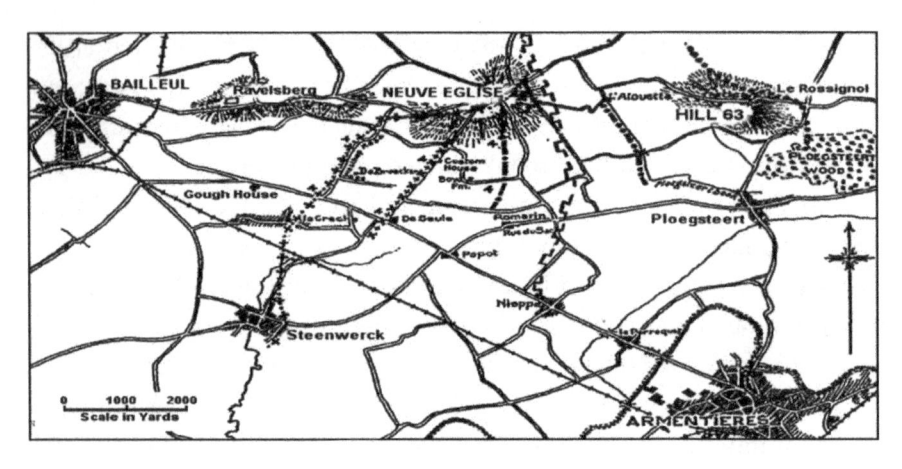

Ploegsteert

Hill 63, being the sole point of high ground in the vicinity, attracted massive enemy fire, which made observing a hazardous business. Poole's faith in Notcutt now paid off decisively. The latter devised a bomb-proof trench. When Poole pointed out that his design was not as laid down in official regulations, Notcutt replied that it was based on his experience as a qualified engineer and that it would do the job.

Just as Notcutt was getting into his stride Poole lost two trusted officers. 'Mac has left us yesterday. He has gone to be adjutant to Colonel Brake. I am very sorry indeed to lose him – he has been a great acquisition in every way and I shall miss him very much.'[43] Captain Apeltre was transferred to Colonel Currie's staff. 'Simmy', as Poole called him, was now able to forewarn about planned inspections. It was little surprise that 114 Battery was well prepared when it was 'inspected yesterday by the General Commanding III Corps – Sir W. Pulteney – who said to me, "You have a magnificent battery I am most pleased with it". It was rather luck he came in just as I was having a shoot with an aeroplane and I had just got the range – so every shot signalled from the aeroplane was a hit. He was most impressed! Thought we never did anything else.'[44]

Leslie Notcutt was now pioneering a way of making better use of the bearings provided by spotter aircraft. He even sacrificed the first hours of

---
43   Poole, Diary, 9 May 1915.
44   Frederick Poole to Alice Poole, 3 June 1915.

his precious home leave until after the inspection.[45] The breakthrough came finally with the Artillery Dial Range Corrector, a device for synchronising the observation data reported from spotter aircraft with the registration of guns on the identified target.[46] It provided a compensating adjustment for the different viewpoint of a given location as seen from a plane as distinct from the ground.

By this time, the Germans were thoroughly annoyed:

> Cleared up in afternoon and went up to 63 with Percy [Notcutt]. They were bursting high-explosive shell over the hill as we walked up and bits were falling all round us. When we got into trench one 'woolly bear' burst thirty yards in front and smothered us with bits, but no one was hit. They then shot over the hill – put a piece which just missed my horse's hoof and covered him with mud.[47]

Events, however, were going Poole's way:

> Colonel Currie who commands our group is off today for a break – he is just being made a brigadier as they are shoving some more batteries under him. I'm very pleased – he is a good man and will do this battery well as he thinks no end of us. Simmy tells me that when he was talking to the Corps Commander the other day, he said that the one man in the country who really understood the role of heavy artillery was Major Poole!!! So you see, if I stay with him, I shall be treated well. No news at all – they were very vicious out at our observing station yesterday; they burst one high-explosive shell just in front of us. We had a hunk of the shell just over our heads into the parapet at the other side which made us think.[48]

Poole learned that he had been promoted to lieutenant colonel on 25 June 1915.

---

45 Amongst General Poole's papers is a photograph with the caption written in pencil 'Notcutt observing': their repeated visits to the observing point on Hill 63 reinforced Poole's belief in one of the army's favourite maxims, 'Time spent on reconnaissance is seldom wasted'.
46 *Royal Artillery Journal*, 45.
47 Poole, Diary, 11 June 1915. The 'woolly bear' was a particularly nasty high explosive shell which released shrapnel and black smoke.
48 Frederick Poole to Alice Poole, 15 June 1915.

Whilst waiting – in growing frustration – for his posting, Poole took the day off to plead his case with Franks, only to have a wasted journey, as No. 1 Heavy Artillery Reserve Group had moved further south beyond the La Bassée Canal. In his absence the Germans struck. 'Yesterday the Huns bombarded our dug-out and trench very heavily – put two hundred shells at it greatly to Percy's annoyance – but they didn't do any harm, so it didn't matter much.'[49]

Having withstood such a test, Percy Notcutt's bomb-proof trench on Hill 63 was considered safe enough for the visiting Prime Minister of Canada:

> Yesterday Sir Robert Borden turned up and had a look over the enemy lines. He seemed a little nervous and there was a general tension. They all seemed jumpy in case they began to shell us. Luckily, it was the quietest day we have ever had, so after a few minutes the general asked me to fire a round of lyddite at the town opposite so that the old man could see it. The shot pitched bang into a house and blew it up, so he saw lots of smoke and dust and destruction and was so pleased that he asked for another. As soon as it had fallen, they all hurried away as fast as they could for fear the Huns would retaliate and that was the end of my interview with 'his nibs'![50]

---

49 Frederick Poole to Alice Poole, 20 July 1915.
50 Frederick Poole to Alice Poole, 22 July 1915.

5

Loos

The forty-six-year-old Frederick Poole was to command III Heavy Brigade consisting of 111, 112 and 113 batteries.[1] The luxury of a motor car did not extend to a newly appointed lieutenant colonel going to join his brigade, so Poole went on horseback. He started at 6 a.m. on 16 August on a ride of thirty miles southwards, accompanied by his interpreter Pierre Morgand.

Poole was back in No. 1 Heavy Artillery Reserve Group. 'I saw Franks today and have a lot of work to do for him … I am very pleased with the whole thing – I shall be worked off my legs for the next few weeks. It is in the air though that, if we have a "boost", I may get a much bigger command – two other brigades in addition to my own – so it might turn into a big thing – but don't say anything about it as it may not come off.'[2] He took an immediate liking to Captain O'Reilly Blackwood, his new adjutant, 'who is very smart and up to date'.[3] He made a point of ensuring Blackwood got his much-deserved home leave. He even forgave Pepper, 'I forgot if I told you I have brought Pepper along with me here. He is a very good servant and by way of being quite a reformed character now!!'[4] He also succeeded in having Notcutt transferred to his new command.

A major offensive – a 'boost' – was being planned in conjunction with the French. They wanted the British attack to draw off pressure from the

---

1 He succeeded Thomas Tancred, who had been promoted to acting brigadier general and given No. 5 Heavy Artillery Reserve Group.
2 Frederick Poole to Alice Poole, 17 August 1915.
3 Frederick Poole to Alice Poole, 19 August 1915.
4 Frederick Poole to Alice Poole, 24 August 1915.

Germans whilst they renewed their struggle to seize back the high ground lost in 1914 that had left Arras, the capital of the Département of the Pas de Calais in Northern France, exposed. In the Second Battle of Artois, from 9 May to 18 June 1915, they had recaptured Notre-Dame-de-Lorette, but only after incurring such heavy casualties that it became known as the *Colline Sanglante* or 'Bloody Hill'.[5] Their objective, in what became known as the Third Battle of Artois, was Vimy Ridge, the dominating escarpment that forms the barrier to the plain of Douai beyond.

The British forces were to attack in what became known as the Battle of Loos over a front of ten miles across the Gohelle Plain from the La Bassée Canal southwards to Lens. Poole was in the southern sector, where the 15th and 47th Divisions of IV Corps were stationed. The French Tenth Army was on his right flank and occupied the heights of Notre-Dame-de-Lorette.

The Gohelle Plain had been worked for coal and was disfigured by large pitheads (*fosses*), by secondary mining shafts (*puits*) and by slag heaps (*crassiers*). The Germans were well prepared and entrenched on the higher ground of the Hohenzollern Redoubt and Hill 70. Poole almost came to grief: 'We had gone up to an observing post and directly we got there they began to shell it with heavy stuff – the second shell fell about two feet away but somehow we all escaped without a scratch … Our OP was up a heap of coal and we were smothered with coal dust, but I had a bath tonight so that's all right'.[6]

The Heavy Artillery Reserve Groups were charged with subduing hostile battery fire whilst preparations were made for the assault; with providing cover for the troops waiting in the trenches; with destroying the barbed wire and fortifications of the enemy trenches in a prolonged preliminary bombardment before the attack; and with blunting the fire of enemy batteries supporting any counter-attack.

As this was a far more demanding challenge than at the Battle of Neuve Chapelle, Royal Field Artillery and Royal Horse Artillery batteries, which previously had been attached to Infantry Divisions and to the Cavalry Corps, were added to the Heavy Artillery Reserve Groups. Their rôle was strictly limited to assisting the heavy guns in subduing enemy batteries; in other words for counter-battery work. Poole interpreted this brief as, 'Our

---

5 The bleeding hill.
6 Frederick Poole to Alice Poole, 19 August 1915.

job is to keep down the enemy's guns in this area and, as they are rather truculent, it takes a lot of doing'.[7]

Whilst attached to the Meerut Division, a Field Artillery battery had been placed under Poole's command for tactical purposes, so he was not entirely a novice in this new dimension of counter-battery work. Nor indeed were the Germans. Poole had been at the receiving end in the Battle of La Bassée, 'A field battery searched for us in the afternoon, but never got very near and were bursting their shrapnel too high'.[8]

Poole took in his stride the responsibility Franks had thrust upon him, 'I'm very pleased with the command I have now. I only hope I will do it well. I should think it was considerably larger than any Royal Artillery colonel out here has got – indeed it is identically the same in peace time in the ordinary division – four brigades of artillery – so if it comes off all right it will be a great feather in my cap'.[9] Notcutt filled in the immediate gap whilst Blackwood was on leave: 'He is working like a horse and doing really well – it's no light work either'.[10]

Poole now had the opportunity to catch up with his brother Arthur, known as 'Babe' in the family, who had been promoted from major to lieutenant colonel in January 1915 and a month later given the acting rank of full colonel. The brothers met briefly when 'Mac and I rode up and found Babe yesterday. He was looking very seedy as he had just been inoculated for enteric, but I expect it will soon wear off. They are pulled back to rest for a few days – as they say being "fattened up for slaughter" as they expect to be put in for attack at the end of it'.[11] Babe emerged unscathed – the only one of the colonels to do so in the 10th Infantry Brigade fighting in the Second Battle of Ypres – and was advanced to acting brigadier general in August.

Sadly, the British Expeditionary Force lacked the experience needed to organise such a large-scale operation. Pressure from the French to meet their requirements, reinforced by political interference, made matters worse. There was a great muddle. Just as Poole was getting into his stride the arrangements for his command unravelled. The 117th Brigade Royal Field Artillery was taken away. Then 72nd Brigade Royal Field Artillery was

---

7   Frederick Poole to Alice Poole, 23 August 1915.
8   Poole, Diary, 28 October 1914
9   Frederick Poole to Alice Poole, 26 August 1915.
10 Frederick Poole to Alice Poole, 29 August 1915.
11 Frederick Poole to Alice Poole, 14 April 1915.

replaced, 'I have had a real hard day – on the go the whole time arranging for three horse artillery batteries who are coming in under me.'[12] Then one of the three batteries in III Heavy Brigade was transferred temporarily to his friend Lieutenant Colonel Herbert Brake.

Poole's troubles continued. Settling into Leahy's Brigade – 21 and 22 Heavy Batteries – got off to a bad start. 'Poor Colonel Leahy has gone sick already – he is pretty bad – I saw him for a few minutes tonight and told his doctor to send him into hospital if he isn't better. He hasn't got much stamina and is too excitable for this sort of life.'[13] It took a week to sort out before he could report that 'Colonel Leahy is a bit better and will get all right now I expect. He is settling down to this sort of life.'[14]

Hard pressed though he was, Poole made a point of comparing his efforts with the French on his right flank: 'I had a most interesting hour this afternoon sitting up in a house overlooking the German trenches and watching a tremendous artillery duel between the French and Germans about three miles away.'[15] With his professional curiosity as a gunner aroused, he found a pretext to visit the French positions. Looking down from Notre-Dame-de-Lorette, a height of 165 metres, he could not understand how in the Second Battle of Artois the fire of the French artillery below could have been so accurately targeted on the trenches then held by the Germans. His questions went unanswered. No one wanted to reveal to an outsider the secret that had provided the edge in such a hard-fought battle.

Even months after the fighting it was still a scene of horror:

> I have just got back from a most interesting trip. I have been to see a battery of ours which has been lent to the French and been through a lot of the French trenches. The place was on the hill where they had all the fighting last May and the casualties on both sides were terrific. We went through some of the old German trenches which had not been altered yet and the effect of the gunfire on them was marvellous. When they were altering the trenches there were some real horrors. One saw a pair of boots sticking out as you walked along and then, when you got near, you saw the corpse it belonged

---

12 Frederick Poole to Alice Poole, 29 August 1915.
13 Frederick Poole to Alice Poole, 3 September 1915.
14 Frederick Poole to Alice Poole, 10 September 1915.
15 Frederick Poole to Alice Poole, 1 September 1915.

to and the smell in parts was indescribable. There were clothes and broken rifles and boots and everything you can think of all mixed up anyhow. It really was most interesting and we got an excellent view all over their trenches. I got a very good German rifle which I hope to get home sometime.[16]

Far from dominating the enemy batteries, Poole found himself reacting to their firepower, 'We live in rather a rush today. I am continually being called with screams for help from the infantry who are being shelled in the trenches and, as it's very thick, it's difficult to find out where the shelling is from. Then in half an hour I have to go off to get to a general of a division who wants to talk about things and at the same time I want to be somewhere else'.[17] The general in question commanded the Seventh Division stationed on Poole's left flank, 'The Huns put in a lot of "frightfulness" shelling our trenches all round so we had a very busy day competing with them. Lunched with General Capper to discuss retaliation'.[18]

Poole's disquiet increased, 'Received orders that the RHA batteries are to rejoin Cavalry Corps and to be replaced by four field batteries'.[19] Time was running short, 'I'm full of work today – my new field batteries have arrived, and I have a lot of work to do in connection with them. They are commanded by a full colonel who was about ten years senior to me in the service – it makes me feel very old to have him under me!!'[20] By contrast the French artillery continued to outperform, 'I watched the French shelling the Hun trenches yesterday – they gave them a real dressing down'.[21]

Poole had been upbeat when he knew that his posting was about to come through, 'Today is a lovely summer day – bright and fresh and west wind. It makes me long for Fowey and a day at sea in the *Maydie!*'[22] The summer was so gruellingly hot that it reminded Poole of his time in India. There were swarms of flies attracted by the heat, and by the detritus of the massive concentration of men, horses, and unburied corpses. He had to go on foot

---

16 Frederick Poole to Alice Poole, 9 September 1915.
17 Frederick Poole to Alice Poole, 14 September 1915.
18 Poole, Diary, 14 September. Major General Sir Thompson Capper would die in battle on 27 September 1915, one of a disturbing number of high-ranking casualties.
19 Poole, Diary, 15 September 15 1915.
20 Frederick Poole to Alice Poole, 18 September 1915.
21 Frederick Poole to Alice Poole, 18 September 1915.
22 Frederick Poole to Alice Poole, 14 August 1915.

on a punishing round of visits to his observing posts and batteries, as riding a horse presented too conspicuous a target for enemy fire. Vigorous walking kept his waistline trim, but his neck swelled out and Alice was asked to send shirts with a seventeen-inch collar.

He had no respite at night. His house, a substantial stone-built structure with the amenities of a bath, a dining room, a cellar and even a garden, was in the line of enemy fire:

> The first shot came into my dreams, the second woke me completely and when I heard the third about twenty yards away, I lost no time in going to ground in our funk pit. They put in about forty altogether and twenty of them were quite near the house. I got a great splinter through my bedroom window and, when I got back to bed about 1 p.m., the whole floor and my bed were all covered with glass.[23]

As the pressure ratcheted up Poole thought of life in Cornwall, 'I hope Pa will be able to stay down some time and get a rest. It would do him a lot of good. Give my love to Sam Rowe and tell him, when I get home, we will have a month's fishing together. I wonder if the boys are going out with him at all. They really haven't had very much on the water this year have they – we must try if all is well to do a bit more next summer. I'm missing you and thinking of you all the time. I do hope I shall be able to get home before so very long'.[24]

The death of the gallant old colonel who commanded the newly arrived 108th Brigade of Royal Field Artillery pushed Poole uncomfortably close to the brink:

> We are beginning an attack tomorrow so I may not be able to write properly – it is late now and I have piles of work to do so can only scrawl a line. I shall send postcards when I can. It's sad one of my colonels – the one commanding the Field Artillery – was killed this afternoon. He was a dear old man and a gallant gentleman – he was killed pulling in wounded men to shelter. I was just going to discuss things with him when I met Captain Blackwood, my adjutant – just

---
[23] Frederick Poole to Alice Poole, 26 August 1915.
[24] Frederick Poole to Alice Poole, 8 September 1915.

coming down from his house covered with blood. He had gone up a quarter of an hour ahead of me and they had been shelled in the house. They heard shouts outside and ran out to carry the wounded in and the poor old man was shot dead. My darling, I hope I shall come through this all right – but, in any case, I will try to do my duty. Goodbye sweetheart, all my love to you and the babies, Fred.[25]

Under such strain, disaster could happen to even the bravest officer. Poole knew how, as the Germans were advancing on Paris in 1914, his brother Arthur had taken command of his battalion in the Royal Warwickshire Regiment and got his men home after Lieutenant Colonel Elkington had had a loss of nerve and wanted to surrender.[26]

Poole was dissatisfied with the results of the preliminary bombardment before the battle started. The 60-pounder guns of the 21st and 22nd Batteries that formed Colonel Leahy's brigade were his most powerful weapon for cutting the wire of the enemy trenches. Poole had already used the 21st Battery before the preliminary bombardment, 'I fired lyddite the best',[27] but there had been massive retaliation, 'We cut some wire on their trenches last night with our big guns and it has made them so furious they are slamming ours badly'.[28]

He tried again on the third day of the preliminary bombardment. This time he deployed the other battery – the 22nd – in Leahy's brigade with field batteries in support. The results were again unsatisfactory, 'Our shelling trenches was effective – wire cutting not so good. The 22nd Brigade and Brigade 108 were both employed on wire cutting'.[29] Poole's disappointment was not a criticism of Colonel Leahy, but a realisation that, as the enemy's entanglements became denser and more sophisticated, new methods would have to be found to destroy them.

On the fourth day of the preliminary bombardment Poole reached an even starker conclusion, 'We have kept their guns pretty quiet. I expect as a matter of fact they are keeping them for the attack; as, if they shot much

---

25 Frederick Poole to Alice Poole, 20 September 1915.
26 Elkington was cashiered, joined the French Foreign Legion and redeemed himself. The officers of Royal Warwickshires included Lieutenant Bernard Montgomery, later a field marshal.
27 Poole, Diary, 13 September 1915
28 Frederick Poole to Alice Poole, 14 September 1915.
29 Poole, Diary, 23 September. The 22nd Brigade referred to here was a battery, not a brigade.

now, we should be certain to knock them out and they know it'.[30]

The infantry went into action on 25 September with great success in the southern sector, 'Attacked at 6.30 a.m. ... Made good progress towards Loos taking all trenches – Loos – Hill 70 and up to the outskirts of Cité St-Auguste'.[31] It was a different story the following day: a repetition of the mistake at the Battle of Neuve Chapelle of failing to reinforce initial success. 'Confusing day – enemy recovered and was aggressive everywhere. ... after a lot of attacking and counter-attacking we ended up by being pushed off Hill 70 and entrenched round Loos ... Disappointing day'.[32]

The action had moved outside the remit of the Heavy Artillery Reserve Groups. 'We are fighting away now but it's at close quarters and there is no job for my guns at present. On the whole things are good, but I'm afraid, as we haven't broken through at once, that we shall not get very far now – they have brought up reinforcements and are doing their damnedest to push us back.'[33] Nevertheless, there was official praise, 'Franks came round in afternoon. He says all First Army staff pleased with work of Heavies'.[34]

Poole used his initiative when the Germans counter-attacked:

> There is still a good deal of shooting, but I am in now sitting at the telephone and running my batteries from there – most of this is not our job – we only put a few shells over the trenches to keep reinforcements from coming up. On the whole quite a good day. No more news, darling. A big shell covered me with mud today – it pitched in a field one side of the road just opposite me. Luckily, I was on the other side of the road! Goodbye sweetheart, Fred.[35]

Firing on enemy troops was, as Poole admitted, 'not our job', being beyond the scope of his brief, which was to engage enemy batteries – counter-battery work – rather than enemy troops. Poole had attended two separate eve of battle briefings because of this demarcation: 'Conference at No.

---

30 Frederick Poole to Alice Poole, 24 September 1915.
31 Poole, Diary, 25 September 1915.
32 Poole, Diary, 26 September 1915.
33 Frederick Poole to Alice Poole, 29 September 1915.
34 Poole, Diary, 30 September 1915.
35 Frederick Poole to Alice Poole, 8 October 1915.

1 Heavy Artillery Reserve in morning – got final orders for attack which begins tomorrow'; and 'Went to Royal Artillery conference of IV Corps in evening'.[36]

The Battle of Loos ended on a sour note: huge casualties, ammunition running out and the Germans unbowed.

---

36   Poole, Diary, 20 September 1915.

1. Frederick Poole, on home
leave from India, 1897

2. Frederick Poole (left) at the wedding of his brother, Frank Poole, and Maud Dawson, Leckhampton, 5 May 1897. Standing behind the bride (left to right) are Gertrude Griffith and Arthur Poole, Frank and Frederick's sister and brother, and Elizabeth Lawrance Poole, their mother

3. Frederick and Alice Poole with bridesmaids, 1906

4. Alice Poole on her wedding day, 1906

5. Beryl Nicholson, Frederick Poole's long-term friend and benefactor

6. Charles and Martha Sabina Hanson outside Fowey Hall

7. Haconby Hall, Lincolnshire, the home of Frederick Poole's sister Gertrude

8. Fowey Hall, Fowey, Cornwall, east façade

9. Fowey Hall, south façade

10. Alice Poole in a landau outside Fowey Hall

11. Frederick Poole (next to mast) and Charles Poole (facing camera) on the *Diana*

12. Torfrey, Golant

13. Frederick and Alice Poole with Charles Poole at his Cambridge graduation

14. Frederick Poole outside Torfrey

15. Alice Poole in old age

16. Frederick Poole at rest

6

Counter-Battery Pioneer

On 16 October 1915, Frederick Poole approached Brigadier General Charles Budworth, who commanded the artillery of IV Corps, with some new ideas: 'Went to see Budworth in evening to discuss counter-battery work generally'.[1] Poole and Budworth, both born in 1869, had begun their careers together: commissioned in 1889, promoted to lieutenant in 1892 and to captain in 1899. Although he had subsequently outstripped Poole, Budworth, who has been credited with pioneering the idea of a 'creeping barrage', was open to constructive suggestions from junior officers.[2]

Poole had come to realise that the French artillery was performing better than the British; but, in the first instance, he concentrated on the British weaknesses which could be addressed. The day before the German counter-attack he had seen the 117th Brigade Royal Field Artillery, which had been under his own command only to be taken back almost immediately, have a severe mauling from enemy fire: 'Went up to OP in trenches – it cleared up and we got an excellent view. Huns very active – considerable shelling – Phipps' brigade badly taken on'.[3] On the day of their counter-attack, the Germans again had the upper hand against the field artillery, though not

---

1 Poole, Diary, 16 October 1915. The two men shared family connections with Durham School, where Budworth's brother Richard was headmaster and Poole's brother Henry second master.
2 Major General Ernest Alexander told Sir James Edmonds, the author of the *History of the Great War*, about the origin of the creeping barrage: 'I rather think I got the tip from Budworth'. Sir James Edmonds, *History of the Great War: France and Belgium, 1916*. When the 15th Division stormed through the village of Loos and took Hill 70 it had the benefit of an early form of 'creeping barrage' from field batteries commanded by Alexander.
3 Poole, Diary, 7 October 1915.

against the heavy batteries: 'Their fire was very effective on our front-line trenches – our casual fire fairly heavy. Our barrages spoilt them – particularly in vicinity of Bois Hugo'.[4] As a result, Poole's command had been reinforced: '63rd Brigade Royal Field Artillery posted to us for counter-battery work'.[5] Budworth listened carefully and things began to move quickly, with Poole taking care to explain his views to his immediate commander. 'Went to see Franks in morning and afterwards Budworth re placing of batteries etc';[6] then, 'Very thick and cold early morning. Lunched with Franks',[7] and 'Franks came round in morning'. Finally, Poole was allowed ten days of home leave.

After his return from ten days of home leave, Poole learned that changes had taken placed of which he was the beneficiary. He was being transferred with III Heavy Brigade plus his field batteries to IV Corps from No. 1 Heavy Artillery Reserve Group, command of which passed to Brigadier General Fiennes Crampton. Franks was posted to Second Army as the GOC Artillery of II Corps, the same position as Budworth held in IV Corps in First Army. In turn, Poole was given his own counter-battery group. He would report directly to Budworth and would now have the authority to call on spotter aircraft when he required them rather than when they happened to be available.

Poole's new headquarters were at the elegant but extremely cold Château Mercier. 'Budworth came in morning and held a conference – quite the "new broom" but I hope we shall be able to carry out his wishes.'[8] 'I have hardly ever had a spare minute ever since I got back here so I have not been able to write at all. This change and reorganisation has meant a lot of extra work and it will be a week or two before we get properly settled down.'[9] Budworth examined III Heavy Brigade in minute detail, 'GOC inspected 111 and 112 in afternoon'[10] and 'GOC inspected 113 in morning.'[11]

The setback at this time was a ruling that captain adjutants holding semi-staff jobs should be redeployed to batteries, which meant that Poole risked losing Captain Blackwood. Snatching a moment from the clatter

---

4 Poole, Diary, 8 October 1915.
5 Poole, Diary, 9 October 1915.
6 Poole, Diary, 18 October 1915.
7 Poole, Diary, 21 October 1915.
8 Poole, Diary, 19 November 1915.
9 Frederick Poole to Alice Poole, 20 November 1915.
10 Poole, Diary, 21 November 1915.
11 Poole, Diary, 22 November 1915.

of typewriters dealing with the endless stream of paperwork, telephones ringing and the unceasing comings and goings in his headquarters, Poole included a brief addendum on a separate piece of paper to his letter home. He made the excuse of wanting to see whether he could manage a typewriter, but it was more of an outburst occasioned by the pain of separation from his family, worry about the ill health that plagued his elder son, and the grim war news:

> Dearest, I am learning to type so this will show you how I am getting on! I think it is rather a fascinating game, don't you? If I can get quick at it, I shall find it very useful, don't you think? It has been a beastly day here – hard frost last night and bitter cold all day and a thick fog, so neither side has been very active. Your dear letters have just come. I was glad to hear that all is well. Just now there is a big strafe going on just to the south of us. It sounds as if the Huns were making a very fierce attack on the French. It is so thick though that it is impossible to see anything, so one can only hope for the best. I will remember what you said about getting a cartridge case for Edward Coates. I will try to send one by a man who will soon be going on leave. I expect you have gone home today. It will be a great joy for the children.[12]

At this point Poole had a stroke of luck. Auguste Pellarin, Général de Brigade and commander of the artillery of the French IX Corps, stationed on Poole's right flank, introduced himself. His interest had been aroused by reports of Poole's visit to the 'Bloody Hill'. 'This morning we had a call from a French general who commands their artillery: he came to establish an entente. I quite liked him, and we parted the best of friends.'[13] It was undoubtedly helpful that Poole spoke fluent French.

Poole was used to directing artillery fire from the bearings reported back from observing posts and spotter aircraft, but only on an ad hoc basis using the data gained on a particular day for the chosen target. He now discovered that the French were running an Intelligence operation to create a sustained picture of the enemy lines and dispositions, based

---
12 Addendum, Frederick Poole to Alice Poole, 22 November 1915..
13 Frederick Poole to Alice Poole, 23 November 1915.

on the mapping coordinates derived from aerial photographs taken by spotter planes. He also learned that their Intelligence gathering stretched well beyond observing posts and spotter planes. It included intercepts from enemy wireless and telephone conversations, interrogating deserters and prisoners of war, analysing captured documents and taking in the findings of raiding parties and spies. Poole was an instant convert to French methods.

After service as an Intelligence Officer in Northern Nigeria, Poole knew how to gather and process information and how to prise out secrets. He was also adept at mastering new skills and techniques. He had quickly recognised the extent of Percy Notcutt's abilities and in a matter of weeks had put them into action to the benefit for 114 Heavy Battery. From August 1915 he had had his own wireless set and recognised how wireless technology could be used to intercept enemy signals. As a camera owner since his time in Nigeria, he was also familiar with photography and immediately receptive to the transformative impact of aerial photography.

Two days after General Pellarin's visit, 'Banting joined and took on duties of Intelligence Officer'.[14] With a legal background, Banting had a sharp eye for detail and a capacity to work under pressure. This was the ideal set of skills for absorbing and analysing accurately the large volumes of information soon generated. While Banting sat behind a desk, Poole was able to be constantly on the move, liaising with aircraft squadrons, checking up on observing posts and inspecting batteries. French telephonists were brought into Château Mercier so that calls were put through without delay and the entente between the English and French began to bear fruit, 'A very active day – Huns began about 9.00 a.m. and kept it up till about 2.30 – Fosse 7 and Mazingarbe took it worst. We kept busy all the time and outlasted them'.[15]

Poole's abilities were now beginning to draw recognition. 'General Budworth told me today that he was trying very hard to have me made brigadier general of either Heavies or Royal Field Artillery. The latter was a great achievement as he is dead against Royal Garrison Artillery Officers getting Royal Field Artillery commands! I don't suppose for a minute that anything will come of it, so don't say anything about it, but it's nice to know

---

14 Poole, Diary, 25 November 1915.
15 Poole, Diary, 27 November 1915.

one's reputation is good.'[16]

Budworth drew Poole to the notice of the commander of IV Corps. 'Sir Henry Rawlinson came to see us and was very pleased with the plan of Intelligence.'[17] Rawlinson's approval had immediate results, 'General Tancred came to see me and stayed looking at things till about 3 p.m'.[18] Despite his seniority, it was Tancred, Poole's predecessor at III Heavy Brigade, who had come to learn. On 6 December, Poole heard that Brigadier General Bland, who commanded No. 1V Heavy Artillery Reserve Group, was being transferred Home and that its 8th, 13th and 19th Batteries would be transferred to his own counter-battery group. He now had 'a 6-inch gun that will shoot miles, 8-inch Howitzers and 9.2-inch Howitzers – all the latest things – and absolutely it. It really now is a very fine command'.[19]

The Intelligence operation raised Poole's profile well beyond his immediate counter-battery mandate. The rapid expansion of the British Expeditionary Force from a small professional army of barely a hundred thousand to an army of some one and a half million men inevitably meant that there was a lack of trained staff officers, whose work was made much more difficult by the primitive state of battlefield communications. One unfortunate result of this was rigidity in orders, which constrained the use of local initiative and had resulted in the critical delays in reinforcing initial success at the battles of Neuve Chapelle and Loos. Poole therefore had a resource to offer which was desperately needed by the overworked staff officers: 'We are getting most important people now – all the staff etc. crowd round here to see us and we really give them the only reliable information they get anywhere.'[20]

Poole worried about antagonising Crampton, who had succeeded Franks at No. 1 Heavy Artillery Reserve Group only to find that it was an empty command. 'I'm going in to see General Crampton to talk over one or two matters. This new brigade I have taken over really belongs to him, so I must see what his views are on certain matters, but I can't go unless

---

16 Frederick Poole to Alice Poole, 3 December 1915.
17 Poole, Diary, 4 December 1915.
18 Poole, Diary, 5 December 1915.
19 Frederick Poole to Alice Poole, 9 December 1915.
20 Frederick Poole to Alice Poole, 9 December 1915.

the Corps Commander comes here first.'[21] In a potentially difficult situation Poole's tact prevailed, so much so that Crampton wanted to travel back with him on their next home leave.[22]

It was an appropriate time to be advancing innovative methods. Lloyd George who had become Minister of Munitions when the Coalition Government was formed in 1915, was getting to grips with the shortcomings in the supply of guns and ammunition. The introduction of conscription was on the way. After the attempt to force the Dardanelles was abandoned, the decision was made to focus on the Western Front. In December 1915 Sir John French was replaced as Commander-in-Chief of the British Expeditionary Force by Sir Douglas Haig, who was determined to make a huge and decisive assault on the German army after the failures of 1915.

Although Frederick Poole's was not the only voice in the debate about the proper handling of artillery, he made an impact by explaining complex subjects in simple terms. As he told his wife on 17 December:

It has been quite a busy day today. Early this morning I had to motor twenty miles to First Army Headquarters to give my lecture. It was quite a success: went off very well – a big crowd there including three generals! I laid down the law well, as I soon saw that I knew more of the subject than any of them, and they all thanked me at the end for a most interesting and instructive lecture![23]

Poole began to stretch his remit beyond the original counter-battery brief from Budworth, 'Had a shoot round St-Eloi at midnight as we heard from a deserter that a relief was taking place then – result unknown.'[24] All the while his confidence increased:

We have had quite a busy day – at 7 a.m. we let off a mine under one they had made in our front-line trenches. This created a bit of a palaver and we had a good deal of shooting at each other. However, it settled down about 9 a.m., so I got away to my lecture at First

---

21 Frederick Poole to Alice Poole, 10 December 1915.
22 In 1914, when Poole had been only a major, Crampton had been acting brigadier general in command at Dover.
23 Frederick Poole to Alice Poole, 17 December.
24 Poole, Diary, 19 December 1915.

Army Headquarters. It went off all right and I got back in time for late lunch.[25]

Poole's relations with the French entered a new dimension. Far from being a slavish disciple of their methods, he earned the respect of Colonel Lefort of the 20th Artillery attached to the 10th Infantry Division:

We have just had a long visit from a French colonel and major who couldn't talk a word of English and our interpreter went off on leave this morning! They stopped to tea and we cemented the Entente splendidly. He likes me because I always shoot hard to help him whenever he asks me! 'Très mordant – un homme d'esprit', he describes me as!![26]

Poole returned the call on Christmas Eve, 'This evening Captain Blackwood and I went to tea with the French colonel of artillery – and we really quite enjoyed it – they were most awfully nice'.[27] Even though it was expected to fight in unspeakable conditions, such as Poole had seen at Loos, the French army fed its officers well and there was even a daily ration of wine, albeit of low quality, for the *poilu* as the infantry soldier was known.

French hospitality was a brief release from the grim conditions of monotonous food, mud, winter cold and sudden death. Glad as Poole was that his two sons had used their pocket money to send him a Christmas present, he thought of his men, 'Tell the boys I have given the cigarettes to some men who work the telephones. They sit up in the OP all day and all night and are always being heavily shelled'.[28] Life was no easier for the brave pilots in the spotter aircraft:

I have lost another of my boys today I am afraid. He was attached to the Flying Corps and was brought down today. I haven't heard whether he was killed or is a prisoner. He was a very good boy – called Formelli – I'm very sorry about it. Things are so lively now – I

---

25 Frederick Poole to Alice Poole, 24 December 1915.
26 Frederick Poole to Alice Poole, 20 December 1915
27 Frederick Poole to Alice Poole, 24 December 1915.
28 Frederick Poole to Alice Poole, 2 January 1916.

don't know when they will settle down – that one daren't think of leave just at present.[29]

There was no Christmas Day truce in 1915. On New Year's Day his house had again narrowly escaped destruction: two shells exploded in the garden and part of one came through the dining-room window. No one under his command was mentioned in the New Year's honours list, even though Poole felt that Captain Blackwood and Major Kelly, a battery commander in III Heavy Brigade, particularly merited recognition. Although desperately tired with the burden of giving high-profile lectures added to the demands of his command, Poole would have to wait another month before his next home leave.

Not only British generals were paying attention to Poole's ideas. The French were also taking an interest and recognising his contribution:

> It has been a fairly quiet day, but I have been very busy. I have had no less than five different generals in here today to see me including the Army Commander!! So, I have been quite in the highest circles. It all takes up a good deal of time. There never was much probability of my being mentioned in these despatches, as it didn't include the last fighting – and of course I had been very well done before and it was time to give someone else a chance. I'm very sorry though that Kelly and Blackwood were left out. I went today to say goodbye to the French artillery general and we had a tender farewell.[30] I hear through my interpreter that he has sent on a recommendation that I and Captain Blackwood should be given the Legion of Honour because we have helped them so well!! I hope it will come off, but I don't expect it will. I've got to go off again next Friday to lecture. I'm afraid it will be a more or less weekly occurrence now for all this winter. It's rather a nuisance, as it wastes a day.

The audience for Poole's lectures was expanding: 'I've just been asked to

---

29 Frederick Poole to Alice Poole, 5 January 1916.
30 Poole was emboldened to ask Pellarin for a *poilu*'s helmet to add to the one he had already secured through his interpreter. Shortly afterwards Notcutt went on home leave and carried the two helmets back as a present to Poole's two children, who were delighted to receive such a novelty. Few British fathers were on such close terms with the French army.

Counter-Battery Pioneer

lecture to some Intelligence Officers from GHQ but I hope to be able to get out of it'.[31] The lecture was to be on counter-battery work, but before it took place Poole rammed home the point that Intelligence gathering had a wider value, 'We have learnt from spies where the officers' club is in a big town just near us, so tonight I am putting ten heavy guns on to the club to give them a round each – it will certainly put the fear of the Lord into them!!'[32] This gave the men huddled in observing posts numb with cold at their monotonous and dangerous task something to cheer about.

Franks asked Poole to speak at Second Army Headquarters. The one person who mattered above all the others in the audience not only thought well of Poole but made a point of passing the message back to him in fulsome terms: 'I've just got back from Second Army – the lecture was quite a success! About twenty generals there including Sir Herbert Plumer – Commander Second Army – who told General Franks "he was very much impressed"!'[33]

On 2 February 1916, anxious to sustain his excellent relations with the French, Poole paid a final call on Pellarin.[34] Poole went on to see Colonel Lefort, his host on Christmas Eve, who came up with an invitation for the following day. He and Captain Banting were entertained to a lunchtime feast of ten courses – it was French cooking at its absolute best, despite the exigencies of war. For Banting it was a well-deserved recognition of his Herculean efforts in building Poole's Intelligence operation, which was at the core of the relationship with the French. Two days later, on 5 February, Poole went on ten days of home leave.

Promotion suddenly became tantalisingly close: 'Headlam GOC RA GHQ came in in afternoon'.[35] John Headlam, who Poole had briefly encountered when taking 114 Heavy Battery into action for the first time in 1914, now held the substantive rank of major general, commanded the Royal Artillery of the British Expeditionary Force and reported directly to its Commander-in-Chief. Budworth, who had prepared Poole carefully the day before Headlam's visit, told him 'in *great confidence* this morning that

---

31 Frederick Poole to Alice Poole, 13 January 1916.
32 Frederick Poole to Alice Poole, 14 January 1916.
33 Frederick Poole to Alice Poole, 22 January 1916.
34 Pellarin died on leave shortly the following month, just sixty years old but exhausted by his long years of military service. As a deathbed request Pellarin asked the priest to bless his cannon.
35 Poole, Diary, 19 February 1916.

it is practically certain that I'm made brigadier general. My name has been sent on home from GHQ for approval – so unless it comes unstuck, we may hear in a week or so – but don't count on it until you hear as nothing is ever certain.'[36]

Even as Poole's path appeared to be smoothed, there was an abrupt turn of events. I Corps took over the section of the line occupied by IV Corps and IV Corps moved south to replace the French Tenth Army, previously on its right flank. Poole was transferred from IV Corps to I Corps and his command was reduced almost to its original size of III Heavy Brigade, consisting of 111, 112 and 113 batteries. Notcutt remained in IV Corps and was promoted to be adjutant to Lieutenant Colonel McCullough, who had formerly been under Poole's command. A hard-working Socialist who disapproved of everything Poole venerated, and a vegetarian to boot, replaced him. Suddenly Poole was no longer in demand as a lecturer, no longer sought out by generals seeking enlightenment and no longer in contact with the French Tenth Army, which had been sent southwards to help stem the German assault on Verdun.

Weeks of hints and rumours followed until finally, 'Orders out posting me to command IV Corps Heavy Artillery'.[37] This promotion was made sweeter by receiving the promised French decoration on 7 April. Frederick was kissed on both cheeks by General Joffre, who commanded the French forces on the Western Front, and was invested as an *officier* of the Legion of Honour. He advised Gertrude his sister that now he would be free from the attentions of French customs should he ever return after the war. In Cornwall, John Treffry, accustomed to British ways, commented, 'I would rather be bit by a pig than kissed by a man'.

Even sweeter was the explanation for the delay in his promotion:

General Mercer came in to see me today – was very pleasant and friendly – he told me that, when they had a conference of all the armies to arrange details two days ago, General Birch of Fourth Army came up with a strong application from Sir Henry Rawlinson that I should be sent to Fourth Army – of course Budworth worked that – but I knew Rawlinson in IV Corps. It's a great advertisement

---

36 Frederick Poole to Alice Poole, 20 February 1916.
37 Poole, Diary, 3 April 1916.

of course. General Mercer refused point blank and said he must keep his best man for his own army commander!!![38]

The assignment given to the Fourth Army, only just formed in January 1916 under the command of Lieutenant General Sir Henry Rawlinson, could not have been tougher: taking the lead in the forthcoming Battle of the Somme. Budworth urged Rawlinson to apply for Poole, which he duly did through his artillery commander, Brigadier General Noel Birch. Although Poole had handled his moment with Rawlinson well, his real relationship in IV Corps had been with Brigadier General Budworth (now referred to as his friend 'Buddy'). On this occasion, Major General Frederic Mercer, who commanded the Artillery of First Army, prevailed and retained Poole. The volunteers and conscripts who had made up for the numerical losses incurred in the unsuccessful battles of the previous year lacked fighting experience, which put a premium on proven officers.

German artillery also knew what it was about, remaining a constant danger. On 14 March it delivered a sharp reminder to Poole, 'We have had a bad time today – they have been taking us on badly – they shelled 111 – knocked out a gun killed one and wounded three. They also shelled 112 and fairly knocked one gun to glory. So, they have had a real joy day with us and we haven't done them much harm'.[39] No one had yet worked out how to break the deadlock on the Western Front.

---

[38] Frederick Poole to Alice Poole, 5 April 1916.
[39] Frederick Poole to Alice Poole, 14 March 1916.

7

Under Fire

Brigadier General Frederick Poole now exchanged the Gohelle Plain for the hills of Artois. For the first time since leaving Hill 63 eight months before he had a full panoramic view of his surroundings. The château de Bouvigny-Boyeffles outside the village of Bouvigny was his new headquarters: 'I have got down to the new place and taken over – all very nice – nice place – nice country – work full of interest. You will be glad to hear it is all right'. The château came with a large garden, stables and a garage with a car for his personal use, although the car struggled on the steep hills.

Poole was reunited with officers previously under his command in IV Corps, not least Lieutenant Colonel McCullough, who obligingly gave up his claims on Notcutt. With Blackwood and Banting coming from I Corps to be his brigade major and staff captain, and with Notcutt stepping into the role of Intelligence Officer, the old team was back together.

British interest in the area was low because of the preparations for the 'Big Push', the forthcoming Battle of the Somme, for which there was no role for IV Corps, as Haig disliked and distrusted its commander Sir Henry Wilson. Budworth had left IV Corps. Poole barely knew his successor, Geddes. Nothing had been done to clear the horrific and evil-smelling condition of the trenches on the 'Bloody Hill'. The batteries left behind by the departing French Tenth Army were equally shocking: 'McCulloch and I started off 9.30 and went all over the south part of the front, Carency, Ablain and Notre Dame, inspecting five French batteries: very bad show, guns prehistoric, detachments slack. We ended up by seeing the OPs on

General Sir Frederick Poole

Notre-Dame-de-Lorette; very good view but very misty'.[1] As Poole could no longer call on spotter planes, as in his previous counter-battery command, he could not know what the Germans might be up to on the reverse slope of Vimy Ridge.

The Germans were not slow in welcoming his arrival:

> We have had an exciting afternoon here. About teatime the Hun took it into his head to shell this village and, as our house is the big one, we got most attention. They got one shell bang into the front door which blew a great hole in the wall and made an awful mess. Another one blew out the room where my French telephonists are – knocked one man endways but didn't hurt him – another into the garage just missed the precious car. They kept it up for about three quarters of an hour but did no real harm – neither men nor horses were hurt. We were all annoyed and hit back as hard as we could, but we had our telephone lines broken and were out of communication for some time.[2]

The shelling had begun after Poole and Lacolle, his interpreter, had climbed up the hill above the château to study the country only to beat a hasty retreat twenty minutes later. The Germans had still not finished when Poole was thinking of going to bed. At 9 p.m. one shell hit the château and another two destroyed the garage. Poole's reaction convinced the French that he meant business:

> Yesterday we did a good retaliation on him including putting forty-six guns of varying sorts on one of his headquarters – letting drive twice during the day – once at lunch time!!! We haven't had anything back since, so I hope he has learnt to let us alone. When I arranged this shoot with the French colonel he was delighted. He laughed till he cried and kept saying 'Mon Dieu, Mon Dieu'. He thought it was the finest retaliation he had ever heard of!! A beastly day today – rain and blow – much worse weather than this time last year.[3]

---

1 Poole, Diary, 6 April 1916.
2 Frederick Poole to Alice Poole, 15 April 1916.
3 Frederick Poole to Alice Poole, 17 April 1916.

The Germans guns were silent for the rest of the day and the following day, when the air cleared, providing good visibility. Poole used the opportunity to observe south westwards across the valley. The trenches at the foot of Vimy Ridge were in the same terrible condition as on the 'Bloody Hill'; they were also exposed to the direct fire from German batteries, which had the advantage of being concealed on the reverse side of the ridge. The General's worst fears about the vulnerability of his right flank were confirmed. Setting up an entente with XVII Corps, which occupied that section of the front, became an imperative.

The result was a meeting at IV Corps headquarters in the Château de Ranchicourt with XVII Corps, which was attended not only by Poole's opposite number, Brigadier General Barron commanding the Heavy Artillery, but also by its overall artillery commander. Poole, who had never visited the area on his right flank, went into the meeting well primed by the French colonel whose confidence he had just won. 'We fixed up a number of points for mutual cooperation and support.'[4]

Poole's Corps Commander, Sir Henry Wilson, took notice. He invited Poole and Captain Blackwood for dinner two days later at the Château de Ranchicourt. Wilson had style. He employed a French chef, was well known for liberal hospitality, was well connected with powerful and influential people, and had a Rolls Royce at his disposal. This was followed by Major General Headlam coming to see Poole in action the following morning:

> This is Good Friday and we have had quite a day of penance! They had a balloon up this morning and had a real good go at our house. They have had six shells bang into it and knocked out half of the front out of it. They haven't hit my room yet, but they have done in the room on the other side of the passage, so if they get another shell through the same hole it ought to get into my little bed! I'm afraid we shall have to shift. It's a nuisance but it means all the wires get cut every time they shell and one can't afford to be out of communication.[5]

Poole's anxiety eased a little when the relationship established with the

---

4 Poole, Diary, 18 April 1916.
5 Frederick Poole to Alice Poole, 21 April 1916.

XVIIth Corps Artillery was put to the test, 'Heavy firing at 7 p.m. on Souchez and XVIIth Corps – scrapping for some time. We opened our new "artillery defence scheme" successfully'.[6]

Even so, when Poole went on home leave from 5 to 15 May, he was afraid that he had not done enough. Notcutt found little opportunity to relax when they travelled back together to London. In Cornwall Alice bore the brunt of her husband's worries. Immediately on his return to the front he wrote to her.

> Darling, you have been a great help to me all the time. I'm so glad sweetheart you are not one of the 'little people' who always want everybody to be sacrificed but their own particular pets. You have been very brave, darling, and if it ever does happen that you are asked to make the supreme sacrifice you will always be proud and not sorry that you can send out your man to help the country – and it will always be a help to me, darling, to know that you will stand steadfast even if I go into the valley of death. God bless you all, darling, your own Fred.[7]

Poole got the reassurance that he was up to the job just two days later:

> I have been very busy all day. General Mercer pulled me out this morning to go and show him a lot of my batteries, so I have been escorting him round. He was very pleased with everything and I am now in high favour!! Funnily enough he talked to me about stopping on after the war. I told him I should like to and he said he thought it could probably be arranged all right, so now I shall be able to tackle him about it and he will back it up when the time comes.[8]

Mercer returned on the morning of 19 May and inspected Poole's French batteries and his new OP constructed on the 'Bloody Hill' with the benefit of Notcutt's expertise.

---

6   Poole, Diary, 26 April 1916.
7   Frederick Poole to Alice Poole, 15 May 1916. This letter has survived in General Poole's papers. A paragraph was omitted when Alice Poole later copied out his wartime letters into exercise books. It is another glimpse of Poole giving vent to emotions that were kept well-hidden and, being such an admission of how much he depended on her, it was too precious for Alice to share.
8   Frederick Poole to Alice Poole, 17 May 1916.

Poole felt in control until he learned that IV Corps was extending its line and taking over from XVII Corps the vulnerable segment at the foot of Vimy Ridge. That afternoon he went to the Château de Ranchicourt to see Geddes. He then had to confer with Lieutenant Colonel McCullough, which involved spending the morning of 20 May viewing the country from an observing post and visiting two batteries. The afternoon was devoted to a briefing from his opposite number in XVII Corps. 'Barron came over in afternoon to tell me about our new area.'[9] The following morning Poole inspected the extension of his right flank. Finally, he briefed Brigadier General Cockburn, who commanded the Heavy Artillery in I Corps and was therefore his equivalent on his left flank. The briefing took place from the vantage point of the 'Bloody Hill' in Poole's OP.

It was time well spent as the Germans attacked ferociously at 3.00 p.m. that very afternoon, Sunday 21 May:

Eighty German batteries were concentrated on a front of only 1800 yards, with an average of 200 shells per battery! Front and support lines were almost obliterated, and communications cut, under a four hours' bombardment. The Germans, it is estimated, rained no less than 70,000 shells on the area. The 47th divisional artillery had four guns knocked out. Our guns replied until, at times, dumps were practically exhausted.[10]

---

9 Poole, Diary, 20 May 1916.
10 Sir Ernest Swinton, *The Battlefields of 1914-18: Then and Now*, i (London, 1937), p. 675. Sir James Edmonds enlivened his *History of the Great War* by including the German perspective of their attack. Its code name was 'Schleswig Holstein', and it was the concept of General Freiherr von Freytag-Loringhoven, Deputy Chief of the German General Staff, who was briefly allowed the experience of an operational command whilst the actual commanders were on leave to recover their health. Freytag-Loringhoven came from an old established family in East Prussia that traced its descent from the Teutonic knights; the family tradition of soldiering was continued under Hitler and after the Second World War.

Freytag-Loringhoven used his air power to prevent enemy planes observing on the reverse slope of Vimy Ridge the huge build-up of munitions, supplies and troops needed to strike his powerful blow. He forbade any reference to his plans being made on the telephone in case calls were being intercepted. His timing was excellent, taking advantage of IV Corps extending its line before it had time to settle in. Complete surprise was achieved. The devastating firepower unleashed was used to capture the shaft entrances to mines being dug in the foothills of Vimy Ridge, which threatened the German position. By not pushing the attack further, the usual stalemate of rising casualties without any material territorial game was avoided.

General Sir Frederick Poole

When the Germans struck Poole was as surprised as everyone else and it was only towards noon on the second day of battle that he could snatch a few moments to give Alice her first situation report,

> I was hard at it all day yesterday and couldn't write. In the afternoon I had taken General Cockburn up to our OP to see the country when the Huns opened a heavy bombardment and after three hours attacked. We have been shooting ever since (about twenty hours); we have all been up all night here and are pretty done. I got my eyes badly gassed again yesterday – they were putting over a lot of gas shell and I had to walk about a mile through it – all our eyes were streaming at the end. It doesn't seem to have done me any harm though: my eye is no worse today and almost clear, so I think it's all right. My batteries did very well yesterday. They kept on firing the whole time although the Huns were strafing them badly. We have had a certain number of causalities but only about three killed. I'm very pleased with them all. I'm dog tired and can't write more.[11]

On the third day of the fighting Poole was still unbowed but on the point of exhaustion:

> All well – no time to write. We have been fighting very hard for three days as far as shooting goes. Our guns have never stopped day or night since 3 o'clock on Sunday morning.[12] We are all dead with want of sleep. The Huns are pitching it in hard. We have a go at them tonight to get back a bit of trench we have lost. I hope it will go off well. My fellows have done really well – they have been heavily shelled and stick it like men.[13]

On the fourth day Poole still was still hoping for a renewed infantry counter-attack to regain the lost trenches, 'Kept on barrage all day till 6 p.m. when slowed off. Pity. Many more batteries coming up and we are to have a

---

11 Frederick Poole to Alice Poole, 22 May 1916.
12 The battle started at 3 p.m. not 3 a.m.
13 Frederick Poole to Alice Poole, 23 May 1916.

big show I fancy'.[14] It was not to be. Although reinforcements were arriving, preparations for the coming Battle of the Somme took precedence.

Franks, who had lent some of his batteries from Second Army to reinforce Poole's command, came with Mercer to assess the situation. Franks was 'looking very pleased with himself',[15] understandably relieved that a near disaster had not happened on his watch and pleased with Poole's efforts. Poole, however, was somewhat dismissive of his immediate superior, 'A lot of palaver in morning. Geddes came very late and so kept me in and wasted my time'.[16]

Having stared into the abyss and yet emerged with honour, Poole's next letter paid a handsome tribute to Blackwood, 'I don't think he had more than three hours' consecutive sleep any night all this week. He has generally worked eighteen hours a day'.[17] It was very much a two-way relationship. Poole knew of Blackwood's family circumstances. Mrs Blackwood was delicate, and their finances were tight, which meant living in lodgings and having nothing to fall back upon when she had to go into hospital for an operation. They had a young daughter for whose welfare the General was concerned. He asked Alice to give the girl one of their children's puppies and to offer to have her to stay during the operation.

Although the most junior of the brigadier generals, Poole was singled out as the one who had excelled during the ordeal of 'Schleswig Holstein': 'Geddes came in in afternoon and told me I was to act as GOC RA of the corps while he is on leave!'[18] Poole now saw a little more of Sir Henry Wilson, 'Went with Corps Commander to an army conference at Headquarters where we were given orders re future movements. Work in office in afternoon arranging details. Dined with Corps Commander at night. Showery – cold'.[19] This time Wilson was putting on a brave face rather than being the confident dispenser of lavish hospitality in magnificent surroundings removed from the fighting: he was in disfavour and not far short of disgrace. Their evening together, however, was a great success.

Wilson and Poole were both affable, genial and optimistic in outlook.

---

14 Poole, Diary, 24 May 1916.
15 Poole, Diary, 26 May 1916.
16 Poole, Diary, 27 May 1916.
17 Frederick Poole to Alice Poole, 28 May 1916. He also spared a rare thought for his aged mother: 'Have you written to Mrs P., for her birthday (31st)? She must be about eighty-six – say I'm busy'.
18 Poole, Diary, 10 June 1916.
19 Frederick Poole to Alice Poole, 14 June 1916.

They were also both French speakers and believed in the importance of collaborating closely with the French. In addition, both were fascinated by politics and admirers of Lloyd George as the one British politician wholeheartedly committed to fully mobilising the Home Front in support of the war effort. They agreed that Lloyd George should replace Asquith as Prime Minister.

Poole's time with Wilson was short-lived. Mercer telephoned with the extraordinary news that, 'It was practically settled I was to get a corps'.[20] The British Expeditionary Force had expanded to some twenty corps, each approximately seventy thousand strong, and Poole was in line to command the artillery of one of them. It was a role second only to a major general's appointment, which was held in France only by those with responsibility for the artillery of an entire army, of which there were now five, and by the artillery adviser to the Commander-in-Chief.

Even before the official announcement on the following day Poole could not resist telling Alice: his elation found an outlet in six exclamation marks at the end of the sentence proclaiming his further promotion. 'It puts me out of the ruck of brigadier generals into the few who are considered for promotion to major general – not that I need think of that yet awhile.'[21]

---

20 Poole, Diary, 15 June 1916.
21 Frederick Poole to Alice Poole, 16 June 1916.

8

Trench Mortars

Poole was posted to I Corps, returning to the familiar territory previously held by IV Corps before it had moved south to take over from the French Tenth Army. IV Corps was now on his right flank and XI Corps on his left. He was still in First Army and so continued to report to Major General Mercer, who commanded its artillery. The corps headquarters was at La Buissière, twenty kilometres west of the Château Mercier in Mazingarbe, which had been his headquarters when commanding the Counter-Battery Group of IV Corps and reporting to Brigadier General Budworth. It was a forty-minute drive by car to the Front Line. The logic of putting senior officers well back from the Front Line was that too many had been killed in the Battle of Loos through direct involvement in the fighting.

Poole lunched with his new Corps Commander, Lieutenant General Sir Charles Kavanagh, on 17 June and the following day moved into corps headquarters. He left behind his trusted colleagues Blackwood, Banting and, for the time being, Notcutt. He had never met his staff officer, Lieutenant Colonel Robert Finlayson, before. Brigadier General Cockburn was suddenly his subordinate commanding the Heavy Artillery of I Corps, whereas previously he had been of equal standing. All that paled into insignificance compared with the astonishing fact that Poole was now running the entire artillery of the corps in which he had served only briefly a few months previously when commanding little more than III Heavy Brigade. He felt, 'It is awkward going over so many people's heads, but I hope to smooth it down'.[1]

---

1   Frederick Poole to Alice Poole, 18 June 1916.

Poole's moment of doubt was fleeting. His hopes of a successful army career after the war strengthened: 'I think I shall try to be brought back to the army now. If they think well enough of me to promote me, they ought to bring me back and I suppose as long as I don't come "unstuck" I ought to have a reasonable career in front of me to make it worth our while. Anyhow they can but say NO. I like this show and am quite pleased with everything.'[2]

Life at corps headquarters was luxurious. The mail arrived in time for breakfast; lunch and tea were available and there were messing arrangements for dinner. Such abundance made him worry about putting on weight and Alice was instructed to terminate the supplies of cakes and other comforts that she and the kitchen at Fowey Hall had been sending, as well as the parcels with luxuries from the food department at Harrods.

Although Poole was out from dawn to dusk inspecting his command at the Front, his sense of reality began to fade before the optimism that permeated corps headquarters. After initial success, the German assault on the French stronghold of Verdun was degenerating into a costly failure; and on the Eastern Front the Austrians were in full retreat before the Russian offensive led by General Brusilov. Poole made a rash prediction, 'I feel more confident than ever that the war will be over this year. I hope before December we shall be home again. With the heavy losses I don't think they can go on long – if only the Russians can make a decent push.'[3] Such optimism struck the right note, 'I went out with the Corps Commander this morning – he wanted me to take him round some of the batteries. He was very pleased with what he saw.'[4]

The British Expeditionary Force, under new leadership after French was replaced by Haig, vastly expanded in numbers, with more powerful guns, and a huge supply of ammunition, was poised to deliver a decisive blow. Haig had concluded after the failed offensives of 1915 that the remedy lay in increasing the weight of the preliminary bombardment even further and relentlessly pushing home the attack until the enemy was exhausted. He overruled Rawlinson's concept for the Battle of the Somme of fighting a series of 'bite and hold attacks' designed to capture specific objectives, having subdued the enemy by an overwhelming concentration of firepower.

An enormous artillery barrage was now in progress, far eclipsing the

---

2 Frederick Poole to Alice Poole, 19 June 1916.
3 Frederick Poole to Alice Poole, 26 June 1916.
4 Frederick Poole to Alice Poole, 28 June 1916.

four days before the Battle of Loos. Poole was a believer, commenting on the fifth day of the artillery bombardment that 'Everyone seems to be full of confidence out here. I've never known such general optimism – a very good sign'.[5] When Captain Blackwood telephoned with the news of a successful raid using gas on the 'Huns', he was delighted that it had 'accounted for quite a lot of the swine'.[6] The gas alone had killed about six hundred of the enemy. Hatred of the enemy stood in the way of a realistic assessment of what the preliminary bombardment before the Battle of the Somme could achieve. Poole had forgotten that the Germans had failed to silence his own guns despite an immense concentration of fire power in operation Schleswig Holstein.

The Battle of the Somme began on 1 July 1916. Reports began to come through of terrific fighting. There was little action in Poole's area, but his mind was turning to new ideas, 'Heath came to see me in office in afternoon'.[7] G.M. Heath was the Chief Engineer of I Corps and his visit may have led to Poole visiting the Trench Mortar School of I Corps at St-Venant north of Béthune. Trench mortars were designed to direct a precise fire capable of destroying the barbed wire entanglements protecting trenches. Being light in weight, they could be relocated with ease and so were less vulnerable to enemy fire. Having failed with heavy artillery, supplemented by field guns, to achieve satisfactory wire-cutting in the preliminary bombardment at the Battle of Loos, Poole warmed to the trench mortar, 'most interesting and great possibilities in it'.[8] He undoubtedly discussed the subject with Finlayson and with Notcutt, who had joined him as his ADC on 10 July. The increased use of trench mortars was one of the many suggestions aimed at ending the stalemate on the Western Front. They had their limitations, however, as was shown after their large-scale use on the Somme.

At this point ill luck intervened:

You would be surprised to get the postcard yesterday and hear I was in hospital. On Friday evening I was perfectly fit when suddenly I collapsed with a most awful pain in my left groin – pretty bad. I got a doctor who put in a dose of morphia and packed me off to

---

5   Frederick Poole to Alice Poole, 28 June 1916.
6   Frederick Poole to Alice Poole, 28 June 1916.
7   Poole, Diary, 5 July 1916.
8   Poole, Diary, 8 July 1916.

hospital. After another dose of morphia there I dozed off to sleep and have been right more or less ever since. They had two lots of doctors vetting me yesterday with a view to operating on me, but they have decided to rest me for a day or two and let me go. It is apparently 'gravel'. It's all right now. I'm tired, sleeping most of the day and night, but I feel fitter today. I was terrified they were going to send me home, but they decided it was only a temporary thing and that a day or two's rest would put me right. Quite a little flutter in the dovecote all together. It would have been cruel luck to have to go sick just now. Well I'm pretty well right now, darling, and hope to come out in a day or two, so you needn't be anxious about me. It's really rather nice having a rest cure – I didn't realise how tired I was!

The Corps Commander was most awfully kind. He told me he was 'perfectly delighted' that I was not to be sent home, so it looks as if he was satisfied with me. Goodbye sweetheart – I shall be OK in a day or two now. Very comfortable hospital. It's great to be a general in hospital – they all bustle and look after one well.[9]

Once he had settled back into his command, Poole went to see at first hand the fighting on the Somme. 'Started off early to see the battle. Went first to Montigny Headquarters of III Corps and saw all Uniacke's orders for Third Corps artillery. Then motored to Fricourt, Mametz, Montauban and saw the whole panorama. There was a good deal of shooting to the south and also round Pozières. Very interesting day. Things fairly quiet here.'[10]

The sequel of that 'very interesting day' was returning to the Trench Mortar School and seeing the new weapon put through its paces. Poole became a convert and started to spread the word, 'Went over to St-Venant in afternoon to see wire-cutting by trench mortars very successfully carried out. Divisional conference in evening – rubbed in trench mortar scheme.'[11]

Military politics suddenly swung in Poole's favour, but only for a few hours. Haig had replaced Major General John Headlam with Brigadier General Noel Birch as the artillery commander of the British Expeditionary Force. That resulted in Budworth succeeding Birch as the GOC Royal

---

9 Frederick Poole to Alice Poole, 16 July 1916.
10 Poole, Diary, 22 July 1916.
11 Poole, Diary, 24 July 1916.

Artillery of Fourth Army. With the Battle of the Somme going badly, Budworth tried yet again to get Poole into Fourth Army but failed.

> Started off in morning to go round new sector of line. About 1 p.m. got telephone message – wanted urgently – came back and was ordered down to Fourth Army at once. Percy and I started off 3.30 – reported at Fourth Army to Budworth. The show had, however, come unstuck. I was to have gone to III Corps, but Tancred had been posted to it. Returned home about 10.30 p.m.
>
> Things not so good down there. Hun is reinforcing strongly – guns and men. I don't think we shall advance much further.[12]

Poole checked what Franks was up to: 'Very fine day – not quite so hot. Motored up to Cassel in morning and lunched with Franks. I wanted to see him to see if they had any new ideas in Second Army. I didn't find they are ahead of us in any way – in many ways behind.'[13] Perhaps Franks did not share Poole's perspective on trench mortars.

On 7 August, First Army came under the temporary command of Lieutenant General Richard Haking, following the departure of Sir Charles Monro to take up a new appointment in India. Poole returned to advocating trench mortars after Haking's disaster at Fromelles on 19 July, when the diversionary attack made by XI Corps with two divisions, to relieve enemy pressure in the Battle of the Somme, had been repulsed with heavy losses. Poole saw Haking at a conference at First Army Headquarters on 15 August and on 18 August he and his Corps Commander, Lieutenant General Kavanagh, dined with Haking. They dined again with Haking on 21 August, just three days later, with Mercer also in attendance, to discuss trench mortars. That morning Poole and Kavanagh had inspected the trench mortar section of the Eighth Division and that afternoon Mercer had visited Poole to talk about the subject. Poole's diary tells us, 'Went with Corps Commander round Sixteenth Division trench mortars in morning. Very good show in every way – long walk.'[14] The following day Poole went on home leave.

Although Poole pressed ahead with his trench mortar crusade after

---

12 Poole, Diary, 25 July 1916.
13 Poole, Diary, 4 August 1916.
14 Poole, Diary, 22 August 1916.

returning from leave on 2 September, leadership changes obstructed him. Kavanagh left on 4 September to take up a new position and there was a hiatus before the eventual appointment of Lieutenant General Sir Hubert Gough to command I Corps. Haking's position as commander of First Army was not confirmed, Lieutenant General Sir Henry Horne being made its GOC on 29 September. Then Poole's first meeting with Horne, on 11 October, did not go well, 'In afternoon Army Commander came over. He perhaps may take over our house for himself! IV Corps ordered south – a great pity it's not I Corps. Geddes came over in afternoon to say goodbye'. Their next meeting went even less well, 'South-west gale, rained hard in afternoon. Things pretty quiet. Army commander came to tea. I lectured him on my ideas of trench mortar organisation, but I don't think he agrees!'[15]

On 21 November 1916, after the end of battle of the Somme, Poole again went on home leave. It was the last he saw of the Western Front. His career took a different direction after he arrived in London on the sleeper train from Cornwall on 1 December, 'Stopped from returning by wire ordering me to report to Sir Henry Wilson for special mission'. On 3 December 1916, he reported to Wilson and learned he was to be sent to Russia, accompanied by Notcutt.

---

15 Poole, Diary, 28 October 1916. It was a disappointment, but it did not stop Poole deciding to send in his application to remain in the army after the war had ended. After a chat with Freddie Mercer on the evening of 30 October, he sent in the application the following day.

9

Proceed at Once to Russia

In December 1916, David Lloyd George forced the issue of who would be best to deliver victory by resigning from the government when his demand for vesting the direction of the war effort in a small council under his chairmanship was turned down. Herbert Asquith, the leader of the Liberal Party, reacted by offering his own resignation as Prime Minister, believing that no one else would be able to form a government and that he could then return to office with his authority renewed. King George V invited Andrew Bonar Law, the leader of the Conservative Party, to form an administration. When the latter refused, Lloyd George stepped in and, to Asquith's surprise, succeeded in forming a coalition and so became Prime Minister.

Lloyd George wanted a clear picture of Russia's reliability as an ally. If Russia was defeated, this would allow Germany to concentrate its strength on the Western Front and might let it achieve the outright victory that it had almost won in 1914. He insisted on an Inter-Allied Conference at Petrograd, as St Petersburg, the Russian capital, had been renamed in August 1914 in response to anti-German feeling. He asked Lieutenant General Sir Henry Wilson to lead the British military delegation to the conference.

In his previous capacity as Secretary of State for War, Lloyd George had already approached Wilson about going to Russia when he was on home leave from the Western Front in November. Lloyd George was wary of Wilson's love of intrigue and political infighting but recognised him as a useful ally. Wilson was persuasive and articulate, comfortable in dealing with Britain's allies and with politicians, and not associated with the costly and indecisive Battle of the Somme. Lloyd George felt that both Robertson and Haig, who had been respectively Chief of the Imperial General Staff and Commander-in-Chief of the British Expeditionary Force since December 1915, needed to be replaced because, under their watch, casualties had been high without any corresponding military gain. He did not believe that they had the imagination and methods to deliver victory.

Wilson decided that there was a rôle for Frederick Poole in Russia and set up a meeting at the War Office, 'I went to see Sir William Robertson and Prime Minister, bringing Poole. Lloyd George wants Poole to go out now and commence collecting information and I think this is quite wise'.[1] Poole was too discreet to refer to the presence of Lloyd George at the meeting but caught the urgent tone that Wilson had contrived to inject at it: 'Sent for to War Office and instructed by Sir William Robertson to proceed at once to Petrograd to make investigations re the employment of artillery, so as to enable Henry Wilson to have some facts at his disposal on arrival of the mission'.[2] These were Poole's instructions:

> Brigadier-General F.C. Poole DSO. You are nominated to attend a Conference of the Allies which is to be held shortly in Russia. Your special duties will be to assist Lieutenant General Sir H.H. Wilson, who will be the senior British Military Representative, in regard to questions affecting the employment of artillery.
>
> We are anxious to render all possible assistance to Russia respecting the provision of artillery, but at the same time there is a limit to our output and to our requirements, and His Majesty's Government are anxious to be assured that any guns we may give will be promptly and efficiently used. You should therefore ascertain carefully whilst in Russia, and as far as possible on the spot, the time required to equip and efficiently man, as batteries, such guns as we may send and to place them on the front; what nature of guns Russia can best make use of; the extent to which road and railway transport is available to keep the guns supplied with ammunition; and in particular whether the state of communications is such as to enable the heavier nature of guns to be used.
>
> You should also enquire whether and when Russia is likely to

---

[1] Sir Henry Wilson, Imperial War Museum, Diary, 16 December 1916.
[2] Poole, Diary, 16 December 1916.

be fully equipped with aeroplanes to enable the fire of artillery to be properly directed.

We have already conditionally promised to supply Russia with a certain number of guns by the end of March next, and we hope that it may be possible to supply more, but you will understand that you have no authority in regard to such supply as this question will be discussed at the conference. Your chief mission is, in fact, to ascertain to what extent Russia will be in a position efficiently to use such guns as it may be possible to give her.

In order that Lieutenant General Sir H. Wilson may, as far as possible, be informed on the above points before the conference assembles, you will at once proceed to Russia and report to the British Military Attaché at Petrograd, who will acquaint you with the arrangements made to enable you to obtain the information in question. You will join Sir H. Wilson on his arrival at Petrograd. It will probably be necessary for you to remain in Russia for some time after the conclusion of the conference so as to complete your enquiries and, in this case, you should keep me informed of the result of your further enquiries.

A copy of these instructions has been sent to Lieutenant General Sir H.H. Wilson.

W. Robertson, General, Chief of the Imperial General Staff
16 December 1916.[3]

The day after the meeting at the War Office, Poole had an interview with Wilson at his home at 36 Eaton Square, in one of the smartest quarters of London. Poole was concerned that Sir William Robertson's instructions made no reference to trench mortars, but Wilson's mind was on ensuring that the military contingent of the British mission to the Inter-Allied Conference would not be outfaced in Imperial Russia. Wilson noted in his diary, 'Poole in afternoon to discuss guns, trench mortars, aeroplanes, etc. He starts for Russia tomorrow if he can with Notcutt and two servants via Bergen'.[4]

---

3   In the author's possession.
4   Sir Henry Wilson, Diary, 17 December 1916. Cox, who was in service at the London home of Poole's father-in-law, was one of the servants. Charles Hanson was anxious to be helpful and no doubt comfortable at shedding a servant, as he was about to become Lord Mayor of London in 1917-18 and move to the Mansion House.

General Sir Frederick Poole

Poole was taking a risk with his career. Being posted to Russia was often a euphemism for getting rid of people who no longer fitted in at home. It had been the poisoned chalice offered to Lord Kitchener, when he was replaced as Secretary of State for War by Lloyd George in 1916, and the solution Lloyd George had tried in his first attempt to get rid of Robertson. When Lieutenant General Sir Charles Barter, a distinguished fighting soldier, fell from favour in the British Expeditionary Force, he was sent as liaison officer to Stavka, the Russian General Headquarters.

Poole's fluency in French was important because it was both the international language of diplomacy and that of people of rank and status in Russia. Even Sir George Buchanan, the British Ambassador to Russia, had no knowledge of Russian. Relatively few people spoke English in Russia, although the Czar and indeed the Grand Duke Serge, to whom Poole would be attached, were fluent in it. The Czar had happy memories from two visits to England and loved reading English fiction, especially simple stories of action and adventure.

The quickest route to Russia in wartime, when Germany controlled the Baltic Sea, was by boat from Newcastle to Bergen and by railway through Norway and Sweden via Oslo (then called Christiana) and Stockholm to Haparanda, within the Arctic Circle at the head of the Gulf of Bothnia. There was a short gap from Haparanda to the beginning of the Russian railway system, with its wider gauge, at Tornea in Finland, then part of Russia.

The General's party left King's Cross on Monday 18 December 1916. On disembarking at Bergen, they were met by a member of the British Legation in Oslo. Being British officers fresh from the Front Line with servants in attendance, Poole's party was conspicuous even while wearing unfamiliar civilian clothes, as required when travelling through neutral countries. Travelling northwards to Haparanda, the General noted, 'Two Americans? Swedes very curious about us – first pumped the servants who said we were commercial gents travelling in hats! Then they tried us'.[5] Unwisely the inquisitive questioners followed Poole's party into Russia, 'Our two friends of yesterday were found to be Hun spies and were brought along under escort – probably to be shot'.[6]

Poole and Notcutt changed back into uniform as soon as they reached Finland and boarded the overnight train for Petrograd. The General's words

---

5   Poole, Diary, 23 December 1916.
6   Poole, Diary, 24 December 1916.

on the picture postcard of Tornea Station he sent to Alice have a certain irony given events soon to come, '24 December 1916. On active service. Safe in Russia! Just off by train to Petrograd – all is well and we are all fit. Merry Xmas to you all'.[7] Cox produced a home-made cake and plum pudding, which the party ate in the train on Christmas Day, but there was nothing stronger to drink than Russian tea. After their train arrived at Finland Station in Petrograd at 11.30 p.m. on 25 December, the General was given a sumptuous room with its own bathroom at the Hôtel d'Europe.

As instructed, on arrival Poole went straight to see Colonel Alfred Knox. Knox had been the Military Attaché at the British Embassy since 1911 and was well informed about the real state of the Russian army, helped by his fluency in Russian.[8] The General went on to the British Embassy, which occupied part of the Saltykov Palace on the bank of the River Neva by the Troitsky Bridge. It had a fine view across the river and a balcony overlooking the Champs de Mars. There Poole spent half an hour with the ambassador, Sir George Buchanan, who told him that 'If I have any trouble to come straight to him and that he will go straight to the Emperor'.[9] Little did the General realise that Buchanan was at this time nerving himself to confront the Czar with the unpalatable message that, unless he accepted limitations on his autocratic power and agreed to reforms, revolution would be inevitable.

After leaving the British Embassy, Poole had a meeting and dinner with Major General Sir John Hanbury-Williams, who had served as chief of the British Military Mission in Russia from the beginning of the war. Like Buchanan, he did not speak Russian and did not have Knox's detailed perspective of the Russian army, but he was comfortable in French and on close terms with the Czar and everyone who mattered at Stavka. The Czar liked him because he avoided the vexed question of political reform. Hanbury-Williams was a tall man with a military bearing which earned him further credit with the Czar, who was apt to comment unfavourably on the fat and the unfit.

Hanbury-Williams had come up from Stavka, where he was normally based, and was staying at the Astoria Hotel. Poole learned that the Grand Duke Serge, described as the Inspector General of the Russian Artillery, was most anxious to see him at once. He concluded that there would be a useful

---

7 Postcard, 24 December 1916.
8 Poole, Diary, 26 December 1916. Knox earned Poole's encomium 'Good man'.
9 Poole, Diary, 26 December 1916.

role for him, 'It seems that there is a great want of a practical gunner to tell these people what is really wanted. Much seems to have been neglected'.[10] Given that every effort had been made so far to smooth his passage from London, it did not strike Poole as odd that Hanbury-Williams would not be accompanying him on his maiden visit to Stavka.

Armed with the credentials supplied by Hanbury-Williams, and wearing the overcoat of a Russian major general complete with sword, Poole departed for Stavka by the overnight train on 27 December. He was glad to be leaving. The Hôtel d'Europe, where he stayed for two nights, and the Astoria Hotel, where he had bought dinner for Hanbury-Williams, were the two best hotels in an expensive city. Even though the accommodation in both hotels had been reserved and was subsidised for those on official business, the demand for tips for every type of service was insatiable and the cost of entertainment and extras high. Poole was, nevertheless, delighted with his reception at Stavka:

> We got down here all right and were met on arrival and been very well done. We live in a big mess with all the GHQ staff – much ceremony, hand shaking and clicking of heels and very good feeling. They don't seem so hard worked as our staff officers! Last night I had a talk to General Gurko, who is Chief of the Staff (practically Commander-in-Chief. The Emperor is nominally). He is clever and talks English well. He is having us sent off south (probably Romania) as soon as possible probably tomorrow, so that we can see their guns in action.
>
> At 12.15 we were asked to lunch with the Emperor. We all stood round the big salon. Much hand shaking and ceremony again. Then the Emperor and Czarevitch came round and shook hands and talked. He was very kind, talked about five minutes to me in good English and about ten minutes again after lunch – very keen to know about guns and very interested. The Czarevitch is a dear little boy – dressed as a soldier – delicate but very merry. I liked him very much. A very good lunch and quite cheery. The Grand Duke Serge was there too and very kind. We had a long talk again. I also had a talk to the Romanian Minister, Count Diamandi, who is most anxious I should go down there (I suppose he thinks they will get some guns!). He is

---
10   Poole, Diary, 26 December 1916.

going to wire to have everything done for us. If we do, I suppose we shall mix in 'Royal Circles' again!! I like this show very much. It's all most interesting. I quite give up hope of hearing from you, darling – it seems one never gets letters in these parts! I shall probably not hear until I get back to Petrograd in about three weeks or so![11]

Poole could not believe that the Czar was being so charming to him, both a stranger and far inferior in rank. He saw the decency in Nicholas II and liked the warmth between the Czar and his son, a boy given to playing pranks on visiting dignitaries but, on this occasion, on his best behaviour. He did not sense the weakness and indecision beneath the surface that made the Czar so ill-equipped to wield such power and the stubbornness that made him refuse to listen to advice that might have averted revolution.

The General's visit, however, made little impression on Nicholas II, who commented laconically in his diary, 'We had many foreigners to lunch today: two Romanians, three Englishmen and one Frenchman'.[12] Remembering his own experiences in Russia, Sir Charles Callwell wrote, 'The Emperor had the gift of putting one completely at one's ease on such occasions, and, being an admirable conversationalist, interested in everything and ready to talk on any subject, it was a pleasure to be with him'.[13]

Little did Poole guess the real agenda at Stavka. A high-level conference was going to take place on 30 and 31 December 1916 to discuss 'forthcoming offensive operations'.[14] The only reason that Grand Duke Serge had been anxious to see Poole before this conference was to discover whether he brought any specific offer of military help. Vassily Gurko, in turn, was anxious to send Poole away from Stavka to the front immediately to avoid any distraction to the conference proceedings. He chose to send him to the south-west sector because it was where the Russians had been successful against the Austrians, in contrast to the string of defeats and retreats inflicted on them by the Germans elsewhere.

Poole left Stavka on 30 December in a private carriage attached to the train for Kiev, where he spent a day sightseeing. At the headquarters of the south-western armies in Kamenetz-Podolsk, in western Ukraine,

---

11 Frederick Poole to Alice Poole, 29 December 1916.
12 Vulliamy, *Letters of the Tsar to the Tsaritsa, 1914-17* (London, 1929).
13 Major General Sir Charles Callwell, *Experiences of a Dug-Out, 1914-1918* (London, 1920).
14 General Gurko, *War and Revolution in Russia, 1914-1917* (New York, 1919).

General Sir Frederick Poole

Poole discovered that General Brusilov, who had commanded a successful offensive against the Austrians in 1916, and his chief of artillery were away. In fact, they were attending the very conference whose existence his Russian hosts had concealed.

A Russian prince accompanied Poole from Kamenetz-Podolsk to the front line. George Chirinsky was a young subaltern in his mid twenties. An officer in one of the smartest regiments, Chirinsky came from an old-established, influential and wealthy family; he even spoke a little English. Chrinsky was impressed by Poole, who was good company, knew his subject well and was hungry for innovative ideas. He was surprised to hear Poole speak familiarly to Notcutt, his junior in age and in rank. Notcutt was even younger than Chirinsky and like him a mere lieutenant. Such familiarity did not exist in the hierarchical world of Imperial Russia

After visiting the Seventh Army, Chirinsky took Poole to the headquarters of Eighth Army in Czernowitz, the capital of Bukovina, then a province in the Austrian Empire, which the Russians had captured in their recent offensive.[15] General Kaledin, who commanded the Eighth Army, only had time for a brief greeting before handing Poole over to Prince Alexander Ouroussov. Chirinsky, who remained with the visitors, managed to interest Ouroussov in Poole's mission and persuaded him to accompany them on their next visit.

It took the General's party four and a half hours to negotiate the thirty-six kilometres of narrow, twisting road in the bitter cold and snow to the remote mountain village where General Andrey Zaionchovsky had his headquarters. Ouroussov and the General went in the leading car; Chirinsky, Notcutt and Hill, the General's interpreter, in the second; and the servants in the third. The General's status had risen with Ouroussov in charge:

> A beastly morning snowing and very cold, so did not go out to see round the town. Russian Xmas Day. At 2.30 p.m. started with Prince Ouroussov in charge of us and had a very cold drive to Seletin headquarters of XVIII Corps. Lovely country – snow mountains covered with pines. We arrived about 7 p.m. and were most hospitably received by General Zaionchovsky, who talks French well and is a most charming man. We had a most tremendous Xmas dinner with

---

15 Bukovina is now in the Ukraine.

the Russian choirs singing, really lovely. A very wet night full of speeches and libations but I got away to bed by midnight.[16]

After the luxury of hotels, sleeping in a small wooden hut was a come down, but Poole emerged smiling and wearing a huge fur coat lent by his charitable hosts. He spent thirteen hours touring the Front Line with the Chief of the General Staff of XVIII Corps

> A day of days. Early start 8.30 a.m. Notcutt and I, Ouroussov and CGS. We motored into the mountain until the road ended and then went on in carriages up a wood road they have made through the forests up the mountainside. After three hours driving, we reached Sarata-Winsaia, headquarters of the 43rd Division. Here we were most hospitably entertained by General Ternavsky, a dear old man, who was up for the first day after a wound in the head. Speeches, libations and kisses! After lunch we drove for three hours in sleighs – very cold. Lovely scenery and got up to the Front – saw three batteries – got shelled. The difficulties they have had to contend with are stupendous. They must concentrate on roads in this area. Got home at 9.30 p.m. We have been 'mentioned' for extreme courage and coolness in inspecting the battery under a heavy fire!!! The Corps Commander has sent on the report and recommended us for decoration![17]

The following morning was spent inspecting trench mortars, Poole's favourite subject, with General Zaionchovsky. There was a final luncheon and a glimpse of the Russian version of the mountain gun, a weapon Poole knew from his service in India, 'Very sorry to leave XVIII Corps, who have been most kind.'[18]

---

16 Poole, Diary, 7 January 1917.
17 Poole, Diary, 8 January 1917.
18 Poole, Diary, 9 January 1917. Andrey Zaionchovsky was not a typical officer of the Imperial Russian Army as he remained in Russia after the Bolsheviks seized power and prospered, becoming a professor of the Military Academy of the Red Army from 1922 until his death in 1926 and establishing a reputation as a military historian. Poole recommended him to Sir Henry Wilson for a British decoration, 'for taking special trouble to arrange that all possible information regarding artillery and trench mortars was placed at the disposal of the artillery mission'. He also recommended an award for Alexander Ouroussov, 'His personal influence in favour of preaching Western methods in the handling of artillery has been very great'. Wilson did not act on Poole's recommendation; nor did Poole receive a Russian decoration for his bravery under Austrian fire.

General Sir Frederick Poole

The Russians remembered that at Stavka Count Constantin Diamandi, the Romanian Minister at Petrograd had made a point of inviting Poole to Romania, promising him a high-level reception. They took the view, however, that, if the British had guns to offer, they should come to them rather than their Romanian ally and therefore put a spoke in Poole's plans,

> Had arranged to look into the system of ammunition supply today and we were to go by a special train to King Ferdinand at Jassy tomorrow morning. All these plans were upset by a wire from Hanbury-Williams saying I must be back at Stavka by 14th at latest. We therefore cancelled our plans and motored back to Czernowitz, two hundred miles, starting at 4 p.m. and arriving at 2.30 a.m. – dog-tired and very cold. It's a great pity to miss seeing Ferdinand, who was particularly keen to see us. They had been wiring about us for a long time. However, we may manage it later on.[19]

A tragic accident then occurred in the rush to catch the train back to Kiev:

> Arrived Kiev midday and went to Continental Hotel to wait for the others. In the evening came a wire to say they had had an accident last night. The car skidded over the side of the road and upset – Hill and one chauffeur killed, Chirinsky badly crushed, Notcutt slightly hurt only. Spent most of the night talking to the headquarters of Brusilov's armies about it and arranging details. Hill's body is starting off to Petrograd tomorrow night to be buried by his people. I supposed all one can say is that the rest of us are very lucky to have escaped accident, as driving for miles through hilly country on roads sheeted with ice is not a very safe pastime when – as in the present case – there is also a thick fog.[20]

Poole had plenty to tell Alice:

> I will begin a letter now as I shall I hope to get to Petrograd in a few days' time and have a chance of posting it there. It's terribly lonely

---

19 Poole, Diary, 11 January 1917.
20 Poole, Diary, 13 January 1917.

in this land. Since I left home, I haven't heard a word of news of any sort – I've never in my life felt so much out of the world. Well, we have had a most interesting trip. We have been in Austria and Roumania and seen the places in the Carpathians where the fighting has been taking place. Everything went right till just at the end. Four days ago, we had fixed to go and see King Ferdinand, who was most anxious to see us. Then came a wire telling me to hurry back to GHQ. So, the visit was off and instead we had two motor drives – one of two hundred and the other of three hundred miles – bitter cold.

The last one was a tragedy. One of our cars turned turtle and Hill, my interpreter, was killed; also the chauffeur. Notcutt was slightly injured and Prince Chirinsky very badly injured. My car was on ahead and we caught the train to Kiev, where I am now, and didn't hear of it till last night. The result is that I am stuck up here. I hope Notcutt will be able to come on tonight and join me here tomorrow and we shall go on to GHQ. It's pretty dangerous driving: the roads are all a sheet of ice, open cars, very hilly. We have driven about 1500 miles – really we are very lucky to have had only one bad smash.

We have been most awfully well treated, like princes everywhere, and have seen everything. I have been mentioned for 'gallantry under heavy fire'!!!! for being shot at when in a battery and I believe Percy and I are to get some decoration!! If I get the one I have been recommended for, it is one which corresponds to the GCMG, a broad button over the shoulder and a star pinned onto one's stomach! So, I shall be 'it' if it comes off! I'm full of admiration for the Russians. The positions they have turned the Austrians out of are very formidable and, considering they have had practically no artillery, they have done marvels. I expect the mission will arrive in a day or two – then I shall get some letters I hope and hear news of you.[21]

Ouroussov's influence was enough to secure comfortable rooms, complete with telephone, in the Continental Hotel, the best hotel in Kiev. Again thanks to Ouroussov, on the Sunday tickets for the opera were

---

21 Frederick Poole to Alice Poole, 14 January. Percy was Percy Notcutt.

forthcoming. Poole took advantage of Ouroussov's standing to obtain a meeting on the Monday with the Grand Duke Alexander, who was the head of the Russian air force, which had its headquarters in Kiev.

When he arrived back at Stavka the General saw he had not wasted the time telephoning on his first night at the Continental Hotel: 'Travelling all day. Much colder as we get north. Arrived at Mogilev at 6.30 p.m. and found the whole of the GHQ staff with a band and escort to pay compliments to Hill's body. They put on two wreaths and played the Last Post. There was no necessity for us to hurry back as the mission has not yet arrived and the first meeting is fixed for Saturday week.'[22]

At Stavka the General again observed an atmosphere of indifference and resignation which made any practical discussions pointless, 'Went with Hanbury-Williams in the morning to discuss the Russian artillery at GHQ – nothing done. The whole thing absolutely futile. They are like a lot of children. Arranged to go on to Petrograd tomorrow. It's only a waste of time being here ... Dull and unprofitable here. I shall be glad to get away.'[23]

Nicholas II had caused deep offence at Stavka by his inattentive behaviour during the two-day conference on 30 and 31 December 1916; and then by his abrupt departure for Petrograd before the conference ended, after he had learned that Rasputin had been murdered. Subsequently, far from taking any warning from Rasputin's assassination, he had made unwise changes in the government, disillusioning even his most loyal supporters and making himself the focus of popular hatred. Previously, he had been shielded personally because the blame had been directed towards his ministers, even though his wife was loathed for coming under Rasputin's influence and accused of secretly wanting Germany to win the war. The Czar's authority was fast draining away.

Hanbury-Williams tried to explain the significance of Rasputin's death, but the General did not believe him. 'Glad to leave here. H.W. is getting melancholic, I think. He is certainly breaking up. The rot he writes about things here passes belief.'[24] As far as Poole was concerned the Czar was a respected and all-powerful figure who had treated him well. He was reluctant to believe that he was the creature of his wife who had fallen under Rasputin's influence. Besides which he was unwilling to rely on Hanbury-

---

22 Poole, Diary, 16 January. Mogilev was the railway station for Stavka.
23 Poole, Diary, 17 January 1917.
24 Poole, Diary, 18 January 1917.

Williams, as the latter had quite unnecessarily ordered his return to Stavka prematurely.

Possibly Hanbury-Williams had had some inkling of the plan to murder Rasputin and consequently had remained in Petrograd to avoid looking the Czar in the eye when the news reached Stavka. Hanbury-Williams makes no reference to Poole in his memoirs but does record how he heard the news of Rasputin's death: 'sitting in my room, I was rung up by Wilton of the *Times*: "They have got him at last, General". I guessed to whom he referred. It was the end of Rasputin. The year 1917 opened with the death of Rasputin as the talk of Russia'.[25]

The British Intelligence Mission in Petrograd was headed by Sir Samuel Hoare, a Conservative MP and later Foreign Secretary. Hoare by some accounts arranged for Captain Oswald Rayner to fire the shot that finally killed the wounded Rasputin as he staggered from Prince Yusupov's home. The General later had a full account of the Czar's final days in power from Hanbury-Williams and, over dinner in Prince Felix Yusupov's palace on the Moika, eventually heard the full story of Rasputin's murder from Rayner.[26]

In Petrograd no one was interested in hearing about the General's visit to the Front Line, as it had ceased to have any relevance. At a private audience on 12 January Sir George Buchanan, with the permission of the British Government, had confronted the Czar about the imperative need for reform but had been turned away coldly. Princess Cantacuzène summed it up, 'Probably our sovereign by this time was so in the habit of receiving warnings that he never gave Sir George's a second thought'.[27] Buchanan's meeting confirmed that nothing could be done to save Nicholas II and that revolution was inevitable.

Poole found himself in a rather different billet to the Hôtel d'Europe. The Dagmar Hotel was dirty, ill-lit, overcrowded and smelly, with people dossing down at night in the corridors and even in the squalid bathrooms. He also felt wretched about the motor accident. Notcutt and George Chirinsky were

---

25 Sir John Hanbury-Williams, *The Emperor Nicholas as I Knew Him* (London, 1922).
26 Unfortunately, Poole never recorded what Rayner told him.
27 Julia Dent Grant Cantacuzène Spéransky, *Revolutionary Days: Recollections of Romanoffs and Bolsheviki, 1914-1917* (Boston, Massachusetts). The Princess knew the world, being a granddaughter of President Grant, marrying into a wealthy Russian family, and making a home in Russia, then being wise enough to send her own children back to America after the Revolution and clever enough to escape with her husband and her jewellery from Russia after the Bolsheviks had seized power.

lucky to be alive and Mrs Hill, the mother of his interpreter on whom he called that evening, was 'very broke up poor woman'.[28] But there was some good news. He visited the British Embassy, collected letters from home and learned that in the New Year Honours he had been awarded the CMG and that Notcutt had been mentioned in Despatches. The CMG was recognition of how well he had done as an artillery officer on the Western Front and signified the importance attached in London to his new responsibilities.

Poole had still not understood that without a proper introduction a foreigner can achieve little in Russia. He should have remembered that he had gone to Stavka with the benefit of introductions from Hanbury-Williams and that his status had multiplied when George Chirinsky had engaged Ouroussov's enthusiasm. Consequently, on the Saturday, he wasted hours waiting patiently to see General Beliayev, the newly appointed Minister of War, but was not granted an interview, 'Don't care much about doing nothing in this country – it bores me stiff. Apparently, there is no definite news yet about the mission'.[29]

A chastened Poole recorded, 'Dined with Knox at night and went over his reports. Very interesting and throw quite a new light on the situation. If the Huns were to concentrate men and guns on this front, I don't see why they should not get into Petrograd'.[30] Knox took charge and, on the Sunday, introduced Poole to General Beliayev and the head of the Artillery Department, General Manikovsky, who put in place a programme of visits for him.

Poole moved from the Dagmar Hotel to the Hôtel de France, 'Much more comfortable and more central'.[31] The Hôtel de France, at 6 Great Morskaya, one of the most fashionable streets in Petrograd, was a fitting address for a British officer wishing to be taken seriously. The street combined luxury, opulence and sin. Its expensive shops and restaurants were a magnet for Society, as well as high-class prostitutes, driven in sleighs and elegant carriages. Fabergé was at 24 Great Morskaya, and Cubat at number 16, 'Those who have had the good fortune to dine there have described the cuisine as the finest they have ever known – in or out of Russia. Decorated in the elaborate French style of the period, there were upholstered armchairs for

---

28 Poole, Diary, 19 January 1917.
29 Poole, Diary, 20 January 1917.
30 Poole, Diary, 20 January 1917.
31 Poole, Diary, 21 January 1917.

every customer. In the kitchen, the chefs were French to a man. The waiters were all Tartars'.[32] Poole would soon be dining there and subsequently enjoying Privato Frères at number 36.

Staying at the Hôtel de France did not come cheap and, understandably, Poole felt worried about money. On the day of his departure, he had drawn an advance of £50 in cash at the War Office and £100 in a banker's draft drawn on Cox and Company, but this did not go far in Petrograd. When Peter the Great had built his capital, he had seen all the strategic advantages of giving Russia an opening to the Baltic, but he had not fully considered the disadvantages of the city being far distant from the main sources of food in the Black Earth region and of coal in the Donbass. Shortages in the capital were becoming critical because the German naval blockade had closed the Baltic Sea; the railway network was breaking down under the pressures exerted by the war effort; further disruption was caused by an exceptionally severe winter; refugees displaced by the advancing German armies were swelling the capital's population; and speculators and corrupt officials were adding to the misery.

As an officer, Poole had a daily allowance of £1 1s. 0d., which bought some 14.7 roubles at the official rate of exchange, but this did not go far in Petrograd where the basic charge for a room in an acceptable hotel was well over 5 roubles per night. According to Baedeker, the cheapest room at the Hôtel de France cost 2.75 roubles per night in 1914, before the rouble had tumbled from its traditional parity of ten to the pound and inflation had taken hold. Writing from the Hôtel de France, Poole was far from his usual cheery self:

> I have got back to Petrograd and found several letters from you and papers up to 3 January. Notcutt is all right again now. He had a bad time, left alone in the middle of the night in the snow with two dead men and one who thought he was dying, and he himself badly stunned and nobody within a mile! However, all's well that ends well … The mission has only just sailed and won't be here for another week. In many ways I hope I shan't have to stay on long here. I don't like this country – it's very lonely and one is lost not being able to speak the language. Also living here is ten times as expensive as at

---

32 Robin Bruce Lockhart, *Reilly: Ace of Spies* (Harmondsworth, 1984).

home and a rouble does not go as far as a shilling and you only get fourteen for £1. So, it's no catch financially.

I'm very busy here seeing arsenals and guns and all sorts of things – some good and some bad. I keep very fit, but it's hard to get exercise and difficult to walk on the streets – it's so slippery! I'm so glad the boys enjoyed their Xmas. Tell them I have got two more rifles and a carbine, which the Russians captured from the Austrians. If I can get them home, they will be a great souvenir. No more news yet about the decoration from the Emperor – it may come off in a few days. Goodbye, sweetheart. All my love to you and the boys.[33]

Poole became more positive as the week progressed. He was busy and getting the more exercise. On Monday, he visited a gun factory in the morning, lunched at the mess in the British Embassy and started to write the report on his visit to the south-west front. On Tuesday, he saw the guns shipped from home to the port of Archangel in North Russia being prepared at Tsarskoe Selo for dispatch to the front line: 'Von Stein the general is young and energetic – first of his type I have seen. Everything is in an awful muddle there, but it is not altogether their fault. Home and Archangel authorities also to blame.'[34]

After his return from Tsarskoe Selo, Poole called on George Chirinsky, who was being nursed back to health in one of the family houses. There Poole saw a dimension of grandeur and magnificence far beyond his experience but only noted that 'They have some lovely old furniture in their house'.[35] The experience gave him a little swagger when he dined with Hanbury-Williams that evening at the Astoria Hotel. Hanbury-Williams knew the world at Stavka, was intimate with the expatriate circle round the British Embassy and lodged well at the Astoria, but Poole had been received in the Petrograd home of the Schirinsky-Schikhmatoff family to see their eldest son.[36] This time Hanbury-Williams was seeking Poole's assistance to prepare for the Inter-Allied Conference.

After briefing Hanbury-Williams in his room the following morning, Poole and Notcutt visited a fuse factory, 'Very interesting – more or less

---

33 Frederick Poole to Alice Poole, 22 January 1917.
34 Poole, Diary, 23 January 1917.
35 Poole, Diary, 23 January 1917.
36 George Chirinsky was in the twenty-sixth generation of a line that stretched back to Genghis Khan.

up to date and they are turning out 1,700,000 per month'.[37] Talking it over with Percy Notcutt, Poole concluded he should put himself forward. So, the following morning, he went to the British Embassy and insisted on seeing Sir George Buchanan, 'I gave him my views very fully. He was much impressed I think. Anyway he suggested I should be kept on to carry them out!'[38]

The General had, however, misread both Russia and Buchanan. The ambassador, who had felt depressed since being turned away by the Czar, could not bring himself to explain that Poole was simply wasting his time. It was an entirely different story to the message he had given Poole on their first meeting, 'If I have any trouble to come straight to him and that he will go straight to the Emperor'.

Knowing that the Allied mission to the Inter-Allied Conference was on the final stage of its journey to the capital, Grand Duke Serge sent for Poole, 'Went round in morning to see Grand Duke Serge and talked hard for an hour. He was very nice and took my criticisms very well – indeed he agreed to all of them. I don't suppose though that much will be done'.[39]

The day afterwards Poole, who had by now grown a Russian-style beard, installed himself again in the Hôtel d'Europe, where the guests for the Inter-Allied Conference were to be lodged as guests of the Russian government. He was ready to begin his campaign to remain in Russia so as to have the opportunity to implement his views on the proper organisation of Russia's artillery.

The General had never been to Russia before and had never had any dealings with Russians. As the train had made its way from the frontier with Sweden to Petrograd, on his first day in the country, he had taken at face value government prohibition, 'The country is strictly temperance – no drinks procurable – tea is the beverage and excellent'.[40] Whilst serving on the Western Front, Poole's geographical horizon was limited to the small area of north-west France between the Channel ports and the Front Line where the British Expeditionary Force was concentrated, interspersed by short periods of home leave. It is hard to imagine less relevant experience for Russia.

---

37 Poole, Diary, 24 January 1917.
38 Poole, Diary, 25 January 1917.
39 Poole, Diary, 27 January 1917.
40 Poole, Diary, 25 December 1916.

10

The Inter-Allied Conference

By early in 1917 Russia had suffered a crippling series of military disasters inflicted by the better equipped and effectively led German forces. This far outweighed any success against the weaker Austrian forces. Huge casualties, retreat and the intolerable pressures on the Home Front caused by the war effort had resulted in growing discontent, a desire for peace and the demand for political change. Czar Nicholas II, however, obstinately clung to his belief in the autocratic rule of the Romanov dynasty. In Britain the House of Saxe-Coburg-Gotha was renamed the House of Windsor, burying its Germanic ancestry under a homely English name and causing the Kaiser to joke that he would have to rename *The Merry Wives of Windsor* as *The Merry Wives of Saxe-Coburg-Gotha*. On Lloyd George's advice, George V took the pledge to abstain from drinking alcohol until the war was won and so set an example to munitions workers spending their wages too freely on drink to the detriment of productivity.

When the British Mission left for the Inter-Allied Conference, it bore a personal letter from King George V to his cousin urging reform. The letter made no impression. If the Czar would not heed his most trusted and loyal supporters, or representations from his closest family members, he had no interest in engaging in any constructive dialogue with the large and high-level delegations sent with the best of intentions to the Inter-Allied Conference.

In the Russian tradition, many of those with wealth took a pragmatic view that a revolution was inevitable and spent the remaining weeks before it came in having as much pleasure as possible. Petrograd had a famous opera and many theatres and was full of excellent restaurants. After his talk with the Grand Duke Serge and a visit to the Hermitage, and collecting mail from home at the British Embassy, the General was at peace with the world. He and Notcutt were finishing a modest and early dinner at a quiet table before going on to the theatre when they saw George Chirinsky sweep in with a party of his young friends, intent on a long and expensive evening. The prince has made a miraculous recovery from the injuries – concussion, shock and two broken ribs – that had confined him to bed just four days previously. It was the beginning of a wild spree to indulge in the pleasures that would soon be extinguished forever.

The foreign delegates were welcomed to the Inter-Allied Conference in Petrograd by immense crowds. Brass bands were at the station to greet them when their train finally arrived from the port of Romanov (now Murmansk) in North Russia on the morning on 29 January 1917. Waiting cars then took them to the Hôtel d'Europe. Meriel Buchanan, the British Ambassador's daughter, caught the atmosphere, 'An endless stream of motors stood at all hours of the day before the Hôtel d'Europe, where the Missions had been lodged. Dinners and dances took place every night; the big royal box at the ballet was filled with French, English and Italian uniforms'.[1] Although the Russians were keen to be good hosts, it was clear from the outset that the conference would be a waste of time.

Poole was an outsider in distinguished company. The political head of the British delegation was Viscount Milner, a member of Lloyd George's small and exclusive War Cabinet.[2] He shared Lloyd George's belief in the impossibility of victory without changing the generals. Lord Revelstoke came as the British financial representative. Not for the first time his family's bank, Baring Brothers, had found itself on the losing side, with heavy exposure to Russian loans. Walter Layton represented the Ministry of Munitions and thus had the practical responsibility for making available any munitions it was decided should be sent to Russia. Lieutenant General Sir Henry Wilson was accompanied by three other generals, senior to Poole and well connected socially, Major General Headlam and Brigadier Generals Clive and Brooke.

Poole did not participate in the first session of the conference, held

---

1   Meriel Buchanan, *Petrograd: The City of Trouble* (London, 1923).
2   Alfred Milner, a key establishment figure, had distinguished himself as an administrator both at home and overseas in Egypt and South Africa.

The Inter-Allied Conference

in the Foreign Office on the very afternoon of the delegates' arrival at Petrograd. Instead, he invited General Headlam for a walk. Headlam, who had seen the chaos at the port of Murmansk when the mission had landed and had endured the slow railway journey over poorly laid track to Petrograd, was receptive to Poole's idea of a British artillery officer staying on in Russia. General Poole was also not among Sir George Buchanan's dinner guests that evening at the British Embassy. These included Grand Duke Serge; Sazonov, the former Minister of Foreign Affairs; and Bark, the Minister of Finance. The latter two both saw the need for reform and were pro-English. Poole did receive a little encouragement before the dinner at the embassy, hearing the Grand Duke Serge telling Milner that he thought, 'I was now half-Russian!!'[3] Afterwards Poole went out to eat with Colonel Knox and General Clive and pushed his idea of staying on in Russia. The following morning Poole outlined his plan to Sir Henry Wilson. He was, however, excluded from the official programme in the afternoon and went instead to attend the funeral of Hill, the interpreter who had been killed.

The grand reception at Tsarskoe Selo on Wednesday 31 January proved a vacuous occasion. Nicholas II was at his charming best and official photographs were taken, copies of which were thoughtfully provided to be taken home as souvenirs. Poole had shed his beard and so, in a galaxy of unfamiliar Slavic faces, looked as conventional as his British contemporaries. If the point had not sunk in fully, the session in the Marie Palace on Thursday 1 February, which again Poole did not attend, showed the Russians at their worst. They made unreasonable demands for munitions, heedless of the practicalities of shipping, of the strain on their existing railway network, of prioritising the most essential items and of the training needed to use unfamiliar equipment effectively. Milner had by now concluded he was wasting his time.

On the following day, Friday 2 February, Milner returned to Nicholas, who remained immovable on the question of reform and uninterested in the proceedings of the Inter-Allied Conference but proved receptive to the suggestion that Poole should stay in Russia. Poole's status rose:

Had long discussion with H. Wilson in morning re my proposals.

---

3   Poole, Diary, 29 January 1917.

Went to see the modern pictures for one and a half hours before lunch. Discussions in afternoon. Dined at Embassy – big dinner – sat between Gurko, Chief of Staff, and Beliayev, Minister of War, and fairly handed it out! Also talked to Grand Duke Serge afterwards. Milner had long private interview with *** today. I hear satisfactory.[4]

Milner had seen the Czar.

Wilson wrote, 'A long interview with Poole ... Dined at Embassy and I sat next Grand Duke Serge and made love to him'.[5] Making 'love' in Wilson's terminology was equivalent to Poole 'handing it out' or in modern parlance using unrestrained flattery. Gurko in his memoirs makes what may be a passing reference to Poole, 'I must acknowledge, however, that these dinners have a good side. They give the guests, between the courses, an opportunity to exchange ideas, to get better acquainted, and to talk over things which would not always be suitable in the meetings'.

After a dinner for the conference delegates at Tsarskoe Selo on 3 February, Poole was singled out for special attention by the Czar:

> The Emperor is very pleased with Milner's suggestion that I should be left behind as expert artillery adviser to the Grand Duke. Henry Wilson went to see the Grand Duke in the morning and asked him his views. He was quite in favour of it and quite pleased to have me, but also saw the difficulties which might be raised by his own officers! It will want much tact. Dined with the Emperor at Tsarskoe Selo at night – very nice and cheery. H.I.H. gave my show a great start by being particularly nice to me and talking to me for about twenty-five minutes after dinner – which sort of singled me out as a recipient of imperial favour!! Had a long talk with H.W. at night. It is to be done, but the difficulties are very great. It all depends on H.I.H. and Serge here and the authorities at home. If I can't do any good in two months' time, I shall take off my hat and go.[6]

The General now required accommodation for his mission and turned for help to Prince Ouroussov. He had already put the prince on the alert

---
4   Poole, Diary, 2 February 1917.
5   Sir Henry Wilson, Diary, 2 February 1917.
6   Poole, Diary, 3 February 1917.

The Inter-Allied Conference

after returning from Tsarskoe Selo on the Wednesday, when they had dined together. Now that he had an official mandate he got down to business, 'Went round to Ouroussov and discussed houses as we want an office'.[7] He also spelt out his new position to Alice:

> After a lot of palaver here, Lord Milner and Henry Wilson have come to the conclusion that the only hope of really getting the Russian artillery up to the mark to be any use in a proper way this year is to leave me behind here to practically reorganize. I am to be expert artillery adviser to Grand Duke Serge and to reorganize and to arrange for the whole system of supply of guns, ammunition and aeroplanes from London to point of delivery to the Hun.
>
> Milner had a heart to heart with the Emperor, and he said he would be very glad to have me if Serge approved. When Serge was asked, he said he would be delighted. So now it is practically settled. My job will last till (1) I find I can do no good; or (2) till I have really done all I can do and put everything on an up to date footing. Of course it is an enormous job and bristles with difficulties. If it comes off, I suppose practically no Englishman, and very few in Allied countries, will personally have done more to win the war than me. That is the attractive part. It's a work of vital importance to all the allies and very much a man's work. If I can do any real good, I shall have been of some use in life.
>
> On the other hand, it is obvious that every single Russian gunner must be dead against me and the slightest mistake or want of tact will ruin the whole show; and one has to contend against a vast inert mass of suspicion and ignorance and intolerance and corruption. It all depends on how far the Emperor and Serge will carry me and on how well they will back me from home.
>
> I have had a very good start. Lord Milner and H.W. are 'booming' me, to all and sundry, as the most up to date practical gunner in the world. Serge has been very nice to me and last night, when we dined with the Emperor, he went out of his way to 'boom' me, as when he came round after dinner, he talked to me for about twenty minutes and markedly signalled me out for attention, which is a very rare

---

7   Poole, Diary, 4 February 1917.

occurrence. So I shall have a good start that way. I expect they will make me a major general. I shall be furious if they don't.

I have applied for Finlayson, and he and I and Notcutt will run the show; and I feel that, if it can be done, we are the people who can do it. If it won't work, I shall give it up in about six weeks or so, but if it goes along, I shall sit here till about the end of May. My headquarters will be here – but my work will reach to Archangel, Odessa, Vladivostok and all along the front – so we shall be doing a good deal of travelling mostly.

It's very hard on you I know, darling, and if I consulted my own wishes, I shouldn't touch the job. But it's big work – big with a B – and it's only right to try; and, if I do fail, I shall fail at a job which is bigger than most men have a chance of trying. So, when you think of it in that light, I know you will approve and think I have taken the right course. I suppose if it comes off I shall be a 'made' man, but it's the work which fascinates and not the hope of material reward. I still think that by August the whole thing will be over – are you pleased at this? It's rather an extraordinary life in two years for a retired major, if you come to think of it, to practically run the artillery of the greatest power the world has ever known!!

Goodbye sweetheart – all my love to you and the boys. H.W. has been a topper. He has helped me to have the courage to tackle the job.[8]

Henry Wilson may have been 'a topper', but he was also a pragmatist. He needed to report to Lloyd George a practical step being taken to improve Russia's fighting capability, and it cost him nothing allowing Poole to go out on a limb with his own reputation. Poole had been astute enough to understand the problems on the surface – such as graft, corruption and incompetence on a massive scale – and the resentment that his appointment might arouse, but he had seen no further. He still had not realised that Nicholas II was a weak man about to be swept away by revolution, let alone the terrifying consequences that would flow from a revolution in a troubled, war-weary country where 90 per cent of the population were illiterate and where anarchy, cruelty and violence broke out when not kept in subjugation by the system.

---

8   Frederick Poole to Alice Poole, 4 February 1917.

The Inter-Allied Conference

The day ended with a valedictory performance from Mathilde Kschessinska, 'Went to the ballet at night – a very fine show. We had the Royal Box so we were comfortable. I have never seen such good dancing in my life, and they are all so well drilled. It is a state theatre. The prima ballerina was having a benefit on her retirement.'[9]

On Monday 5 February Wilson telegraphed to the Chief of the Imperial General Staff:

> I am leaving General Poole and Lieutenant Notcutt in Russia. Poole will create an organisation for the more rapid delivery of guns and ammunition, the training of some Russian personnel, the formation of trench mortar and aviation schools, and, generally speaking, will assume responsibility for all artillery, aviation and munition material which we send to Russia. He will also act as expert artillery adviser to the Grand Duke Serge, and so far as he can, he will put Western ideas into the Russian artillery.

If Wilson's telegram fulfilled all Poole's expectations, meeting the Grand Duke Serge the following day brought him down to earth. Having originally supposed that Serge was an all-powerful figure in the artillery, Poole began to realise that his practical authority was limited, that he was at best interested in having a quiet life and was at worst untrustworthy. In fact, Serge had stepped down as the Inspector General of Artillery of the Russian forces in 1915, an office inherited from his father in 1905, having been implicated indirectly in a corruption scandal. His position at Stavka was nebulous, as he had little influence with Nicholas II as the Czarina did not approve of him, and he had no department to run. Being 'expert artillery adviser' to the Grand Duke Serge was therefore a position without meaning. Serge simply referred Poole to Beliayev, the Minister of War, and, after reporting this back to Sir Henry Wilson and Milner, Poole relieved his frustration over a dinner with Prince Ouroussov. It ended at a late hour after much alcohol had been consumed.

Sir Henry Wilson and Viscount Milner duly had a meeting with Beliayev. Poole learned that 'He is delighted about the idea of my staying and says he will do everything possible'.[10] In the evening, Wilson and his

---

9   Poole, Diary, 4 February 1917.
10 Poole, Diary, 7 February 1917.

entourage departed by train for a tour of the Front Line and Moscow. By this time General Headlam had succumbed to the abundance of hospitality and, according to Poole, was feeling 'quite seedy – in bed all day'.[11] When Milner set off for Moscow with Buchanan, Poole was left to see what progress he could make in his own right.

Beliayev's words proved to be a mere *politesse*. Whilst waiting to see him, the General penned an angry letter to Alice, which brought to light just how forthright he had been at his meeting on 6 February with the Grand Duke Serge, 'I was quite frank with Serge. I said if I feel I am not doing any good I'll let you know and clear out, as I don't propose to stay here and be an ornament!!'[12] Poole had a further disappointment afterwards, going to see a self-contained flat within Prince Ouroussov's house on the Fontanka. The prince, scenting Poole's desperation, proposed an exorbitant rent, but could give no guarantee as to when the flat would be available. He also required him to provide the furniture necessary to turn it into an office.

Poole dined with Mr and Mrs Hill, the parents of his interpreter who had been tragically killed. It was a 'very pleasant dinner'.[13] Perhaps Hill's father told the General a little more about the ways of Russia. Having learnt that accidents were frequent because of reckless driving in atrocious weather conditions, the General drew an appropriate conclusion by later instructing his ADC to sit next to the driver with a loaded revolver and issue the warning, 'Drive slowly or you will be shot'.

Poole went again to Beliayev's office, but to no avail. After an evening at the opera, he was drawn into a lavish dinner: 'Went on to Ouroussov afterwards and didn't get home till 1.30 am'.[14] Finally, on the third attempt, Poole saw the Minister of War, 'In afternoon had an interview with Beliayev, which was satisfactory. He expresses himself delighted that I am coming and asks me to keep him posted with all my views'.[15] More of the same insincere platitudes came when Poole went to the Artillery Department to meet General Alexey Manikovsky, 'who was very pleasant and glad that I was staying. He seems quite inclined to be helpful'.[16]

---

11 Poole, Diary, 7 February 1917.
12 Frederick Poole to Alice Poole, 8 February 1917.
13 Poole, Diary, 8 February 1917.
14 Poole, Diary, 9 February 1917.
15 Poole, Diary, 10 February 1917.
16 Poole, Diary, 11 February 1917.

The Inter-Allied Conference

Poole piled the pressure in vain on Prince Ouroussov to produce accommodation for his mission. 'Prince Ouroussov has a big house here, about as large as a Belgrave Square house. We may be going to get a flat in there, which will do for an office and also to live in; but it's quite uncertain we shall be able to get it as the government are likely to commandeer the whole house.'[17] The government itself was unable to help because the demands of the war effort far exceeded the additional space gained by requisitioning hotels, offices and private houses. The influx of refugees from the advancing German armies also meant that hotels were packed, while the supply of rental accommodation had dried up. The problem was only resolved after the Revolution when the wealthy were either dispossessed by the Provisional Government or were desperately anxious to secure foreign tenants on nominal terms to protect their homes from being plundered.

The General considered taking the flat being vacated by Sir Samuel Hoare, who was returning home on the conclusion of the Inter-Allied Conference. It was too small, however, and too expensive. Whilst palaces and embassies had grand reception rooms, servants slept in the passageways and the sanitary arrangements were rudimentary, not least in the British Embassy. There was certainly no space available for the General in the embassy itself.

Meanwhile the partying of the young Russian aristocrats continued apace, 'Chirinsky came round in the evening. He has been ill again, but as his idea of resting seems to be to sit up all night it's not to be wondered at!'[18] Chirinsky shrugged it off and insisted on inviting Poole for dinner the following evening, which the General accepted on condition that it would end at an early hour. Poole began to realise why Milner had concluded that nothing could be done to help the Russians, 'Long artillery conference in the afternoon – got things squared up a little, but we can't possibly give them all they ask for. Even if we did give it there would not be tonnage or freight available to hump it all.'[19]

Finally, even the General's energy abated, 'Quiet day nothing very much doing.'[20] The following day Sir Henry Wilson and his entourage returned from their tour of the Front Line and a visit to Moscow, exhausted after

---

17 Frederick Poole to Alice Poole, 13 February 1917.
18 Poole, Diary, 13 February 1917.
19 Poole, Diary, 14 February 1917.
20 Poole, Diary, 16 February 1917.

bounteous hospitality and muttering vague platitudes for Poole's benefit about Russian interest in trench mortars. Poole had another late night, 'Dined with Knox. Went on to a show given by the Mayor of Petrograd at the Town Hall. Rather a good show and supper at the end and didn't get home till 2.30 a.m.'[21]

Sunday came and Poole decided it was time to go easy on the good living, 'We have been very gay this week out every night. Last night I didn't get to bed till 2.30. Tonight, I am engaged to dine out with a Prince Obolensky – a very cheery fellow – who "drinks very good" to use the expression of my "bear leader"! It seems a tremendous beano, so I am trying to get out of it and go to bed early instead'.[22] Prince Ouroussov, however, made short work of the General's protestations and insisted on a visit to the gypsies as the guest of Prince Obolensky, 'Busy all day and pretty tired. I had meant to go to bed early, but at 8.0 p.m. Prince Obolensky came and hauled me out to dinner. We then joined a large party and drove out at midnight to Villa Rodé to the gypsies where we remained all night. I didn't get home till 6.00 a.m.! I don't like these Russian customs; it's too strenuous a life for me. The amount of money these people spend on their "busts" is simply appalling'.[23]

The Inter-Allied Conference finally came to an end after a last round of feasting and a lavish distribution of medals. Somehow the General convinced himself about the value of the exercise, 'On the whole it has been a success, and will I hope have very good results'.[24]

Poole then went to investigate the situation at Archangel, the main port of entry in North Russia for munitions and supplies. He left on 27 February, after a terrific struggle with the Russian authorities to gain the appropriate documentation, and arrived back in Petrograd on 5 March, staying this time at the Astoria. He tried to settle matters at Tsarskoe Selo, but found himself stalled again:

Had a very busy day writing and seeing people all the time. Went to see Manikovsky in the afternoon. He was very pleasant but couldn't get much of a move on him. He is afraid to tackle the Tsarskoe Selo question as he does not, I gather, wish to bump up against Serge.

---

21 Poole, Diary, 17 February 1917.
22 'Frederick Poole to Alice Poole, 18 February 1917.
23 Poole, Diary, 18 February 1917.
24 Poole, Diary, 21 February 1917.

The Inter-Allied Conference

> Went down to embassy in evening and had a long talk to Knox. I have now made up my mind not to go away until someone is here to take my place.[25]

General Manikovsky was a serious soldier who knew well the issues at Tsarskoe Selo but recognised their sensitivity.[26] The scandal of guns urgently needed at the Front Line but left idle at Tsarskoe Selo had been uncovered long before by a visiting French mission led by Albert Thomas in January 1916.[27] The Czar himself had highlighted the issue in two letters to the Empress, yet even this had not stimulated Serge into action. This puts the scale of the challenge facing Poole into context.

Poole tried again, 'Wrote to the Minister of War re delay in turning out batteries. It is beginning to be time they put some ginger into it!'[28] Beliayev's qualification for promotion to Minister of War after the murder of Rasputin was that he had not incurred the displeasure of the Empress. He was already at the end of his tether when Knox taxed him with Russia's military shortcomings: 'I saw Beliayev at 9.45 p.m. and found him much depressed. He said he would do all that was possible to hasten the conveyance of stores from Romanov, and he begged me to avoid alarming people in England into possible refusal to continue the dispatch of munitions to the port. He felt everyone was against him in the fight for order, but he would continue to do his duty as long as Minister'.[29] On 8 March Poole tried yet again but still got nowhere:

> Fairly busy all day. Went to Artillery Department in afternoon to talk to von Stein and was confronted with a room full of generals and colonels who tried to prove what they were doing in the way of organization was beyond reproach! As usual, after a few minutes they got away onto technical details. If only they devoted the same energy to getting batteries turned out they might move mountains.

---

25 Poole, Diary, 6 March 1917.
26 Manikovsky was also politically aware. His career continued under both the Provisional Government and the Bolsheviks before he was killed in a railway accident in 1920. Before his death he had begun writing an analysis of the shortcomings of the Russian war effort. This was posthumously published in 1937.
27 Rodzianko, *The Reign of Rasputin* (New York, 1973).
28 Poole, Diary, 7 March 1917.
29 Sir Alfred Knox, *With the Russian Army, 1914-1917* (London, 1921).

Am not satisfied, but perhaps the fact that I have raised the question will be effective.[30]

The following day Poole wrote a report for Sir William Robertson, Chief of the Imperial General Staff. He had met many important people and had some interesting experiences, but after more than two months he had achieved nothing. His hoped for promotion to the acting rank of major general had not come through and his pay and allowances were insufficient to cover the ruinous cost of living in Petrograd. The only tangible reward had been the lavish distribution of Russian medals when the Inter-Allied Conference ended. Poole received the Imperial and Royal Order of St Stanislas, first class (with swords) and Notcutt the Order of St Anne, third class. Notcutt, who had not fully recovered from the car crash, and Poole's second servant went home with the mission. Poole was left on his own 'except for my Russian Prince Ouroussov – and my embryo ADC who comes in for an hour or two during the day to work – so it's very dull. It will be much better when I can get settled down properly and really get started. I have a cable that Finlayson has got home and will be sent out here shortly'.[31]

Wilson, who had had painful personal experience of setbacks in his own career, wrote in his final report to the War Cabinet on the Inter-Allied Conference, 'Officers sent out to Russia run a serious chance of being forgotten or overlooked, and their military prospects suffering thereby'.[32]

---

30 Poole, Diary, 8 March 1917.
31 Frederick Poole to Alice Poole, 25 February 1917. Ever active in networking with the rich and well-connected, Sir Henry Wilson had asked the General to take on Sir Victor Warrender, a youth in his eighteenth year, who had just inherited a baronetcy and a large fortune, as an ADC. Finlayson had returned from France.
32 Sir Henry Wilson, Papers, Imperial War Museum, G. 132, Allied Conference at Petrograd, January-February 1917, dated March 1917.

11

The March Revolution

Frustrated by the official channels, General Poole decided to cast his net more widely. His Intelligence gathering began in earnest after meeting a British expatriate, 'Had a long talk in the evening with Marshall, a civil engineer, as to the industrial situation'.[1] Two days later he made his way to the Great Morskaya and lunched at Cubat with the Ginsburgs.[2] This was soon followed up with: 'Dined with Ginsburgs at night. Very pleasant dinner'.[3] Baron Ginsburg was a business contact of his father-in-law's. By moving in these circles Poole met Alexander Guchkov, a prominent businessman who was active in politics and keen to promote a peaceful transition to democratic government. It would prove significant because, after the March Revolution, Guchkov was appointed Minister of War in the Provisional Government. Poole referred obliquely to Guchkov when later writing home, 'The new Minister of War is a man whom fortunately I had taken up before – a good businessman and a pusher, so I shall get on well with him'.[4] Poole makes no further reference to the Ginsburgs but continued to see the Marshalls until they left Russia for England in September 1917.

Poole also discovered an expatriate called Lessing, 'He is a useful fellow and knows the language and is in touch with labour conditions'.[5] Lessing,

---

1   Poole, Diary, 15 February 1917.
2   Poole, Diary, 17 February 1917.
3   Poole, Diary, 22 February 1917.
4   Frederick Poole to Alice Poole, 20 March 1917.
5   Poole, Diary, 25 February 1917.

who might otherwise have been sent home to fight on the Western Front, introduced Poole to his most valuable civilian contact in Russia, Poliakov, an entrepreneur well connected in financial and industrial circles. Lessing took Poole to dine *en famille* with the Poliakovs on 22 March.

Hungry for information, Poole established relations with newspaper correspondents who did not rely on official sources, among them Claude Anet, who later published an account of his time in Russia. Poole himself had the knack of the good reporter, of being present at crucial events, keeping a cool head when there was every reason to panic and emerging with a clear picture of their significance, 'The situation here is bad. No bread can be got by the people here – entirely through chaos and corruption on the railways. Riots in the streets yesterday – Cossacks out to keep order. Nothing very bad so far, but if it develops will turn out badly'.[6] Rumours abounded. Harold Williams, the correspondent of the *Daily Chronicle*, 'says he is sure the whole thing is engineered by the government of whom high officials are pro-Hun and want to force Russia into making peace. This may be, and probably is, incredible. Nevertheless, there are a great many well-informed people who believe it!'[7]

An American journalist called Arno Dosch-Fleurot spotted the General on the Nevsky Prospect watching desperate attempts by the government to quell rising popular unrest on Saturday 10 March. Although the police remained loyal to the government, the crowd sensed that the allegiance of the Cossacks was wavering. The latter made several charges to clear the Nevsky Prospekt but did not use their sabres and whips. The crowd took courage. Their numbers were swollen by workers from the huge Putilov works, where management had retaliated to wage demands by a lockout, and from other factories which had stopped work. Dosch-Fleurot makes it clear that the General was no stranger to him:

Coming down the Nevsky I encountered an English officer of my acquaintance, General F.C. Poole, and we stopped in the middle of the wide sidewalk before the Singer building in the Nevksy to watch a crowd following and cheering a Cossack patrol. We were still lost in conjecture when we noticed people about us turn and run quickly

---
6 Frederick Poole to Alice Poole, 8 March 1917.
7 Poole, Diary, 9 March 1917.

The March Revolution

towards the building. A squad of mounted police, sabres drawn, was charging around the corner into the Nevsky on the sidewalk. General Poole reached the wall in time. I did not. Someone jumping back knocked me over and I went down before the charge. 'You're all right', I heard Poole's voice, 'Well bred horses won't step on you'. One went right over me, but the General was right. I was glad, though, there was only one file.[8]

By now Poole was now thinking that only extreme measures could restore the situation:

Went to embassy and to see Bury [the railway expert sent out by Lloyd George] in morning. Latter holds out no great hopes for immediate improvement of railways. Practical solution for present needs is to place orders in America for new locos and wagons which will all help as soon as they arrive. Riots much worse today – cavalry charged several times and killed a few. Infantry shooting on Nevsky. I walked up very quickly and kept near the horses! It would be sad to end one's days killed in a riot in Russia. Situation is really serious now, but I hear they hope to have bread in tomorrow. Putilov and the other factories closed for the present. The whole thing is neglect on the part of government officials. The remedy would be to hang one or two.[9]

On Sunday 11 March the General still clung on to the hope there might be one final chance of the Government re-establishing its authority:

A very serious day. Shooting seems to have been indiscriminate all day and as far as I can hear there were a lot of casualties killed or wounded. A machine gun was shooting near Nicholas Station at one time. The bread question ought to be more or less solved now. It is certain that there is enough flour in Petrograd if it were only distributed on some method. Putilov is to open for some departments tomorrow and to begin work properly on Tuesday. I

---

[8] Arno Dosch-Fleurot, *Through War to Revolution: Being the Experiences of a Newspaper Correspondent in War and Revolution, 1914-1920* (London, 1931).
[9] Poole, Diary, 10 March 1917.

haven't heard yet about the other works. The Nevsky was closed all the afternoon: no trams, a few people allowed to cross it, but no up and down thoroughfare. If only the works open again that will settle the whole question.[10]

This last chance, however, was missed. On Monday 12 March the floodgates opened. The troops went over to the people and the Revolution took hold. It was a terrible day for Poole that began with the news of the death of his close friend Beryl Nicholson and stretched far into the early hours of the following morning:

> Went to embassy in morning and got cable with news of Beryl's death on 3 March, which knocked me badly. At the same time Knox told me that the soldiers had gone over *en masse* to the people and that they had seized the Artillery Department and most of the town. The police were all killed or fled. The Palais de Justice burned, the prisons opened and three thousand men let loose; and during the day the Revolution gained ground and took the whole town. At night they took the Upper Senate: established a Provisional Government under Rodzyanko and started in. We had an unpleasant night at the Astoria as at 1.30 a.m. we thought they were coming to loot the hotel. We Britons were put down in the hall to meet the mob to try to quiet them! However, they let us alone – we got to bed at 3.30 a.m.[11]

After a brief respite, the Astoria Hotel had another invasion:

> At 8.30 a.m. the mob rushed the Astoria, said they had been shot at, which was I fancy true. They shot a lot and smashed up all the lower part of the hotel. I only saw one colonel dead and one woman badly shot – but they let loose a lot. They treated the allies well: they took my revolver but otherwise did nothing to my kit. Things looked awkward for a bit as they wanted to burn down the place and, as many were drunk, we never knew that we shouldn't be shot. At midday we

---

10 Poole, Diary, 11 March 1917.
11 Poole, Diary, 12 March 1917.

The March Revolution

got out, went to the Europe; very perilous – indiscriminate shooting everywhere. The new government gradually began to take hold and are being recognized, I fancy. A lot of shooting at night but otherwise things pretty orderly. I stayed with Lessing at the Europe and it was quite quiet there.[12]

Alice would have read this report in the *Times* of Friday 16 March:

> British Officers' Promptitude. Tuesday Afternoon. While some sailors with a band were on their way to the Tauris Palace, a machine gun, secreted on the top floor of a military hotel formerly known as the Astoria, where a number of English officers reside, opened fire, whereupon the mob stormed the hotel and wrecked the ground floor. General Poole and our other officers promptly took steps for the protection of the women and children, who were all saved. The Russians speak with the highest admiration of the coolness of our officers. The delinquent who fired on the sailors was killed.[13]

There was a particularly dangerous moment when Poole seemed to be pointing a gun, but fortunately it was only his pipe.[14]

Leaving the vandalised Astoria, Poole had a hazardous journey to the Hôtel d'Europe, where he took refuge in Lessing's quarters:

> I've had a terrible time here the last few days – a revolution and much bloodshed. I quite sympathize with the people. The soldiers joined the people and the revolutionaries have won so far all along the line. It may be a good thing if the government can get the people back to work – otherwise disaster. They have looted the drink and opened the prisons so are a bit out of hand now. Luckily, they like the English; so, unless we are shot by accident, we shall be safe.
>
> They rushed our hotel yesterday morning – shooting blindly and smashing up everything. We thought we were 'for it' but they treated us very well. I was very pleased with Cox. He quite kept his

---

12 Poole, Diary, 13 March 1917.
13 *Times*, 16 March 1917.
14 According to an anecdotal account passed down through the family, when the General put the pipe into his mouth the crowd, seeing their mistake, roared with laughter and the tension was defused.

head and passed through a very unpleasant half hour with me when we both expected to be shot any minute.[15]

Poole was not only witnessing the Revolution in Russia, but also experiencing a revolution in his own fortunes. He had also just heard of the death of his close long-term friend, Beryl Nicholson, who left him most of her estate. 'I have had a wire from Pa telling me of Beryl's death. I have told Pa that, if possible I should like the house to be left as it is till my return; Sinclair to be kept on, if he will stay as caretaker. I want his welfare assured; he had been with her all his life.'

When Beryl had told him of her intentions it had seemed a far distant prospect, as she was only fifty:

> My dear, I made a new will the other day and left you most of my fortune and all my possessions! Hope letters won't be a bore but should like you to have them – in memory of our long and wonderful friendship. I had to have some legacies and hand Nicholson LSD back to their family, but rest is for you and you are sole executor. You see Alick is gone and feel I can do what I like with it. When you come there are one or two things I want to explain. You must come and have a long talk if you can.[16]

Now, just seventeen months later, she was dead, broken-hearted at the death of her nephew Alick on the Western Front in December 1914. The inheritance made Poole financially secure in his own right, which meant that he could act independently in Russia without the career officer's fear of alienating the powers that be.

On Thursday 15 March Poole tried to find out who, if anyone, was now in control. At the British Embassy Bertie Stopford was struck by his presence. 'In the hall I met General Poole, who asked if I had any news. I repeated what I had heard at the Foreign Office that the situation was most critical. He said, "That is just what I told the Ambassador".'[17]

Although everyone was expecting revolution, when it came no one knew what to do or how it could be controlled. The parliament, known as

---

15 Frederick Poole to Alice Poole, 14 March 1917.
16 Beryl Nicholson to Frederick Poole, 4 November 1915.
17 Bertie Stopford, *The Russian Diary of an Englishman: Petrograd, 1915-1917* (1919).

The March Revolution

the Duma, proved to be powerless. It had been established by a reluctant concession from Nicholas II, who had come close to being overthrown in 1905 after Russia's humiliating defeat in its war with Japan. There had been a general strike in the capital and the workers had formed a Soviet or council to seize power and had encouraged workers in other cities to follow suit. Unrest and disorder spread throughout the land. The 1905 Revolution was suppressed only because the upper classes and the army remained loyal and had no qualms about using force. In 1917, in contrast, the Czar had few or no effective defenders when the test came. As popular discontent welled over, power passed to the workers and soldiers. The Petrograd Soviet came back into being before the Duma, led by Alexander Rodzyanko, could persuade the Czar to abdicate and a Provisional Government could be established. The Petrograd Soviet, however, had no wish to participate in the Provisional Government or take responsibility for the government of the country. It called for the formation of Soviets throughout the country and in the armed forces, seeing itself as the vanguard of the Revolution.

Alexander Kerensky had emerged as the leading figure among the Social Democrats, which was how the General referred to moderate elements on the left. As a public speaker, Kerensky was capable of commanding the attention of large audiences enjoying the unfamiliar experience of liberty. The situation, however, created a dilemma for Kerensky. He sat in the Duma and had accepted the Provisional Government's invitation to become Minister of Justice, but he was also deputy chairman of the Petrograd Soviet. If he threw his weight behind the Provisional Government, he would lose his support in the Petrograd Soviet; but if the Provisional Government could not establish its authority there was a real danger of anarchy.[18]

General Poole got an early insight into the seriousness of the situation when he had an interview with Kerensky on 15 March:

> Went round to the Artillery Department in morning. They are just coming back there – all very frightened! Saw Manikovsky, who was most depressing about the Social Democratic Party and wants us to come in. Went to embassy and discussed with the ambassador. Wired home urging Labour Party to cable out to

---

18 Richard Abraham Alexander Kerensky, *The First Love of the Revolution* (New York, 1987). 'General Poole ... buttonholed Kerensky on 2 March to ask when war production might resume'. 2 March was 15 March by the Western calendar.

Social Democrat Party telling them to work, etc. Went down to Duma and interviewed Kerensky, who is head of Social Democrat Party. He has just been made Minister of Justice and is not too safe, as his party are getting suspicious. I put my points in front of him. He agreed as to the gravity, but said the whole thing was out of hand. If they take steps to compel the people to go back to work now, they will upset the whole thing. He is really afraid. If the extreme Social Democrat Party gain more ground, we shall see (or rather we shan't), but others who are safe will. I fear that will outdo the excesses of the French Revolution. It all hinges on whether Rodzyanko can hold them or not.[19]

Equally prophetic was Poole's prediction for the monarchies of Germany, Austria and Turkey:

That poor Emperor what a chance he had. If only a week ago today he had sent a wire and done what he ought to have done, he could have been a demigod today. It's marvellous to think that in three days the strongest and most powerful king in the world is overthrown and deposed by a handful of students and socialists. It will make the other kings see that they set their houses in order, especially Wilhelm – he will go next![20]

The General summarised:

Things are still in the balance. There is a strong Social Democratic Party, who are for stopping the war. If they gain ascendancy the bottom will fall out and we shall probably fall into anarchy. If, on the other hand, the moderates can master the situation all will be well. The pendulum swings up and down – no one can say how it will end. It's most amusing the hand we all take in this: I spend all day at the Duma now and interviewing ministers and telling them what to do! I am so perturbed about all the works still being shut. If it goes on the Huns will be here in a month, if they want to come.[21]

---

19 Poole, Diary, 15 March 1917.
20 Frederick Poole to Alice Poole, 18 March 1917. Wilhelm was Kaiser Wilhelm II.
21 Frederick Poole to Alice Poole, 18 March 1917.

George Bury also brought a grim message from the new Prime Minister, Prince Lvov, that the government was 'like straws floating on a turbulent stream'.[22]

Poole decided to tackle the Petrograd Soviet on whether it would allow the Provisional Government to continue the war. He interviewed Nikolay Chkheidze, Chairman of the Petrograd Soviet, and some of his Social Democratic colleagues, and even attended a meeting of the Social Democrat committee. He departed noting, 'Their views were on the whole quite satisfactory. They are quite willing to go on with the war until the Hun throws up his hand, which is after all what we want. Chkheidze is a strong man – quite interesting – reminds me of John Burns'. Burns had been an early trade unionist, best known for the success of the London dock strike of 1889, and subsequently as a politician on the left wing of the Liberal Party, which marked him out as a radical rather than an extremist. Poole was treated respectfully by the Soviet and indeed provided with a car formerly belonging to the royal family: 'It is a beautiful quite new 60/80 Delauney Belleville with everything of the very best and two men on the box!'

Later that day the British Ambassador brought Poole an anonymous letter appealing for help from officers who were being held captive in miserable conditions by the sailors who had taken control of the naval base at Kronstadt and were running it as an independent fiefdom.

> Mr Ambassador, You have been kind enough to recognise the new government and that's why we allow ourselves to approach you for your protection because we have no other option. We implore you to direct your attention to the absolutely impossible state of naval officers, prisoners of the sailors at Kronstadt. They are dealing with us even more fiercely than our prisoners in Germany, and yet you are certainly aware of how much the whole universe is revolted by these monsters. The arrested officers do not even have straw for their beds, nor even planks of wood; they are forced to sleep on beds which have only rings of iron. As food they receive only bread and water; it is demanded that they sing *La Marseillaise* and those who are not in a position to do so are obliged to remain for two hours on rifle discipline as a penance.

---

22 Poole, Diary, 24 March 1917.

At present, the sailors have refused the government permission to transfer these officers to one of Petrograd's prisons, under the pretext of their necessity for their service to the fleet. However, if it continues on the present course, these officers will no longer be able to do anything at all, not just fulfilling their heavy and exhausting fatigues. If the Allies want to keep the Russian fleet, it is absolutely essential to take care of the fate of the imprisoned officers and come to their aid as soon as possible.

The names of those who address you, Ambassador, are unknown to you, but they are Russian people who implore your help.[23]

On 29 March Poole raised the matter with his friend Guchkov, now the Minister of War, who told him that the Provisional Government was powerless to help the imprisoned naval officers. Afterwards, with the benefit of Guchkov's goodwill, he went on to introduce himself to Nekrasov, the newly appointed Minister of Ways and Communications, thereby moving on to the territory occupied by George Bury before his return to London to report back to Lloyd George on the state of the Russian railway system. The General now found people were beating a path to his door. The British Military Attaché from the Caucasus, where Russian armies were fighting the Ottoman Empire, came. So did General de Candolle, who was concerned about the South Western Railway, which was the lifeline on which Romania depended for outside assistance.

Poole decided the time had come to brief Sir Henry Wilson, 'I wrote to H.W. giving an account of all the doings up to date and saying that in my idea if the Huns attack seriously they should have a chance of taking Petrograd. I base my views on 1. Discipline question; 2. Labour question and 3. Expressed wish for peace of many of Social Democrat Party. I hope I am pessimistic'.[24] With this report Poole established his credibility on Russia with the powers that be at home,

My dear Poole, Your letter of 5 April was most interesting reading. I had several copies made and gave them to Sir Douglas Haig, to Nivelle, to Esher, to Foch and so on. Most interesting. So, write me

---

23 The original is in French. Translated here from a letter in the author's possession dated 14 March 1917 (27 March by the Western calendar).
24 Frederick Poole to Alice Poole, 5 April 1917.

your news again. We like it so much because we know it is the true, as well as the inside, story of what is going on. How little we thought when I first told you, at my house, of the trip it would turn into all this. Of many weak spots, the navy seems the weakest, and will be all the more when the ice goes.

As regards your rank and allowances, I was shocked to hear that these things had not been settled and wrote at once to CIGS asking what the devil was the delay. I may have to go to London for a day visit and if I do I will make a point of seeing about it … I am with French GHQ trying to keep the peace for the moment, but my address is GHQ. When I got back from Russia there was considerable trouble, so I was packed off at once. The French politicians, and indeed, a little, the French nation and army are getting a trifle on an edge, but I think they will be all right when the Boches give ground quicker. [25]

---

25 Sir Henry Wilson to Frederick Poole, 26 April 1917.

12

The Provisional Government

At first after the Revolution there had been some semblance of a gradual return to normal life. Despite the pessimistic prognosis he had sent to Sir Henry Wilson, even Poole admired the Provisional Government's handling of the ceremony to honour those who had lost their lives in forcing the Czar to abdicate:

> A day of burial of the victims of the revolutionary party. Enormous processions all day from different quarters of the city, concentrating on the Champs de Mars. Everybody was a bit nervous of what would happen, but it all went off well. Admirably organized in a most orderly crowd. I heard of no disturbances whatever and the only police in the city were the militia. So it's a great triumph for the government.[1]

Further reassurance came when the great festival of the Russian Easter was celebrated in the traditional manner with the churches full. Poole, who had been intent on retiring to bed after seeing the midnight procession in the Kazan Cathedral, found himself celebrating with his hosts. 'At 1.30 a.m. had to have an Easter supper here: hard-boiled eggs, ham and a sort of creamy cake. All I'm told typical Russian Easter fare!'[2] Next morning he went 'to church in morning at English Church. After came back to lunch

---

1 Poole, Diary, 5 April 1917.
2 Poole, Diary, 14 April 1917.

with the Marshalls, who I met there. Lovely warm day. For the first time since I have been in Russia I walked out without a coat on. Went to embassy and got letters on way home.[3]

Yet soon enough it became apparent how much life had changed and how difficult it was for the formerly privileged classes to cope. There was no one to keep order in Petrograd. The Czarist police force had been disbanded, the jails had been thrown open, criminals and deserters were roaming the streets and the large garrison of troops had become little more than an undisciplined rabble intent on mischief and without any respect for their officers. On 24 April George Chirinsky's family decamped to Moscow in the belief that they would be safer there. Prince Ouroussov was on a different tack:

> Went into Ouroussov's at about 11 p.m. and stayed at his party till 2.30 a.m. Too many young aristocrats there who sit and wring their hands at the situation and do nothing to help. Their one idea is to join the British Army! Their idea of their own value to us differs slightly from mine. If they can't manage their own men, they certainly couldn't tackle ours.[4]

Poole returned two days later to dine with Ouroussov, but the evening was not a success and they drifted apart.

America welcomed the March Revolution as the first transitional step from the absolute rule of the Romanovs to a democracy, with the opening of a huge opportunity for trade in a large economy at an early stage of development. The USA, now an ally of Russia in the war, was ready to offer massive assistance in the form of financial credits, supplies of munitions and technical expertise to regenerate the railway system, providing a dimension of support that was well beyond the capacity of Britain and France after their manpower and resources had been drained by three years of costly and unsuccessful warfare.

Powerless as it was, the Provisional Government did its best. On 4 April 1917, the day when Congress voted to declare war on Germany, a Russian general visited Poole and proposed the establishment of a committee to

---

3   Poole, Diary, 15 April 1917.
4   Poole, Diary, 19 April 1917.

The Provisional Government

coordinate the purchasing of armaments from the Allies and the consequent prioritising of the shipping required: 'In evening General Michaelson came to see me to find out my views about starting an Anglo-Russian Commission here to decide on all orders. It will be useful if – and only if – we cut out a lot of the useless committees at home. However, I expressed my approval in principle. He will let me have his detailed proposals later'.[5] Poole learned from his new friend, Nikolay Nekrasov, the Minister of Ways and Communications, 'They are now going to squeeze America for all they are worth'.[6] The General's spirits rose, 'America will make a big difference out here – both for money and supplies. It will help to put Russia on its legs again'.[7]

Boris Bakhmeteff, the assistant Minister of Trade and Industry following the Revolution, was dispatched to the USA as the new ambassador of the Provisional Government, accompanied by a large retinue chosen to impress. Lieutenant Riggs, the Military Attaché at the US Embassy in Petrograd, accompanied Bakhmeteff to Vladivostok. Poole recorded, 'He suggests, and I agree, that the best thing is to concentrate on the supply of wagons and locos and establish a mission at Vladivostok',[8] and 'Riggs came in in afternoon. The Russians have agreed to his proposals re America and now I hope we shall see an improvement in the Siberian Railway'. In return, President Wilson now sent a fact-finding mission led by Senator Elihu Root and a railway commission headed by John F. Stevens. He had already appointed a new ambassador to Russia, David Francis.

The difficulties of supplying Russia were, however, immense. Shipping worldwide was scarce because of wartime demands and the losses inflicted by enemy submarines. The closure of the sea routes through the Baltic and the Dardanelles forced Russia to depend on just three ports: Murmansk and Archangel in north Russia and Vladivostok in the Far East. Murmansk, also known as Murman or Romanov, was an ice-free port because of the warm current from the Gulf Stream, but it had a primitive and unreliable single-track rail link, built over inhospitable terrain, which had only formally opened in late 1916 and was full of shortcomings. Archangel was ice-bound during the winter months, which limited navigation to barely seven months of the year; and, although the rail link was double-tracked, it did not run across the

---

5 Poole, Diary, 4 April 1917.
6 Poole, Diary, 10 April 1917.
7 Frederick Poole to Alice Poole, 14 April 1917.
8 Poole, Diary, 6 April 1917.

North Dvina River to connect with the town and the port. Vladivostok was ice free, but far distant and dependent on the Trans-Siberian Railway, which was single-tracked for most of its length. With roads in a primitive state and rivers ice-bound in winter, Russia depended on its railways to function, but by 1917 the Russian railway system had been reduced to a very poor condition through overuse, insufficient maintenance and a particularly harsh winter. The age-old conundrum of Russia's centres of population being distant from its natural resources was compounded into a problem of nightmare proportions by the demands of the war effort against Austria and Germany, made worse by the extension of the Front Line far to the south beyond the Caucasus down to the Black Sea to fight the Turks.

The General's optimism was short lived: everywhere there was corruption, delay, excuses, incompetence and a general lack of leadership in a country descending into chaos and disorder. Although conditions had improved marginally at Tsarskoe Selo, it was only because of the beneficial impact of the British officers he had installed there. Poole also returned to Stavka, 'Thank goodness I am not here permanently – It would drive me mad'.[9] He did his best the following day, but with limited effect:

> Went with Hanbury-Williams and had long interview with General Denikin, Chief of Staff. I made a report to him as to the situation of the artillery given from the Allies and urged him to take drastic steps to ensure it being put early into the line. He had been well primed with excuses, but I was able to tear them all to pieces and I really hope I have done some little good. He had no idea even that the 9.45-inch trench mortars were in the country. I suggested that Gaydon should take them to the Front. He is going into the question of sound rangers. On the whole I am quite pleased and feel I have done a little good.[10]

The Grand Duke Serge was still at Stavka, 'In afternoon I was sent for by Serge and had a long talk to him. Poor chap he is very down on his luck – a sort of prisoner and deadly dull. He was very glad to see me and we discussed things generally'.[11]

---

9 Poole, Diary, 27 April 1917.
10 Poole, Diary, 28 April 1917. Gaydon was one of Poole's officers.
11 Poole, Diary, 29 April 1917.

The Provisional Government

After Stavka Poole went on to Moscow accompanied by a Russian colonel, 'a "live" man and helps a lot. He quite upholds the "get going anyhow" theory I am always preaching.'[12] 'In afternoon had long discussion with Gruzinov about artillery generally and the necessity of speeding up. My visit has had the effect already of making them produce a thousand horses, which they said two days ago were unobtainable. We have fairly put the wind up the whole place.'[13]

Whilst in Moscow, Poole met the Platonov family, friends of Robert Bruce Lockhart, the British Consul in Moscow, and Valentine, who commanded the small contingent of British aeroplanes sent to Russia. 'Went up to Platonovs at night – on to supper and variety show there – then to see the gypsies. Home at 3.30 a.m. dead tired.'[14] In due course Sacha Platonov would become one of Poole's ADCs.

Back in Petrograd on 5 May, Poole learned that Bratiano, the Romanian Prime Minister, was there. Romania had entered the war overconfidently in August 1916 only to find its invasion across the Carpathian Mountains into Hungarian Transylvania repulsed. This was followed up by the Central Powers occupying the whole country, apart from the province of Moldavia. Had it not been for Russian reinforcements, Romania would have been totally defeated in 1916. Bratiano had arrived with a large delegation to see whether it could still count on Russia.

> Had interview with Bratiano in morning at Winter Palace. He says Romania wants to make an attack and what can we do to help them by way of heavy artillery. Am trying to get some 6-inch for them and will see when I get down there what they are like. Knox came in and we had a long talk. Lunched at embassy. Shipping likely to be cut down, which is a pity. Tried to see Guchkov in afternoon – no use – appointment for tomorrow.[15]

On the next day, 'Knox and I went to see Guchkov with a proposal to run a beano for him against the Huns, with the basis for it a concentration

---

12 Poole, Diary, 2 May 1917.
13 Poole, Diary, 3 May. Colonel Gruzinov was the Commander-in-Chief of the Moscow Military District, a post he held for just one month.
14 Poole, Diary, 3 May 1917.
15 Poole, Diary, 7 May 1917.

of every one of our guns, but he was in bed very seedy'.[16] The hopeless predicament of the Provisional Government had reduced Guchkov from the man of dynamism, optimism and purpose into a pitiful wreck. It was less than two months since 15 March when Czar Nicholas II had abdicated and the Provisional Government had taken office.

One of the few positive contacts that the General made was with Albert Thomas, the French Minister of Armaments, who had arrived with a large entourage in Russia to assess the situation with a large entourage on 22 April. He also brought a letter of recall for the French Ambassador, Maurice Paléologue, who had been too intimately connected with the Romanov dynasty to be credible with the Provisional Government. Although Thomas and Poole held diametrically opposed political views, they were united by the conviction that nothing else mattered but winning the war and that the ingredients of success were courage, energy, and initiative. Poole hit it off immediately with Thomas, 'a real good man – keen and quick'.[17]

Sir George Buchanan had asked Poole to call on Thomas, as he was otherwise engaged at a farewell luncheon given by the Italian Ambassador for Paléologue. The luncheon left Buchanan depressed and when Poole dined at the British Embassy that evening it was a gloomy occasion: 'The sands are running out as far as our government is concerned and unless there is a speedy change, we shall cut off all supplies'.[18] His assessment was bleak:

> We seem to live in a rush and never have time to do much. One never knows, however, if one's work is any use. These are such unsatisfactory people and there's no doubt that the majority of them want peace more than anything. They can't keep concentrated on anything for more than a few months. I should never be surprised to see the whole show crumble up in the next few weeks.[19]

The Romanians, however, were keen to fight on and had little difficulty in persuading Poole to see what was happening for himself, 'We ought to be very well done as they are anxious to get something out of us and we are

---

16 Poole, Diary, 8 May 1917.
17 Poole, Diary, 11 May 1917.
18 Poole, Diary, 11 May 1917.
19 Frederick Poole to Alice Poole, 11 May 1917.

travelling down with Bratiano, the Prime Minister. So Ferdinand ought to pull out a big decoration for us I think!!!'[20]

On the afternoon of 13 May, Poole joined Bratiano's special train at Stavka, accompanied by George Chirinsky and Victor Warrender as his ADCs. Warrender's godmother, Queen Victoria, was the grandmother of the Queen of Romania, creating a connection with the Romanian royal family. On the evening of 14 May Bratiano's train stopped at Kiev, where there was a long delay. Summer had now arrived, the linden trees were in blossom. Kiev looked beautiful and Poole's Romanian hosts made the most of the occasion:

> Travelling all day. Very well done by Bratiano and the Romanians. Arrived Kiev 9.30 p.m. and waited till midnight. Then motors to meet us and we went for a drive round Kiev and then to dine at the Continental Hotel. It really is a beautiful place in summer – more so than one would have thought possible when seeing it in winter. Had a long talk to General Prezan, who is very anxious to make a big offensive. He showed me his plans and really, if his men have any drive in them, it should afford fair hopes of success.[21]

Poole was more cautious after reaching Jassy, the capital of Moldavia, where the government and the royal family had fled after the Germans had swept over the Carpathians and captured Bucharest:

> Lunched at embassy. In afternoon called on General Ragoza, commanding troops in Romania under the king. He was frankly pessimistic. Said his people would not take offensive 1. because they felt they were too weak in artillery; 2. because of unrest caused by the discipline question and general wish for peace; and 3. because they were more interested in question of getting land than of fighting. He said he only had forty-seven heavy guns on the front of the Fourth Army and practically no aeroplanes. Then went on to Prezan, who is perhaps unsoundly optimistic. He wants to make an attack but doesn't seem to have worked out details:

---

20 Frederick Poole to Alice Poole, 11 May 1917. Ferdinand was King Ferdinand of Romania.
21 Poole, Diary, 14 May 1917.

ammunition, aeroplanes, horses. He was sketchy on all these points.'[22]

On his return to Jassy, the King and Queen of Romania invited Poole to lunch. The General was decorated as a 'Grand officier de la Couronne de Roumanie, a very pretty order – ranks with our KCMG';[23] Chirinsky and Warrender were also decorated. Poole still felt overwhelmed after returning to Petrograd:

I enjoyed the lunch very much. Sat next to the Queen and just opposite the King. They all talk English, so it made things easy. The Queen has been a most beautiful woman but is now beginning to age. Still she looks very lovely dressed as a nurse. They were both most simple and friendly and it was a very pleasant experience. When I said goodbye to the King after we had had a long talk after lunch, he held my hand for about three minutes as if we were the dearest of old friends.[24]

Poole tried to secure assistance for Romania, but the problems of delivery were almost insurmountable. Kiev was 823 miles from Petrograd and 532 miles from Moscow, let alone the additional distance to north Russia. Razdyelnaya, the junction on the South West Railway for Jassy was 361 miles south of Kiev and just forty-five miles north of Odessa on the Black Sea. Razdyelnaya was a further 141 miles distant from the frontier town of Ungheni, which was a bottle-neck. 'At Ungheni, the frontier railway station, the congestion was indescribable. The whole needs of a nation, and a nation destitute of everything, had to pass over this solitary line.'[25] The line continued the final twelve miles to its own terminus at Jassy: it was unconnected with the Romanian railway system, which anyway did not have the Russian broad gauge.

---

22 Poole, Diary, 16 May 1917.
23 Poole, Diary, 26 May 1917.
24 Frederick Poole to Alice Poole, 4 June 1917.
25 Mrs Gordon, *Roumania Yesterday and Today* (London, 1918).

13

Petrograd and Moscow

Prince Lvov tried to make the best of the unenviable situation of being a Prime Minister without power. He persuaded leading members of the powerful Petrograd Soviet to become ministers in a coalition administration, hoping that they could transfer to the Provisional Government the authority and standing they enjoyed in the powerful Soviet. This proved hopeless, however, as they had no experience of holding office

Alexander Kerensky was moved from Ministry of Justice to succeed Guchkov as Minister of War and Marine, in the belief that his undoubted energy and his popularity with the masses would revitalise the armed forces. Kerensky toured the front line, where he was deceived by the rapturous reception he had from troops inspired by his oratory. He came to believe that the army was ready to mount the offensive that Russia's hard-pressed allies were demanding on pain of cutting off any further aid. He also ignored numerous warnings from loyal and conscientious serving officers about the complete collapse of discipline, leading to the disintegration of Russia's fighting capacity. This collapse played into the hands of the Bolsheviks. After three years of war, Lenin's programme of peace, bread and land had an instant appeal, made even more forceful when advanced with what amounted to an open invitation to those who had not to steal with impunity from those who had.

In fairness to Kerensky, the Revolution released not only forces of disorder but also bursts of enthusiasm and pride that were easy to misconstrue. As General Poole noted, 'Went to station in evening en route to Stavka and found the most terrible chaos: a draft, the first, was leaving for the front and the enthusiasm was enormous; so much so that we couldn't get along and so missed the train and returned'.[1] Finlayson, a serious soldier, also told Poole after visiting the front line that he was 'Quite pleased with his trip. He is of opinion that they mean to fight all right and that the attack is being well worked out and will be a success'.[2] Poole, however, went on to note, 'Bad reports of labour situation from south both in Kharkov and Donetz basin. The men are making impossible demands and won't abate them. Government is weak and won't handle the matter, so all points to a crash here'.

During the General's absence in Romania a team of British officers led by Colonel Byrne, sent by the Ministry of Munitions, arrived in Petrograd. Byrne saw the need for vigorous action, rightly alarmed by the behaviour of Trotsky, who was returning from exile on the same train to join Lenin and the Bolsheviks in Petrograd.

The uncertain and anxious atmosphere of the time is captured by Christopher Thomson, who had been recalled as British Military Attaché in Romania and left Petrograd for home on 6 June:

> At the embassies of the Allied powers there is a not unnatural nervousness; no one knows what is going to happen. As a matter of fact, they never did know what was going on, but now they admit their ignorance ... In the hotels, foreigners have rallying spots where they arrange to gather in case of attack by night ...The streets are crowded, also the churches and the two cathedrals. I attend these latter on account of the singing. Moreover, one sees the people, or at least a large number of them, in a frame of mind that makes me, even at this eleventh hour, wonder whether there will be a real red revolution ... Lenin is here and very active. I haven't either seen him or heard him. The French journalist says he will be arrested shortly and that everything is going well.[3]

On his first day back in Petrograd, Poole wrote, 'Found we had shifted our office to the palace in the Moika and had shifted our house to a charming

---

[1] Poole, Diary, 26 April 1917.
[2] Poole, Diary, 4 June 1917. Finlayson had only arrived in Russia in April and had not had much of an opportunity to grasp the true picture.
[3] Christopher Thomson, *Smaranda* (London, 1931). The French journalist was Claude Anet.

place in Galernaya nearby. A really nice house, which is offered to us free, to save it from plunder. Had long talk to Banting. In evening dined with Byrne and discussed things generally. He is very nice and strikes me as exceedingly capable.'[4]

Next day Poole went to the British Embassy where, in a long talk, the normally reserved and distant Sir George Buchanan complained about how he was being treated: 'He is being virtually superseded by Henderson and is very angry about it.'[5] Arthur Henderson had been just sent out by Lloyd George in the belief that a Labour politician might have more credibility with the new and unpredictable political leaders thrown up by the Revolution. Poole also had another talk with Colonel Byrne: 'He thinks, and I agree that, if we can't run the munitions of the whole country, there is no use in him being out here and he ought to go home in a few months.'[6]

Meanwhile Sir Henry Wilson's promises were being more than fulfilled. Poole's promotion from acting brigadier general to acting major general was announced on 26 May. He was also made a brevet colonel, entitling him to the substantive rank of full colonel as soon as a vacancy arose. Notcutt was given the Military Cross. On 5 June Poole received a telegram announcing that his pay had been increased to £1250 per annum.

Although he had expressed his disappointment to Poole, Buchanan concealed his anger about being superseded and handled Henderson astutely. He demonstrated immediately the strength of his own position by giving a dinner party at the embassy on 2 June, the day following Henderson's arrival in Petrograd. The guests included not only the Prime Minister and Foreign Minister of the Provisional Government, Prince p. 135. Para 3, line 7, Mikhail Tereschenko and Emile Vandervelde, but also Albert Thomas and Georgy Vandervelde, who were Socialists of similar or greater stature than Henderson. Thomas, the French Minister of Munitions, had just returned from a tour of the Front Line with Kerensky. Vandervelde was about to leave on a similar tour. They were all fluent in French, whilst Henderson could speak only English. Of the other guests only Tereschenko spoke English. They were all exercised by the fast-moving and threatening developments they were witnessing at close hand and had little use for the experience of a Labour politician from a stable country used to democratic change.

---

4   Poole, Diary, 1 June 1917.
5   Poole, Diary, 2 June 1917.
6   Poole, Diary, 2 June 1917.

General Sir Frederick Poole

The following evening Buchanan hosted a dinner at the British Embassy at which General Poole urged Henderson to ask Prince Lvov, the Prime Minister, to hand over control of 'the munitions of the whole country'. A few days later Buchanan went on holiday, leaving Henderson to experience at first hand how complex and dangerous the Russian scene was.[7] By this time Poole and Byrne were doing their best to help preparations for the coming Kerensky Offensive. The General 'made arrangements for Moscow trip,'[8] and 'went with Byrne in morning to call on Manikovsky … He gave me a free hand to ginger up matters at Moscow'.[9]

The General and his entourage, including Banting and Chirinsky, arrived in Moscow by the overnight train from Petrograd and were met at the station by 'four artillery officers and two cars – so came in with a great splash!'[10] They were driven to the National Hotel and an open-top motorcar was placed at their disposal.

Moscow was the natural point from which to supply the entire Russian Front Line except in the north, which was better served from Petrograd. It had become the hub of the Russian railway system with lines radiating to all parts of the country, including Archangel in the north, Petrograd in the north west, Kiev in the south west, the Crimea, Rostov-on-Don and Caucasus in the south, and Vladivostok in the east. The Black Sea Express and the Caucasus Express passed through Moscow on their journeys from Petrograd, taking advantage of the line that bisects the city. The circular railway around Moscow connected with convenient points outside the city for guns to be collected, assembled and parked, for harness and horses to be gathered, and for artillery batteries to be loaded onto trains and dispatched to the Front. It gave access to the Khodynka Field on the north-west side of the city which was used for military manoeuvres and which provided a landing ground for aircraft. In the vicinity were a large military barracks and the workshops where British personnel prepared aircraft and the French assembled guns shipped in via the port of Archangel.

---

7   Poole, Diary, 8 June 1917. 'In afternoon Byrne and I had a talk to Henderson, who is now most optimistic. I hope with sufficient grounds'.
8   Poole, Diary, 7 June 1917.
9   Poole, Diary, 9 June 1917.
10 Poole, Diary, 11 June 1917. Although the waiters throughout the city were on strike, the General's party dined agreeably that evening at the only restaurant functioning normally. It was at the top of one of the tallest houses in Moscow, 10 Maly Gnezdnikovsky Pereulok, in a side street off the Tverskaya, and afforded a magnificent view.

On the Monday, Poole, Banting and Chirinsky motored out to Cherkisovo. It was then a village beyond the circular railway to the north east of the city and a point of assembly for artillery. Soldiers who had ceased to care about discipline after the Revolution were suddenly on good behaviour, 'In afternoon we motored out to where the artillery is forming. There are forty-eight guns there now – a lot of excellent material there. I made the men unload two guns and run a gun up the hill to the gun park and they worked magnificently ...'[11] Poole continued:

> Went off in morning to the workshops, where we saw a lot of French working really hard at the 120 pounders. They have some five hundred officers and men out here and are doing the equipping themselves. The workshop is well run and is quite a good show. I had the committee on the mat over the harness for the 4.5 and 6.0 pounders. Then we went on to the railway siding and there saw a great mess: two guns and a mass of wagons for 6.0 pounders and 4.5. Raised a storm and promised a train and party for tomorrow to shift the mess ...[12]

On Wednesday, the General was pleased with the British contingent at the Moscow aerodrome, but his suspicions were aroused about their pay and conditions. He got Banting, who relished untangling complexity and getting at the truth, to investigate: 'In morning went up to aerodrome, where I had a good impression. All our work seems very good. Had a great morning with the Russian paymaster over the men's pay. Banting downed him in the end'.[13]

Poole professed himself satisfied on returning on Thursday, 'Went out to railway junction siding in morning – no confusion there. About thirty 4.5 wagons or trucks. Nothing belonging to us. At Gyll siding they have cleaned up well and that alone shows we have done some good down here'.[14] Verkhovsky, the incoming commander of the Moscow Military District, agreed to 'carry out any policy I indicated as regards the guns'.[15] The General

---

11 Poole, Diary, 11 June 1917.
12 Poole, Diary, 12 June 1917.
13 Poole, Diary, 13 June 1917.
14 Poole, Diary, 14 June 1917.
15 Poole, Diary, 16 June 1917.

also noted that 'Manikovsky is sending off people right and left. Two generals arrived today to look into the matters we raised'.

Poole found time for a little relaxation in Moscow. Chirinsky took him round to see his parents and he visited the Kremlin. Neilson, a brother officer attached to Colonel Knox, introduced Poole to his father-in-law, William Cazalet, 'At 5.30 p.m. started out with Neilson to his pa-in-law's dacha – about twelve miles out. Very nice place indeed. Mrs Neilson very nice. Had dinner and motored home about midnight after promising to put off our return for a day and sleep there on Saturday night. Cazalet not very pessimistic, rather pessimistic-optimistic, that is, as regards labour'.[16] Poole returned on the Saturday, 'Motored down to Khimki to spend the night with Cazalet – all very comfortable, very nice people'. He made the most of the weekend, 'Stayed down at Khimki all morning'. In the afternoon Currie, one of Poole's officers, based in Moscow, 'motored down so we borrowed his car to get back in and so saved a nasty trip by train'.[17]

William Cazalet was the proprietor of Muir and Merrilees, which enjoyed the prestige and reputation of Harrods at its zenith. It was nationalised after the Bolshevik takeover and became known as TsUM (Central Department Store). Cazalet held strong views about how little Britain cared about, let alone comprehended, the workings of commerce in the Russian market compared with Germany. Poole took the opportunity to draw Cazalet out on the subject, rightly apprehensive that, if Germany forced Russia to make a separate peace, Germany would gain control of its economy and thus have the resources to win the war.

Poole departed on Sunday 16 June by the 9.20 p.m. train for Petrograd after he 'had final talk with Byrne and decided to establish a branch office in Moscow, probably under the consul with expert assistance'.[18] Byrne, who had arrived on Thursday afternoon, remained in Moscow. The day after his return to Petrograd from Moscow Poole had a follow-up meeting with Henderson, who was now acting as the de facto British Ambassador; Sir George Buchanan was still on leave with his wife and daughter. The General

---

16 Poole, Diary, 13 June 1917. In a photograph taken during the visit a relaxed General Poole can be seen with a pipe in his hand standing in the garden of Cazalet's spacious dacha, flanked by his host on the left and Banting on his right, with a contented dog in the foreground. Further to the right stand Neilson and his bride. In 1916 Neilson had married Cazalet's daughter Helen.
17 Poole, Diary, 17 June 1917. The railway station at Khimki was the first stop for through trains from Moscow to Petrograd.
18 Poole, Diary, 16 June 1917.

found Henderson 'more optimistic than before' and learned that 'He wants to arrange a conference with us and Lvov and Kerensky and thinks that after that I might go home'.[19] Henderson was considering remaining in Russia and thought that Poole could carry a message back to the War Cabinet in London about the vigorous regeneration of the ailing Russian war effort.[20]

There was good news from the American Military Attaché Riggs who 'came in after dinner. He is just back from Vladivostok. The Americans have made a start and are hopeful of being able to do some good'.[21] Poole followed this up quickly:

A day devoted to the Americans. Went to Winter Palace in morning and had first a long talk to Bertron, who is the finance man, then to General Scott. We then lunched and had long talk to Elihu P. Root, who is quite a live man. Then in the afternoon another hour with Bertron, who is very good. He is quite alive to all Russian tricks. They will find it difficult to get round him. In the evening gave a dinner at Donon's to the Railway Commission people and went into the situation there. They are all at the top of their job in America, so I found them a most interesting crowd. Scott is a past number. Judson is the live man of the military party.[22]

On 22 June there was a conference of the Allies at the British Embassy. Poole, however, was otherwise engaged in smoothing the path for General Michaelson's committee: 'Had long interview with Michaelson in morning and cleared up several outstanding matters. He hopes to have his show properly running in a few days. Lunched with French Military Attaché and discussed with French and American members of the Michaelson Committee what line of policy we would adopt in working'.[23]

The next day Poole went back to the Winter Palace. Nothing had been achieved at the Allied conference because Henderson had failed to give a

---

19   Poole, Diary, 19 June 1917.
20   Poole now felt that when he came home, 'it will be a case of being in town practically all the time, I'm afraid, as I shall be so busy'. He wrote that he wanted smart civilian clothes, 'Bring up my best blue suit and a bowler, also my brown suit'. Frederick Poole to Alice Poole, 19 and 24 June 1917.
21   Poole, Diary, 19 June 1917.
22   Poole, Diary, 21 June 1917. Senator Root's mission was accommodated at the Winter Palace in grand style, though not perhaps in much comfort
23   Poole, Diary, 22 June 1917.

lead and the Americans had merely listened politely. The only positive note in Poole's diary entry concerned Brigadier General Judson, who would be staying on as head of the American Military Mission to Russia and thus be his opposite number. 'Lunched at Winter Palace with American Mission, had long talk with Judson, who seems sound'.[24] Poole then explored a different tack, 'In afternoon drove to Tsarskoe Selo and dined with Poliakoffs ... Home 1 a.m.'[25] Poliakov's grasp of Russian financial and industrial matters made a lasting impression on him.

From Poole's perspective events now took a new and sharply different turn for the worse. Sir George Buchanan arrived back at the British Embassy in Petrograd refreshed from his holiday and determined to reassert his authority and to sideline Henderson.[26] Buchanan was the doyen of the diplomatic corps and a baronet, with a wife with high social connections, whereas Henderson had no Foreign Office experience and came from a far humbler background.[27]

The General's initiative faltered, 'Had interviews with Sir George Buchanan, who is just back from three weeks' leave and looking much better; also with Henderson, who is really a weak, disappointing man when one really gets in touch with him'.[28] It was Buchanan, rather than the confused and uncertain Henderson, who went to see Prince Lvov the following day, 'In a conversation which I had with him on June 27, Prince Lvoff assured me that my fears as to Russia being unable to continue the war were groundless, and that, now that the government had the requisite forces at their disposal, they were determined to maintain order'.[29]

Poole knew that Prince Lvov's message was meaningless, 'Had a meeting of Michaelson Committee in afternoon. Not very satisfactory. He is suspicious and dead against us; accuses England of letting him down. I give him back, in proportion of his countrymen's incapacity to handle the goods

---

24   Poole, Diary, 23 June 1917.
25   Poole, Diary, 23 June 1917.
26   Buchanan had an unmarried daughter of marriageable age and was dependent on his earnings to maintain his position in society, as he had little in the way of private means. Buchanan was not prepared to be superseded in a post close to the top of the diplomatic profession which carried a salary of £8000 p.a.
27   *The Russian Year Book* (1911).
28   Poole, Diary, 26 June 1917.
29   Sir George Buchanan, *My Mission to Russia* (London 1923).

we send them, as much as he bargains for, and so it goes on'.[30] There was, however, little to be done. 'Henderson is away at Moscow and nothing can be settled till he comes back'.[31]

Poole hoped to influence Samuel Bertron, the financial expert on the Root Commission.[32] He 'lunched with Riggs and Bertron but did not discuss much as we were all busy and had to run on'.[33] The following day, 'In afternoon Bertron came round and we had a long discussion. I'm very keen for them to take a strong line and insist on supervision of any stuff they send out. They are a little alarmed at the vastness of my ideas!'[34] After his initial alarm, Bertron took note of the General's position. There is a letter from Bertron to Colonel House, the trusted adviser of President Wilson, suggesting the case for Russia having a dictator until the promised constitutional assembly could be elected and convened.[35]

On the Sunday Poole 'lunched at Winter Palace and afterwards had long talk with Bertron, Holbrook and Darling about the Murmansk line. The Americans are now interested and will chip in I fancy'.[36] Darling was the chief engineer of the Northern Pacific Railway. On their journey from Vladivostok to Petrograd the Americans, who were used to operating huge railway systems over challenging terrain, had already experienced the chaotic state of the Trans-Siberian Railway. They were naturally receptive to combining their expertise with the practical experience that the British and French had already gained from their involvement in the railway to the ice-free port of Murmansk in North Russia.

Poole was well briefed on the Murmansk railway. He had met Lieutenant Colonel Battine, a British officer who reported to Nekrasov, the Russian Minister of Ways and Communications, 'He seems to be not a bad fellow at all and has evidently done some good at home for the railways'.[37] Subsequently Poole 'had interview in morning with Battine and the Russian

---

30 Poole, Diary, 28 June 1917.
31 Frederick Poole to Alice Poole, 29 June 1917.
32 Born on 26 February 1865, in Mississippi, Samuel Bertron had become a prominent New York banker, founding before his thirtieth birthday Bertron and Storrs in 1894, which later became Bertron, Griscom and Co.
33 Poole, Diary, 28 June 1917.
34 Poole, Diary, 29 June 1917.
35 Samuel R. Bertron to Edward M. House, June 18, 1917, Edward M. House Papers, drawer 3, cited in Theodore Catton, *League of Honor: Woodrow Wilson and the Stevens Mission to Russia* (1986).
36 Poole, Diary, 1 July 1917.
37 Poole, Diary, 21 April 1917.

in charge of construction work on Murmansk line. He has got the whole thing tabulated and, if he works up to programme, will make a very good job of it. Battine will be useful to see that things are going on properly.'[38]

The lunchtime discussion on the Sunday generated enough enthusiasm for the General to organise a dinner that evening to gain the French perspective on the Murmansk railway from Major du Cassell, who worked alongside Battine, 'Bertron and the French engineer dined with us at night and we discussed plans for improving output.'[39] The General's enthusiasm mounted, 'I have seen a lot of the American Mission out here and am now working in close touch with Bertron, their big financial expert!!'[40]

On the morning of 2 July Poole saw Sir George Buchanan, again in command at the embassy, and afterwards Henderson, back from his visit to Moscow with nothing to say and feeling ill. In the evening Buchanan held a dinner party at the embassy where he let Poole hold forth to Senator Root and US Ambassador Francis. They had the perspective of experienced politicians who had achieved high office, Root having been Secretary of State and Francis the Governor of Missouri. Their perspective counted far more than the financial expertise and pragmatism of Bertron and the practical knowledge of the railway experts. They were, however, unconvinced by Poole's message. This was unsurprising as President Wilson had no intention of letting America involve itself in the running of the Russian state. The General concluded, 'Dined at embassy to discuss matters with Americans. Had long talk to Senator Root and Governor Francis and told them my views. They are too gentle in their ideas.'[41] One can imagine their scepticism as the General expounded on 'the vastness of my ideas!' and Buchanan's well-concealed satisfaction as events moved further his way. The discussion was not pursued after dinner and Poole 'Ended up with a conversation with Young, who is sound and progressive.'[42]

The General now returned to the safe ground of smoothing the path of the Michaelson Committee, which was perfectly acceptable to the Americans. Its formation had been a Russian initiative and its aims were

---

38 Poole, Diary, 12 May 1917.
39 Poole, Diary, 1 July 1917.
40 Frederick Poole to Alice Poole, 2 July 1917.
41 Poole, Diary, 2 July 1917.
42 Poole, Diary, 2 July 1917. G.M. Young later wrote the classic *Victorian England: Portrait of an Age* (1936).

entirely consistent with their objective of helping Russia as an ally without interfering in its internal affairs, 'In morning had meeting at American embassy with Senator Root and Mr Francis to discuss American cooperation on Michaelson's committee.'[43] Albeit unconvinced by the 'vastness of my ideas,' the Americans remained friendly and hospitable. They invited the General to the Fourth of July celebrations at the US Embassy.'[44]

Having failed with both Henderson and the Americans, the General's thoughts reverted to Poliakov. Before attending the Fourth of July celebrations, Poole 'Had long talk with Poliakoff in morning re his working for us'.[45] He may also have consulted Byrne, who had just returned from Moscow, but we only learn that Byrne was 'quite satisfied with his trip'.[46] Poole briefed Byrne at a farewell dinner on 10 July before he returned to London.

With an eye for timing, Buchanan chose the morning after the Fourth of July celebrations for the dénouement. The Americans were feeling a little jaded and looking forward to returning home, exhausted after extensive travel, meetings, conferences and the abundant hospitality organised by their Russian hosts, ever skilled in avoiding conclusions that were not wholly to their advantage. Poole was feeling miserable because of a prolonged attack of toothache. Now unchallenged, Buchanan presided over a conference of the Allies at the embassy. This produced pious platitudes and left a subcommittee to produce a note to the Provisional Government that would obviously be ignored. He used Henderson to tell Poole that the time had come for them both to return and produced a telegram from Milner summoning Poole home. As recorded by the General:

> Dentist early. Teeth still bad. Had a long conference of all the Allies at embassy in the morning to enquire into the possibility of Russia increasing her output of war material. Too much hot air and too little drive. In afternoon we had another subcommittee meeting to draft a note to present to the government. Too much milk and

---

[43] Poole, Diary, 3 July 1917.
[44] Bessie Beatty, an American journalist, was also invited and made a point of referring to the sandwiches made from white bread, which had become a delicacy in a city short of food outside the exclusive preserve of restaurants like Donon. Bessie Beatty, *The Red Heart of Russia* (New York 1918).
[45] Poole, Diary, 4 July 1917.
[46] Poole, Diary, 3 July 1917.

water! Henderson told me he thought I'd better go home with him. Sir George agreed. In afternoon came a wire from Milner also saying I'd better go home. Dined with Marshalls at night.[47]

Poole's verdict on the departing Root fact-finding mission was right enough at the time: Russia would swallow vast quantities of American aid without making the effort to save herself. Between March and November 1917, the Government of the United States opened credits of $187,000,000 to Russia under the rule of the Provisional Government, a remarkable figure to fritter away on a country soon to be torn apart by civil war and famine.[48] 'Went round in morning to Winter Palace to say goodbye to Americans. Their mission has tried hard, but has I think not done half so much as it might, because they have been bluffed by the Russians. They have believed their promises of amendment. They will promise everything and do nothing unless made to.'[49]

According to Sir George Buchanan, at a farewell dinner party on 12 July, Henderson 'suddenly burst out laughing, and on my wife asking what had amused him, he said, "It's all so funny! It's you, not I, who ought to be going!"'[50] The poor man, an innocent in Russia, had still not understood how he had been comprehensively outmanoeuvred. The General was also there: 'Had long talk with the ambassador in afternoon to get final instructions from him'.[51]

On the way back, Claude Anet introduced the General and Henderson to Joseph Noulens, the incoming French Ambassador. They met in the immaculately clean restaurant of Haparanda Station where food was laid out in a buffet style, providing a welcome return to civilised living after crossing the border with Russia. It was 14 July, the day when France celebrated the storming of the Bastille in 1789.

---

47 Poole, Diary, 5 July 1917.
48 American-Russian Chamber of Commerce, *Handbook of the Soviet Union* (1936).
49 Poole, Diary, 8 July 1917. In the longer term, the General had underestimated both the Americans and Samuel Bertron. The USA was early in establishing trading relations with Communist Russia and played a significant part in the regeneration of its economy. Bertron became a director of the American-Russian Chamber of Commerce.
50 Sir George Buchanan, *My Mission to Russia* (London 1923).
51 Poole, Diary, Thursday, 12 July 1917. After the dinner Poole and Henderson slept in the train, which departed at 6 the following morning.

17. Sir Frederick Lugard, Frederick Poole's chief in Nigeria

18. Cartoon of Sir Frederick Lugard

19. The *Corona*, Lugard's official yacht, in northern Nigeria

20. The end of the line at Zungeru, the capital of Northern Nigeria

21. Frederick, Alice, Charles and Robert Poole, September 1914

22. Frederick Poole in the trenches

23. Percy Notcutt in front of a dug out

24. Percy Notcutt observing from a trench

25. General Sir Henry Wilson, General Poole's patron
(National Portrait Gallery)

26. Frederick Poole

27. General Poole in the Carpathians, January 1917

28. British officers at the Inter-Allied Conference. Centre of front row (left to right), General Poole, General Hanbury-Williams and Colonel Knox

29. General Poole in Moscow with Princess Turkestanoff, June 1917

30. General Poole in Moscow, June 1917

31. General Poole with British and Russian officers and artillery, Moscow, June 1917

32. General Poole with a Russian officer and horses, Moscow, June 1917

33. Guns abandoned outside Moscow, June 1917

34. General Poole at William Cazalet's dacha at Khimki, June 1917. Left to right, Captain Neilson, his wife (Cazalet's daughter), Captain Banting, General Poole and William Cazalet

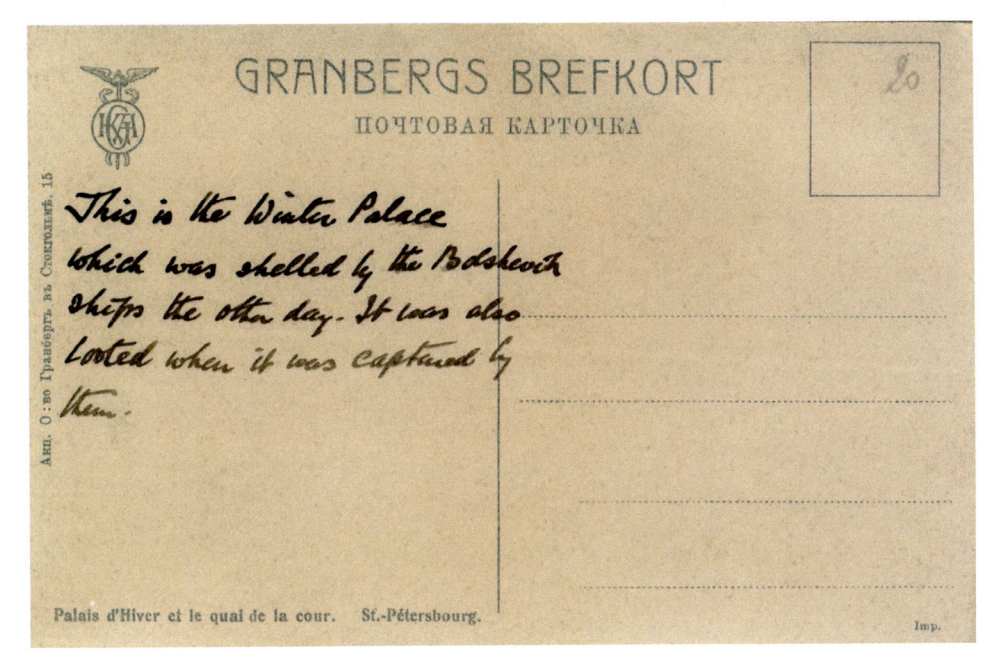

> This is the Winter Palace
> which was shelled by the Bolshevik
> ships the other day. It was also
> looted when it was captured by
> them.

35. The Winter Palace, November 1917

36. General Poole's party after crossing the lines in the Finnish Civil War to safety, March 1918

37. General Poole on HMS *Glory*, July 1918

38. General Poole, flanked by his Cossack bodyguard, Archangel, August 1918

39. Parade at Archangel, August 1918

40. Allied troops in Archangel, August 1918

41. Anton Denikin, the main leader of the White Russian forces in south Russia (second left), looks on as General Poole salutes a guard of honour, January 1919

42. General Poole arriving by train to meet General Krasnov, December 1918

43. General Poole with General Krasnov, December 1918

Peter Krassnoff Ataman of the general-lieutenant African Don Bogaevsky

MENU.

28 Décembre 1918.

Soupe purée à la reine
Patés divers.
Esturgeon stelli fère à la amèricain.
Rosbif à l'Anglaise.
Salade de pomme de terre.
Pouding Nesselrodé.
Café. Fruits. Liqueurs.
Cruchon.

44. Banquet menu, 29 December 1918

14

Coups

In early July 1917, after Germany routed the Russian offensive launched by Kerensky, the Bolsheviks launched a coup d'état against the Provisional Government. It failed because the Cossack troops in Petrograd remained loyal. On 20 July Prince Lvov resigned as Prime Minister, exhausted after four months in office and unwilling to take the harsh measures needed to crush the Bolsheviks. He was also confronted by the Ukraine's decision to secede from Russia. In his place, Alexander Kerensky became Prime Minister and appointed General Lavr Kornilov as Commander-in-Chief of the Russian army. A rift soon developed between the two men which came to a head at a conference, with representatives from all shades of opinion, held in Moscow in August to debate the future of Russia. Kerensky, eloquent as ever, and Kornilov, less eloquent but surrounded by a personal guard of Cossacks and greeted with acclaim by the wealthy, both presented themselves as the saviours of Russia. The conference reached no conclusion, but Kerensky became determined to get rid of Kornilov.

Knox, who had returned to England on leave, brought news of this before General Poole started on his second visit to Russia on 4 September. The General's party left for Aberdeen on the night train from St Pancras, after he and Banting had taken an early dinner with Alice at the station hotel. From Aberdeen the party crossed the North Sea and reached Oslo on 7 September. There Sir Mansfeldt Findlay and his wife made the General welcome at the British Legation. The party arrived in Stockholm feeling stiff and tired at 9.00 on the morning of Sunday 9 September, after sitting up all night in a crowded compartment.

Poole called on the British Minister to Sweden, Sir Esmé Howard, and met the Russian Chargé d'Affaires at the station before continuing north on the night train, which was almost empty, as no one wanted to go to Russia. Their train reached Haparanda early on 11 September. There they were greeted by Marshall, the local British consular official, and, after crossing the Finnish frontier at Tornea, by Grove, the British Consul in Helsinki. Grove brought a telegram from Sir George Buchanan urging Poole to go no further. Kerensky had broken with Kornilov at a cabinet meeting on 8 September, which went on into the early hours of the following morning. He took the line that Kornilov was planning a coup, but all his colleagues refused to believe him and resigned. Kerensky went to bed in his room at the Winter Palace after sending a telegram to Kornilov dismissing him as Commander-in-Chief of the Russian army. Kornilov, aggrieved and feeling unjustly treated, then embarked on a military coup.

Despite Buchanan's advice, the General pressed on, 'I decided that if it is so serious my place is with him and with my officers in Petrograd, so shall go on and I wired him accordingly'.[1] On the same day, Cossack troops sent by Kornilov reached Gatchina, only thirty kilometres from Petrograd. 'Apparently Kerensky has deposed Kornilov, but the latter declines to budge and is starting a show of his own at the head of the Cossacks. If he is strong, he ought to win.'[2]

Louise Bryant, travelling on the same train, wrote a description of the threatening atmosphere this news created at Tornea Station, with passports and baggage being checked and rechecked. She was escorted into a 'small, cold, badly lit room, guarded by six soldiers' where she was invited to strip and be searched by 'a stocky Russian girl'. Despite being advised by British officers not to proceed, she boarded the train where she saw Poole:

> Next to my compartment was a general, super-refined, painfully neat, with waxed moustachios … Rough, almost ragged soldiers climbed aboard continually, looked us over and departed. Often, they hesitated before the general's door and regarded him suspiciously; never at any time did they honour him with the slightest military courtesy. He sat rigid in his seat and stared back

---

[1] Poole, Diary, 11 September 1917.
[2] Poole, Diary, 11 September 1917.

at them coldly. Everyone was too agitated to be silent or even discreet. At every station we all dashed out to enquire the news and buy papers.[3]

When the train reached the last station in Finland, Poole decided to proceed with Cox and Banting and send back his other three officers. The soldiers they had encountered were under no control and ready to turn on anyone whom they suspected might be harbouring sympathies for Kornilov. According to Bryant, 'the tension was deep and ominous. We were suddenly afraid to enquire the news of the crowds on the platform. There were literally hundreds of soldiers, their faces haggard, in the half light of late afternoon. The scraps of conversation we caught sent shivers over us'. When the train then crossed from Finland into Russia, there were unpleasant moments. The passengers had to get out after midnight and wait in the cold for passports and baggage to be examined. This did not apply to the General, who still had the pink diplomatic passport provided by the British Legation in Stockholm on his first visit to Russia.[4]

In Petrograd the General learned that Kornilov had failed, 'The whole show was planned at a time when the country was not ripe for revolution. There was no attempt at secrecy. They trusted in the Cossacks, who are a broken reed'.[5] Kornilov had no legitimate objective, since there was no rebellion against the government to crush, as had been the case in July. The difficulties of his men's advance were great because the railway workers were obstructive, which meant they had to move across country without adequate supplies. Kornilov himself, who should have been with them, capitalising on their personal bonds of loyalty to him, had remained at Stavka.

After just two days back in Petrograd, Poole got to the root of a matter that is still debated today, 'It seems now that Kornilov and Kerensky were in collusion at first, but that when the news got round Kerensky got frightened and carted Kornilov'.[6] Although Kerensky survived, his standing was much diminished. Kornilov was put under house arrest but guarded by his

---

3 Louise Bryant, *Six Months in Red Russia* (New York, 1918). Louise Bryant was the wife of John Reed, the author of *Ten Days That Shook the World*,
4 Poole, Diary, 12 September 1917. 'Met by Lessing at Bieloostrov'. Lessing, who was fluent in Russian, had prepared the way and arranged accommodation at the Astoria Hotel in Petrograd.
5 Poole, Diary, 13 September 1917.
6 Poole, Diary, 14 September 1917.

General Sir Frederick Poole

own men with no question of bringing him to the capital and putting him on trial for treason.

The only positive feelings Poole expressed were about the Bolsheviks. He felt that they had acted decisively and wisely in organising effective resistance to Kornilov's attempted coup, while not repeating their mistake in July of making a premature and unsuccessful bid for power. The Bolsheviks 'got to hear of the plan as everyone in Russia was talking about it. They sat quite tight and gave no excuse for interference'.

When the General went to the British Embassy on Saturday morning, he found them 'much perturbed' and expecting 'a rising tonight or tomorrow'. He suggested, as the government had 'no troops to send upon which it can rely, that the embassy send for two of our submarines from Helsingfors which could give a sufficient guard for the embassy'.[7]

Unfortunately, the General tells us nothing about his meeting with Lieutenant General Barter other than 'Barter came in and we discussed matters generally'.[8] Barter had replaced Hanbury-Williams as the British military representative at Stavka and was on close terms with Kornilov. He had accompanied Kornilov to the conference in Moscow.

By this point the power of the Bolsheviks was growing fast in Petrograd, so much so that Kerensky considered relocating the Provisional Government to Moscow. Trotsky was released from prison on 17 September and on 23 September became chairman of the Petrograd Soviet, which was now dominated by the Bolsheviks, who were totally opposed to any accommodation with Kerensky. On 18 September Poole noted in his diary:

> All quiet, but an undercurrent of unrest everywhere ... Poliakoff came in afternoon and we discussed matters generally. The city here is absolutely bankrupt. It has a deficit of 10,000,000 roubles monthly and now the banks are declining to finance more. This will probably lead to riots. The country is also bankrupt. They will probably have to take drastic measures soon.[9]

He tried to reassure Alice:

---

[7] Poole, Diary, 15 September 1917. Helsingfors was Helsinki.
[8] Poole, Diary, 17 September 1917.
[9] Poole, Diary, 18 September 1917.

Coups

I have been most awfully rushed ever since I got back here so that I have hardly been able to write at all. Things are in a funny situation out here and the position is so often changing that it's difficult to forecast what is going to eventuate. The Kornilov rising is definitely squashed and as far as that goes the government is that much stronger. On the other hand, it has bumped up against the Maximalists and has now definitely broken with them. Thus, they live in fear of a rising from their side, as they have considerable power and backing, and if a successful rising came off the results would be deplorable as the whole country would be plunged into anarchy. There are now rumours of a whole shift of all government and departments to Moscow, but I don't know if it will come off. They would be in a stronger position there. If they do go, I suppose we would have to move also.

I have now shifted into Colonel Byrne's old flat. We are most comfortable there – a really good cook and lots of food. It's all quite luxurious.[10]

On 29 September, however, General Polovtsoff left Petrograd, depriving the Provisional Government of its last hope of a disciplined formation that could afford protection.[11] Polovtsoff could no longer rely on the loyalty of his Cossack troops, who were now anxious to protect their own families and left for their distant homes in the south of Russia. On arrival there the division melted away and Polovtsoff went into exile.

A trip was being organised for Poole to be shown the new munitions plants built in the interior by General Hermonius. These were meant to be an insurance against the risk of existing munitions plants being overrun by the advancing German army.[12] The trip had been sanctioned while Poole was in England. On the day of his departure from London, he had gone to the 'Ministry of Munitions and saw Bingham in morning – good interview'.[13] General Hermonius was well known to Bingham, the Deputy Director of Artillery at the War Office. Hermonius's purchasing responsibilities for

---

10 Frederick Poole to Alice Poole, 19 September 1917. The Maximalists were the Bolsheviks.
11 General P.A. Polovtsoff, *Glory and Downfall* (London, 1935).
12 Poole, Diary, 19 September. 'We are to start Sunday for our trip with Hermonius'.
13 Poole, Diary, 4 September 1917. Major General Sir Francis Bingham served as Deputy Director of Artillery at the War Office and subsequently as a member of the Ministry of Munitions Council.

armaments needed by the Russian army had brought him to London earlier in the war.

The General entertained Hermonius before they set out. 'In evening we gave a big dinner (twelve) for Hermonius, which was quite a success. The old man enjoyed it I think.'[14] It paid off, 'In morning Finlayson and I went to see Manikovsky who was very pleasant. Hermonius has been booming me and I see the results! Then went to see Verkhovsky, the new Minister of War, and had a most satisfactory interview. He will do us well if he stays in.'[15] Poole also informed Alice, 'On Sunday night Banting and I and Victor start off on a trip with General Hermonius to see some works etc. We shall be away for about a fortnight. It ought to be rather interesting, as we go over a good bit of Russia right down on the Volga in the south.'[16] George Chirinsky could not come, as he was ill. Before leaving on his tour, Poole had had a long meeting with Poliakov. Possibly, it was then that the arrangements were initiated for the General to investigate the industrial scene in Moscow on his way back to Petrograd.[17]

Poole's party travelled in style, 'Started for Moscow 9 p.m. by Caucasus Express. Special coach. Very comfortable.'[18] The carriage was roomy thanks to the broad gauge of the Russian railways and its accommodation was self-sufficient, with sleeping compartments for the officers, washing facilities, living room and a kitchen provisioned with supplies of food and drink no doubt expertly served. The reserved coach was insulated from the mass of travellers starting to overwhelm a railway system already brought to breaking point by the demands of the war effort. There was now a disorderly mass of deserters, soldiers returning home from war and peasants carrying food for sale in the cities. Many were taking advantage of their sudden freedom since the Revolution to travel in whichever part of the train they could find a footing to wherever their fancy took them, without the nicety of paying their fares or carrying documents authorising travel. The distinction between first-, second- and third-class carriages had been swept away.

The journey was undoubtedly an ordeal for the stream of once secure

---

14 Poole, Diary, 20 September.
15 Poole, Diary, 22 September 1917.
16 Frederick Poole to Alice Poole, 20 September 1917.
17 Poole, Diary, 23 September 1917. As was often the case, there is a complete absence of detail about the meeting with Poliakov.
18 Poole, Diary, 23 September 1917.

and wealthy families, intent on escaping from the grim conditions in the capital to well-appointed spa towns such as Pyatigorsk, Mineralnye Vody and Kislovodsk in the Caucasus. There the climate was healthy, food was plentiful, servants could be found and living conditions were still not unlike those before the Revolution. On the train, however, they had no protection from abuse and foul language, being swept away from their seats, reduced to standing in crowded corridors reeking of sweat, being stripped of their valuables, and having their luggage pilfered

The Caucasus Express, according to Bradshaw's August 1914 guide, departed daily from the capital at 9.30 p.m. with restaurant and sleeping cars and took ten hours and forty minutes to cover the 404 miles to Moscow, with an average speed of thirty-eight miles per hour. This represented high-speed running on a railway system where long-distance trains normally averaged between twenty and thirty miles per hour. The line between the two cities was built dead straight thanks to an autocratic whim of Czar Nicholas I. Passing over level ground, it was better laid than elsewhere on the Russian railway system. On this occasion the journey took thirteen and three-quarter hours. There was only a brief stop in Moscow for the train to be reformed with the carriages carrying those starting from there.

The next phase of the journey to Tula proved remarkably quick, taking about three hours to cover the 121 miles. At Tula the Caucasus Express continued southwards on its journey to Vladikavkaz in the foothills of the Caucasus Mountains, but the General's coach was attached to a train heading eastwards to Siberia. The track was poorly laid so the going was rough. The train took twenty-four hours to cover the 621 miles to Samara on the left bank of the Volga River. The train passed through Penza and crossed the Volga over the magnificent Alexander Bridge at Syzran, built between 1875 and 1880 and, according to Baedeker, taking six minutes to cross. Poole and his party had travelled 1146 miles in some fifty-five hours.

Poole's inspection began at Samara:

> Arrived Samara early in morning. At 9 a.m. started off to see fuse works, which are in a great block of buildings about twenty minutes' drive out of the town. They have developed enormously during the war – now employing 12,000 hands and their output ought to be 40,000 fuses a day. Owing to labour troubles, though, it barely reaches 30,000 now. It is a thoroughly modern, well-equipped,

General Sir Frederick Poole

well-ventilated works and is practically self-supplying as they make lathes, tools, everything – good organization and well run.

At 6 p.m. embarked on a most comfortable river steamer for Simbirsk, which lies about 250 versts upstream. The Volga here is a magnificent river about three quarters of a mile wide now at low water.[19]

The day at Simbirsk was long on feasting, libations, speeches and sightseeing:

Arrived Simbirsk 9 a.m. A very pretty and prosperous town, which begins on the side of the hill and extends westwards behind it. There is a fine new railway bridge across the Volga here one and a half versts long. We were met by the general's ADC and taken across to the eastern side of the Volga in a launch. Then we were met by carriages [with] very good horses driven by Austrian prisoners and taken out to the works. This is a small arms and ammunition factory but is not yet completed. The main buildings are half finished and will not be covered in before November. They are well off for machinery, but the power generating plant has not yet arrived. The organization is not good. The buildings will be magnificent. The whole thing has been planned on an absurdly large scale. When complete they hope to turn out 15,000,000 per day. We had a very good lunch at the works with speeches! In the afternoon we crossed to Simbirsk, had tea with the general and were then driven round the town in his motor. It is really a nice town, and here and there most lovely views of the Volga. At 9.30 p.m. we caught the boat for Samara.[20]

Poole so enjoyed his trip on the Volga that, had it been springtime, he would have liked to have continued to its mouth in the Caspian Sea. His hosts had wisely chosen the river's most attractive segment, known as the Bow of Samara, where the Zhigulév Hills force the Volga to make a pronounced diversion eastward and provide spectacular scenery reminiscent of the Rhine. On the left bank the monotonous steppes that stretch towards Siberia give way to hills and on the right bank there were steep thickly wooded

---

19 Poole, Diary, 26 September 1917. In 1924 Simbirsk was renamed Ulyanovsk in his honour on the death of Vladimir Ilyich Ulyanov, better known as Lenin, who was born there.
20 Poole, Diary, 27 September.

slopes interspersed with ravines. These had formed a lair in former times for outlaws looking for rich pickings from unwary river travellers.

The Russian Year Book 1916 advised, 'The Caucasus and Mercury Steamship Company which runs regular services on the Volga ... has put into commission four new and luxurious passenger steamers fitted with diesel engines working on naphtha'.[21] The 1915 edition carried an advertisement with the reassuring statement, 'First- and Second-Class Quarters isolated from Third-Class and Deck Quarters'.[22] The General's party would have enjoyed an excellent dinner in the first-class dining-room, perhaps catching the distant sound of music and the singing of voices from the lower orders packed behind the forecastle before retiring to the drawing-room in the bow, which had well-cushioned armchairs and, for the more reflective, polished writing tables. They would have passed a comfortable night in commodious cabins, equipped with electric light and washing facilities, before waking up for a hearty breakfast. The pre-Revolutionary standards that had been swept away elsewhere were still in force, although this was soon to change.

The rest of the General's trip was by railway. He left Samara on Friday 28 September and retraced his steps westwards to Penza (243 miles), branched off on a subsidiary line to Tambov (215 miles) and turned westwards again to Kozlov Junction (45 miles) on the main line from Moscow to Rostov-on-Don, which he followed southwards to Voronezh (111 miles). Then it was back to Moscow (366 miles) and finally to Petrograd (404 miles). The whole journey, including the steamer trip, was no fewer than 2842 miles over ten days, which gives some idea of Russia's formidable size and was remarkable given the unsettled conditions.

Poole's carriage was uncoupled from the afternoon train from Samara to Penza so that he could inspect a powder works built near the railway line. Impressive as the plant was, the Russian general officially in charge had lost his authority:

> These are well laid out and fairly complete. They turn out 15,000 tons a month of toluol. The work is good – about 15,000 men and women employed. The position of the officers is not happy, I gather. When we were there the general was asked why he had allowed us

---
21 N. Peacock, *The Russian Year Book 1916* (London, 1916).
22 N. Peacock, *The Russian Year Book 1915* (London 1915).

into the works without the leave of the committee!! There is also a factory for making primers and detonators – well equipped and well run. On the whole I was very pleased with all I saw.[23]

After the visit, the General's carriage was attached to the overnight train to Penza.

Arrived Penza 12.30 p.m. We were met by a special messenger from Manikovsky to Hermonius. The former has been put in charge of the anti-aircraft defences of Petrograd and, not unnaturally, finds them inadequate. He therefore prays Hermonius and me to do our best to get him at least eight anti-aircraft guns from England. We both write telegrams and all is well.

Penza is a fuse works in embryo. Most extravagant buildings all on a palatial scale regardless of expense. When finished (in about one year) it will be one of the finest places in the world. But it is all such a pity that they don't see how much better to have run up wood huts in a few weeks so that they could make fuses, which are necessary. Reports of agrarian troubles all over the country. All quiet in Petrograd. Started for Tambov at 6.30 p.m.[24]

Poole's party in its comfortable carriage was insulated from the old order in the countryside now being violently overturned. By this point landed estates were being invaded by peasants burning, looting and murdering, seizing cattle and valuables, and appropriating land for their own use.

At Tambov the General found a sylvan setting: 'Train very late, so we did not reach Tambov till 3.30 p.m. We were then fifteen versts away from the works. We had a special engine to pull our coach most of the way there and then finished up on a narrow-gauge railway. It is most beautifully sited in a pinewood.'[25] The General's party left Tambov at 10.30 p.m. and reached the busy Kozlov Junction, notorious for both delays and congestion, where they turned southwards on the main line to Voronezh. Kozlov Junction was the starting point of the railway via Tambov to Saratov, where it crossed the Volga River and continued south eastwards.

---

23 Poole, Diary, 28 September 1917.
24 Poole, Diary, 29 September 1917.
25 Poole, Diary, 30 September 1917.

Coups

Arrived Voronezh 10 a.m. and went off to inspect the works. These are just outside the town – for making fuses for high explosive shell. They are not yet completed and will probably not function before the end of the year. They are planned on an enormous scale, prodigal of expense … Voronezh itself is rather a civilized town [with] well laid out, broad streets. It is one of the old border towns against the Tartar invasion. It was also here that Peter the Great began to build his fleet which he sent by river to Moscow. It seems strange, as it is a very tiny river. Started 11 p.m. for Moscow.[26]

When the train reached Moscow:

Started 8.30 a.m. and went into Mitishi State Auto Works. Very fine works, nearly completed and just beginning to function. Their chief job will be repairs. There are already 250 lorries in for repair. The concern is run by the Siberian companies under Marshall; a very good show. Much trouble with workmen and wages excessive. We then went to see the Arbo Auto Works – Ryabushinsky is the owner – a very good and well-equipped works. At present they are putting together the machines coming from England, but in about six weeks they hope to begin construction themselves – about sixty a month. After this we looked for another works but couldn't find them … [27]

In 1916, in the typical Russian way, the government had decided it was time to create an automobile industry and so ordered the construction of six plants, one of which was the Mitishi State Auto Works inspected by the General as it was coming on stream. Arthur Marshall was an expatriate businessman who had made his living before the war by importing agricultural equipment to Siberia. He now headed the British Engineering Company of Russia and Siberia, formed in 1915 to coordinate the import of engineering components and equipment purchased by the Russian

---

26 Poole, Diary, 1 October 1917.
27 Poole, Diary, 3 October 1917. In Communist times the factory produced the Zil limousines favoured by elite members of the party. Pavel Ryabushinsky was the head of a wealthy Moscow-based family with industrial and banking interests.

Government.[28] At this early stage, the new plant was an assembly operation, hence the connection with Marshall, who organised the delivery of components, parts and sub-assemblies from England.

Back in Petrograd, Poole summarised his trip:

> I have just got back this morning from a most successful trip and, as there is a bag out tonight, I will send a few lines to tell you I am still alive! We have travelled for hundreds of miles right down to the south of Russia – very comfortable. We had our own special coach and just hooked it on to any train we liked. We had two days steaming up and down the Volga and in most comfortable ships, which I especially liked. We saw some very good works, but the labour conditions are very bad and depressing all over the country. I don't know how it will all end; but, unless they find a strong government who can and will govern, there will certainly be a big débâcle before many months.[29]

A 'big débâcle' was indeed about to happen, but it came in just over a month rather than in many months.

Poole's priorities on his return are clear, 'Meeting of Michaelson Committee in afternoon – much hot air, very little accomplished. Lessing dined with us last night'.[30] The Michaelson Committee, set up to coordinate the purchase of armaments from the Allies and the consequent prioritisation of shipping, had ceased to be relevant with Russia now spent as a fighting force. On the other hand, Lessing was an integral element in Poole's dialogue with Poliakov and assessment of Russia's resources. On Monday 8 October, he took Lessing with him to see Verkhovsky, the Minister of War, and over dinner briefed him before he departed for home so that he could bring the authorities in London fully into the picture. Poole was also ready to take his relationship with Poliakov a stage further, 'Poliakoff and Kamenka dined with us at night and we played bridge'.[31] They dined in the comfortable flat with its excellent cook taken over from Colonel Byrne and afterwards playing bridge, a game Poole relished for relaxed and informal talk.

---

28 Leeds Russian Archive.
29 Frederick Poole to Alice Poole, 4 October 1917.
30 Poole, Diary, 4 October 1917.
31 Poole, Diary, 10 October 1917.

Coups

Boris Kamenka was President of the Azoff-Don Commercial Bank and one of the five directors of the Russian Corporation in Russia. The others were Alexey Putilov, President of the Russo-Asiatic Bank and owner of large industrial undertakings, including the huge Putilov works in Petrograd; Alexander Vyschnegradsky, Managing Director of the International Commercial Bank of Petrograd; Ernest Grube, President of the Commercial Bank of Siberia; and Jacques Outine, President of Banque d'Escompte of Petrograd. They were at the centre of the Russian banking system.

The General was in possession of knowledge and contacts bound to be of interest to Russian financiers. Quite apart from what he had learned during the tour organised by General Hermonius and from his engagements in Moscow, Poole was on intimate terms with Russian and Allied military circles in Petrograd and had many contacts at Stavka. He was involved with the Allied missions to improve the railways, with conditions in the Caucasus, with the beleaguered state of Romania, with measures to suppress contraband trade with the enemy, with the aerial defences of Petrograd, and with much else besides. The Caucasus was of great interest to his guests, as the wealthy Russians congregating there might in time offer the hope of averting Russia's descent into anarchy. From Poliakov's perspective, the evening allowed him to demonstrate to Kamenka that he had access to Poole and that, if business eventually could be done with the British Government, Poole would be a key intermediary.

The mood in the capital at this point is captured by E.H. Keeling in *Adventures in Turkey and Russia*. Keeling had escaped from captivity in Turkey and managed to sail across the Black Sea to Sevastopol with two other British officers, Captain R.J. Tipton and Lieutenant H.C.W. Bishop.[32] Poole met the three officers in Petrograd on Saturday 13 October and was impressed by them. Keeling was an exceptional man, insisting on returning to Sevastopol, where he tried unsuccessfully to organise a force to pick up other officers who were trying to escape from the Turkish coast. He finally left Sevastopol for Petrograd on 16 December 1916 and reached England in January 1918.

Keeling's analysis of Petrograd is chilling. There was barely enough to eat and outside the bakeries were long queues for the meagre ration of what passed for bread. This was before the onset of winter in a capital without

---

32 E.H. Keeling, *Adventures in Turkey and Russia* (London, 1924).

reserves of coal and wood for heating and electric light. The harshness of life was brought into relief by the high living still available to those with money and position. General Poole, for instance, dined at two of the elite restaurants that continued to thrive: at Privato Frères on 25 October with Finlayson, who was jubilant at the prospect of leaving Russia; and at Contant on 29 October with the French Military Mission. Otherwise, conditions were worse than before the Czar had been forced to abdicate. As Keeling described it, the Bolsheviks knew how to work up popular discontent to their advantage, 'Kornilov's attempt to seize the capital was used with ever-increasing success to embitter the people against Kerensky (who knew more about the attempt than he admitted), and against the Cadet Party and the bourgeoisie as a whole. All of these were branded as Counter-revolutionaries and Royalists, though none really desired to restore the old régime'. [33]

The General's next trip was to Stavka and Kiev, travelling with a British officer and the head of the American Military Mission in a reserved coach, 'In afternoon Rane and I started off for Stavka – Judson also going down, so we had a large party. Very comfortable.'[34] At Stavka Poole was not impressed: 'Find our people here are not doing very much – too much talk, too little action.'[35] His verdict on the Russian Inspector General of Artillery was in the same vein, 'He seems very helpless, poor devil, but tries to do his best. The whole show though is pretty rotten.'[36]

Poole and Rane then travelled on to Kiev in the special carriage of General Mikhail Dragomirov. 'Met by the O.C. and taken to the Continental. He is a depressing old gentleman and holds out gloomy hopes for the future. He says the troops are absolutely out of hand. He has 50,000 and can't depend on one of them! He thinks in a short time we shall all have our throats

---

33 The Cadets were the Constitutional Democrat Party.
34 Poole, Diary, 17 October 1917. The clue about the real objective of the trip comes from an item amongst General Poole's papers held by the Liddle Hart Centre for Military Archives, King's College, London. A 'Report on Work Done in Russia to End of 1917' by Captain G. Hill indicates that Kerensky intended Stavka to be a final bastion for reasserting his waning authority. 'Was ordered by Lieutenant Colonel Maund, RFC, to Stavka at the summons of General Barter to attend the Russian Aviation Conference to which the French specialists were also invited. This Conference sat for about five weeks and was composed of officers from every Aviation and Artillery Branch of the Armies in the field, and its technical problem was to introduce Western methods into its very badly organized services. Underlying this Conference, which was attended by Kerensky, was a strong political movement, which, however, came to nothing.'
35 Poole, Diary, 18 October 1917.
36 Poole, Diary, 19 October 1917.

cut!'[37] The party's return journey was comfortable, 'At 9 p.m. took the train for Stavka. I was lucky as I got a very fine coupé in the Minister of Food's private carriage'.[38] They arrived at Stavka on Monday afternoon and stayed overnight. After seeing a trench mortar demonstration, the party left for Petrograd, 'We were very lucky as we annexed the special coach, which we had travelled in from Kiev, so we came up like kings'.[39]

The General was unhappy when he returned to Petrograd, 'Sir G.B. is going home to attend the Paris Conference. If only the government would take a firm hand and put in a strong man here!'[40] Poole poured out his feelings to Alice:

> I do hope it won't be very long before we can finish off this show and settle down at home again. I'm bound to say though that it doesn't look much like it at present, though out here one can never tell for a week ahead if these heroes will stay on in the war. I'm quite convinced that they won't be any more use as a fighting force. They don't tackle the question in the right way and our diplomacy is not of the strong, energetic type to drive them to take action. I believe if we sent out here 'Winston', the Americans 'Roosevelt' and the French 'Albert Thomas', we could get great results and that is the only possible solution.

Poole's letter ended, 'I'm very busy here. One's work seems to grow daily. Banting is a marvel. He is at it day and night and really accomplishes the impossible. I'm glad we are kept so busy. It would be deadly otherwise'.[41]

Russia by now was suffering from a general feeling of war-weariness. There was also a loss of belief in the possibility of an effective government being established until a democratic election was held and the people could choose their own representatives for a parliament that would determine how Russia would be ruled. The General concluded, 'They are all surrounded by a sort of wall of torpor, which nothing can penetrate'.[42]

---

37 Poole, Diary, 20 October 1917.
38 Poole, Diary, 21 October 1917.
39 Poole, Diary, 23 October 1917.
40 Poole, Diary, 26 October 1917.
41 Frederick Poole to Alice Poole, 28 October 1917.
42 Poole, Diary, 30 October 1917.

Poole himself had reached a milestone, 'Three years to the day since 114 received its first baptism of fire'.[43] He was now an acting major general with a brief far different from the compass of an artillery officer. In this he had little constraint on his freedom of action.

---

43 Poole, Diary, 2 November 1917.

15

Dealing with the Bolsheviks

Frederick Poole's life entered a different phase after the Bolsheviks seized power. Two unsent postcards in his papers indicate that he was not unnerved by the experience of living through what seemed one more revolution, 'St Isaac's Cathedral – I live about five minutes from here' and 'This is the Winter Palace which was shelled by the Bolshevik ships the other day. It was also looted when it was captured by them'. His travels outside Petrograd, however, ceased altogether and his three ADCs left him. George Chirinsky went to Moscow to protect his family. Sacha Platonov made his way with his wife Natasha to the relative safety of the Caucasus; and Victor Warrender went home on leave to see his family before going to fight on the Western Front.

Prior to leaving, Victor Warrender, drawing on his own experience of a friendship with a Russian princess which had become uncomfortably intense, warned the General not to become too friendly with a Russian aristocrat called Baroness Cassandra Accurti. The friendship began when Poole dined 'with our next-door neighbours at night – Baron Accurti. Very nice people, with a dear little twelve-year-old girl, who is violently anglophile. She was allowed to stay up especially to see us'.[1] That is the only mention of Baron Accurti. Two days later Baroness Accurti decided that Poole was a man to trust.

> Just before dark they put the bridges up over the Neva. The Bolsheviks held the far side and the government held this side. The government

---

1 Poole, Diary, 4 November 1917.

fairly terrified out of their wits – most despondent messages flying about. The Bolsheviks in absolute control, but too afraid to take control. We had a party here, but our guests were too frightened to come. We went in next door to the Baroness after dinner – found them very collected but expecting the worst. She handed over to me a pocketful of most lovely jewels to keep for her – worth about £20,000. A great tribute to the accepted idea of British honesty.[2]

The General, normally meticulous on matters of rank, referred to Baroness Acurti as 'the Countess' when writing to Alice:

We are in the middle of great excitements again and Petrograd is at war! The government have gone on with their footling, futile policy, doing nothing and giving way to every demand of the Bolsheviks, so at last the Bolsheviks have come out in force and want to take over the whole show. If they do get the upper hand, they will probably ask for peace at once. At present things are in a chaotic state and there has been no actual fighting. Government are in control of the situation on this side of the river. The Bolsheviks have got the other side and there is a cruiser anchored in the middle of the Neva and it is doubtful which of the two sides it is backing!! Everybody here seems terrified and all are expecting the worst to happen. (I mean among the Russians.)

I went into our neighbours in the flat just opposite ours last night to hearten them up. They are very nice people and have a dear little girl, just twelve years, who is madly in love with England and the English. The Countess asked me if I would take her jewels for the night, as she was afraid the place would be searched. So she handed over to me a pocketful of the most beautiful diamonds and pearls, which I tied up in a hanky and kept in my coat pocket all night!! We estimated they were worth about £20,000! It's interesting to show the complete trust they have in British honesty. But I was glad to hand them back, as it would be awkward to lose them and unhealthy for me if anyone knew they were in my pocket.[3]

---

2   Poole, Diary, 6 November 1917.
3   Frederick Poole to Alice Poole, 7 November 1917.

Dealing with the Bolsheviks

Poole returned Baroness Accurti's jewellery after there was no sign of a mob descending on their building. This was in stark contrast to the riotous events of the March Revolution which had overthrown Czar Nicholas II. There is no reference in Poole's papers to disorder in the capital until a month later when 'The Winter Palace was looted last night and all day there was a drunken orgy in the square. Many drunken soldiers firing in all directions and the whole place reeking with broken wine bottles. This is a bad sign. It's the first time they have got out of hand'.[4]

The mood had changed. The city was in a state of apathy. Its inhabitants were exhausted by privation and were longing for the war to stop. They desperately clung to the hope that, when the Constituent Assembly finally met, there might be a new government that would restore some form of stability. The Provisional Government had put in place a democratic franchise, the first in Russia's history, but the election had not yet taken place. Meanwhile the Bolsheviks shrewdly concentrated on securing the key points in the capital, avoiding any action that might have rallied active support for Kerensky, the legitimate head of state. Kerensky himself had left the city and was trying to organise a counter-coup.

Trying to make sense of this confused and volatile situation, on the morning of 9 November the General went to see Colonel Raymond Robins, who was with the American Red Cross and was on close terms with the Bolshevik leaders. He then called on David Soskice, who had been Kerensky's secretary and had remained in the city. Poole concluded, 'The bulk of the political feeling is against the Bolsheviks and there are many who think they will shortly collapse. On the other hand, the Bolsheviks have practically all the power in the shape of rifles and most of the energy, and in my judgement most of the brains, and I'm inclined to back them to win out, if only they will keep the people supplied with food'.[5]

When Kerensky's counter coup petered out there was no further appetite in Petrograd to challenge the Bolsheviks by force. Although there was considerable opposition to them, it took the form of strikes and passive resistance. The railway trade union, Vikzhel, tried to persuade the Bolsheviks to compromise and form a coalition government. It was a force to be reckoned with as it could have cut off the food and other necessities on

---

4   Poole, Diary, 7 December 1917.
5   Poole, Diary, 9 November 1917.

which the capital depended. In March it had stopped the royal train carrying Czar Nicholas II returning to Petrograd from Stavka to make a final attempt to save the Romanov dynasty. In September the union had denied passage to Kornilov's Cossacks heading for the capital to overthrow the Provisional Government. Fortunately for the Bolsheviks, Vikzhel decided not to exercise its power when this might have been politically decisive.

The Bolsheviks were much weaker in Moscow than in Petrograd and their bid for power there was fiercely resisted. 'Saw Marshall, who is just up from Moscow where there has been a lot of fighting and many casualties. Apparently, it's a state of anarchy there.'[6] The turning point in Moscow came when the Bolsheviks captured the army depôt with its huge stores of armaments and food, after which they negotiated a truce which gave them control of the city but allowed their opponents to leave, many going to the Caucasus.

Stavka, the General Headquarters of the Russian army, which did not recognise the Bolsheviks, had significant resources at its disposal and no intention of accepting their orders; but when both Petrograd and Moscow came under Bolshevik control the will to fight at Stavka collapsed. The Bolsheviks took it over without any resistance. Poole wrote to Alice on 23 November, still hopeful that an election would take place:

> We are all still very fit, but it's sad getting no news of you. All the mails are stuck up somewhere between here and Stockholm, as there has been a strike on the Finnish railways. I hope that in a day or two now we will get something in.
>
> Things are still quiet here. They have not yet managed to form a government, but they are pushing along all arrangements to make a Constituent Assembly. So they will have the elections in a short time. They are now taking steps to see if they can arrange an armistice with the Hun to discuss peace terms. They have asked all the ambassadors 'to order' their respective governments to do likewise. The C-in-C here, General Dukhonin, rather jibbed when he got the order, so he was immediately fired out and replaced as C-in-C by a revolutionary whose rank is second lieutenant.
>
> If it wasn't all so sad, it would be too comic for words. So far we

---

6   Poole, Diary, 14 November 1927.

have plenty of food here, and it is coming in pretty well. We have difficulties ahead with the works, which are beginning to close down for shortage of coal and raw material. When we get a crowd of out-of-work Bolsheviks roaming about, we may have trouble. I shall be glad when the time comes to say goodbye to this distressful country.[7]

After his exasperation with the 'wall of torpor, which nothing can penetrate' that had engulfed the Provisional Government following the failed Kornilov coup, Poole was impressed by the determined way the Bolsheviks were handling matters:

Everything is still quiet here. The elections are now going on! No arrangement – no excitement – no disorder. The Bolsheviks take the sensible line and say that if any government is elected whom they don't like, they will kill them!! They can do it too, as they are the people with the guns. It all makes things much simpler if you say to the electors, 'You elect whomever you like, but let them take care that they do exactly what we tell them', and it gives the government their programme ready-made.

Unless a miracle happens, or Germany doesn't want it, I fancy we shall be out of the war by Xmas or January. So, if all goes well, I may be home again before long. I keep very fit – not overworked, as half the government offices are doing nothing. I've got a lot of tobacco out via Lessing. Many thanks, darling. Don't send any more. I've got too much now.[8]

Poole's next letter to Alice continued in the same vein,

Really it is absolutely right for Russia to get out of the war. With the state the country is in it is absolutely impossible for her to carry on, and every single man out here except for a few Russian blusterers are in favour of an immediate peace at any price. It would be far better if we Allies made a virtue out of necessity and gave her absolute carte blanche to do what she likes. She will do it anyhow and our present

---

7   Frederick Poole to Alice Poole, 23 November 1917.
8   Frederick Poole to Alice Poole, 27 November 1917.

attitude does no good at all and is absolutely playing into the hands of the Germans for after the war policy.[9]

On the following day the General made his views clear in a letter to Colonel Byrne in London:

We won't recognise the Bolshevik Government. We threaten that if they make peace it will have terrible results for them. The result is that the Bolsheviks now dislike us and humiliate our government by pinpricking British subjects out here. If we want to help the Hun, we are being successful. It all fits in with the Hun anti-British propaganda. If it goes on it will tend more and more to drive them into German arms.[10]

Poole's main concern now became how to get his own men home safely. He decided that the key man to avoid antagonising was Trotsky, who had been incensed by the arrest in England of his friends Georgy Chicherin and Peter Petroff for stirring up anti-war propaganda. In retaliation Trotsky had introduced a quota system whereby each person allowed to leave Russia had to be balanced by a Russian being permitted to return. He then raised the stakes by nominating Chicherin as ambassador and Petroff as counsellor at the Russian Embassy in London.

Trotsky was suspicious about the Allied missions, which had reacted to the Bolshevik takeover of Stavka by moving to Kiev: it was the capital of the Ukraine and the Ukraine had declared itself independent from Russia. Poole knew that Trotsky's suspicions were well founded, 'Later on Keyes came in. He is full of the possibilities of the Ukraine scheme. I don't share his optimism.'[11] Poole was not convinced by Terence Keyes, who was attached to the British Embassy, because he himself had first-hand knowledge of the situation. He had been to Kiev shortly before the Bolshevik seizure of power in Petrograd and had taken Captain Rane with him. Subsequently, he had sent Rane back to Kiev to make a further reconnaissance and concluded, after Rane's return to Petrograd, 'The Ukraine government don't recognize the Bolsheviks. Apparently, they have very little strength – more like a

---

9   Frederick Poole to Alice Poole, 3 December 1917.
10 Michael Kettle, *The Allies and the Russian Collapse*, i, *March 1917 to March 1918* (London, 1981).
11 Poole, Diary, 6 December 1917.

glorified county council'.[12]

Poole summed up for Alice, 'I am quite sure that under no circumstances will Russia take any more part in the war', adding, 'No news here. We are not very popular with the Bolsheviks, as we are not recognising them as the proper government and they don't like it, but they are behaving fairly well except that no English are allowed to leave the country!!'[13]

On 10 December Poole found an ally in Victor Stanley, the Naval Attaché at the British Embassy, 'No news. Rumours of fights between Bolsheviks and Cossacks, but not much in the way of fighting I fancy. Stanley dined with us and we went to a concert – balalaika playing – really a very fine show. Had long talk to Stanley. He shares in my views at the diplomatic inefficiency out here and we are planning combined action to get a move on in the right direction'.[14] Two days later Poole took action, 'I sent Bobby to Smolny in afternoon to see what undiplomatic methods would accomplish as regards allowing my own people away and found Trotsky most reasonable'.[15] With the departure of Victor Warrender for home, Bobby – otherwise unidentified – had become Poole's ADC, chosen because of his strong nerves and capacity for diplomacy. It cannot have been easy for a British officer to penetrate the headquarters of the Bolsheviks, secure an interview with Trotsky and achieve what he wanted.

Bobby found Trotsky 'most reasonable', partly because Poole had prepared the way by steering well clear of any involvement with elements that could be construed as counter-revolutionary. Poole well understood that the Bolsheviks meant business, 'Lenin has found a very simple way of arranging the Constituent Assembly. He orders the arrest of all Cadets and anyone else personally disagreeable to him!'[16]

Poole's initiative paid off, 'The restriction on the exit of Britishers is removed', which meant that plans could be made for evacuation.[17] He had produced the result that had eluded Sir George Buchanan when he had dispatched Captain Aubrey Smith, the translator on the British Embassy's staff, a few days before.[18]

---

12 Poole, Diary, 28 November 1917.
13 Frederick Poole to Alice Poole, 7 December 1917.
14 Poole, Diary, 10 December 1917.
15 Poole, Diary, 12 December 1917.
16 Poole, Diary, 12 December 1917. The Cadets were the Constitutional Democrats.
17 Poole, Diary, 13 December 1917.
18 Buchanan refers to Captain Smith's efforts with Trotsky in his memoirs, as does Lloyd George in his account of the First World War, but not to Poole's intervention.

Trotsky remained suspicious but Poole carefully avoided giving cause for complaint. 'Snowing all day. In morning Rane and I went down to the Artillery Department and saw Orloff, who is now in charge. No news there and nothing doing. Trotsky wants to know what my people at Kiev are doing – but our consciences are clear.'[19] Others had been less wise, not least his American colleagues 'Found them in great distress as apparently they have been found out in giving aid to Kaledin!'[20] Kaledin had been among the generals arrested for participating in Kornilov's attempted coup. After the Provisional Government had been overthrown, the plotters had all escaped and were now in south Russia raising forces to fight the Bolsheviks. General Kaledin had been elected the Ataman of the Don Cossacks.

On the same day, 'Keyes came in in evening and we talked politics.'[21] During their conversation on 22 December the General persuaded Keyes that his contacts would be helpful. So much so that on the following day Poole drily noted that he had 'Had interview with Poliakoff and Keyes in morning.'[22] The meeting was arranged at short notice and took place on a Sunday. In retrospect, the weekend marked the beginning of Poole's involvement in the execution of the British Government's decision to acquire for cash the principal banks in Russia.

Poole was now thinking of returning home:

I don't know when this letter will go, but I fancy that the troubles over our couriers are more or less settled up now, so it may not be very long before it starts. A happy New Year to you, sweetheart, and all good luck for 1918. It looks more like peace now with this last offer from Germany. It may be that before very long we shall be talking over terms. In any case it won't be very long before my work

---

19 Poole, Diary, 20 December.
20 Poole, Diary, 22 December 1917.
21 Poole, Diary, 22 December 1917. Keyes and Poole had both served on the North-West Frontier, shared a fondness for bridge and were good raconteurs. As a twenty-year-old newly commissioned officer, Keyes had first seen action in the Tirah Expedition on the North-West Frontier in 1897 and been mentioned in despatches; in 1903 he had entered the Indian Political Service; in 1915 he had been promoted to major and fought against the Turks; and in 1916 he had commanded an expedition to forestall attempts by German agents to foment unrest against British influence and disrupt the shipping on the eastern shore of the Persian Gulf. According to the *London Gazette*, the mission set out in April 1916 and returned in February 1917 having had a 'trying march', an understatement for overcoming conditions of extreme hardship over dangerous territory.
22 Poole, Diary, 23 December 1917.

out here will be over, and as soon as I can square up everything I shall try to be off. I'm sending home a good many of my people. One or two will be going next week. I'm sending another box of spare clothes etc. home in a day or two either by Major Oke or Captain Whittet. In it you will find some toys for the boys, which are sent them by Baroness Accurti – very nice ones; also a very nice tea cloth, which was given me for Xmas by the Poliakoffs; also two rather nice sort of bead necklaces, which the Baroness gave me. I am also sending by the sea route a package of swords, which will turn up sometime. One is mine, one is Notcutt's, one is Finlayson's; and the other one has no owner, as far as I know. When they arrive, send a line to Finlayson and Notcutt and let them know you have their swords and they will do the rest.

There is no news here. All is pretty quiet. The Bolsheviks have just taken over all the banks and all the balances therein, which will make things a little awkward for some wretched people. They don't get any out of me I'm glad to say! This place is full of Huns now. We have a deputation of Hun naval officers in here, who are arranging naval details, and Hun commercial travellers are everywhere, getting going at once. I keep very fit, although I hate this cold and snow. We have rumours of a general strike in the future. The result will be no water, no light and probably no heat and food!!! So, if that comes off, it won't be so cheery.

I'm very anxious to hear what you think of the boys now you have got them home again. Goodbye, sweetheart. All my love to you and the boys.[23]

Poole's efforts in Russia had not gone unnoticed. On 21 December he was presented with the grand cordon of the order of St Anne as a token of appreciation for his work on the Michaelson Committee. A warm citation referred to Russia now entering a state of civil war. In the 1918 New Year Honours he also received the CB. Finlayson, who had returned 'jubilant' at leaving Russia for the Western Front in November 1917, was made a CMG. Captains Banting and Rane were promoted to the rank of brevet major.

---

23   Frederick Poole to Alice Poole, 29 December 1917.

General Sir Frederick Poole

Poole had seen a lot of Baroness Accurti and her daughter since the first meeting the night before the Bolsheviks seized power.[24] She had even begun to teach him Russian. Tamara Accurti had just reached an age when she could converse intelligently with an adult, but she was tactful enough to withdraw when the General wanted to be alone with her mother. Tamara was a very pretty girl, well-educated and skilled at drawing out the General on subjects close to his heart. Enclosed with his letter for Alice was one for his two boys:

> I am sending you home some Russian toys next week, which are sent to you as Xmas presents by Baroness Accurti, who lives next door to me. She has a little girl, twelve years old, who speaks English, French and Russian very well. She always likes to read your letters. Her name is Tamara and she is very nice and a great friend of mine. I hope you have got good reports from school. I shall be anxious to hear all about how you have got on …[25]

One of the gifts was a Russian doll which cannot have been as exciting for boys aged eight and ten as the previous bounty, which had included two soldiers' helmets from their father's friends in the French army. The traditional matryoshka doll can be unscrewed to reveal a smaller doll within and in turn yet smaller dolls. It is a reminder that Russia was not a simple place and that there were many layers of meaning to be discovered inside it.

---

[24] On 28 November, 'Dined at Accurtis and had a séance – rather successful'; 5 December, 'Dined with Accurtis at night'; 9 December, 'Dined with Accurtis at night'; 16 December, 'Dined with Accurtis at night'; 19 December, 'Dined with Accurtis at night'; 23 December, 'Dined with Accurtis at night'; and 26 December, 'Dined with Accurtis at night'.

[25] Frederick Poole to his sons, Charles and Robert Poole, 29 December 1917.

16

Buying the Russian Banks

The British Government did not take notice of General Poole's advice to recognise and work with the Bolsheviks. Instead, it dispatched a young diplomat called diplomat, Robert Bruce Lockhart, with the vaguest of instructions. Poole's verdict on Lockhart, who was eventually arrested by the Bolsheviks, was 'He is a smart little man – with a little too much wind in his head at present, but the best man out here now'.[1] At the same time, the British Government pursued other initiatives which achieved nothing apart from teaching the Bolsheviks never to trust the British.

One of the more bizarre of these British initiatives was an attempt to buy the Russian banks to prevent Germany gaining control over Russia's resources. Terence Keyes, now a lieutenant colonel, advised the British Government to proceed, through a middleman called Jaroszynski, with an ambitious plan to purchase the key Russian banks and to provide the financial support to fund forces in south Russia opposed to the Bolsheviks. Jaroszynski was of Polish extraction and no doubt a persuasive talker. On 17 January 1918, Keyes had wired London recommending that the British Government advance a rouble loan worth a 200,000,000 rouble loan (worth £5,000,000) to enable Jaroszynski to buy the five main Russian banks. This would allow him to set up a bank in south Russia to issue bank notes. It would also provide the Don Cossacks and volunteers opposing the Bolsheviks with fifteen million roubles.[2]

---

1   Poole, Diary, 6 February 1918.
2   Kettle, *The Allies and the Russian Collapse*, i, p. 202.

Two days later, on 19 January, Keyes sought Poole's reassurance, 'Keyes came up in morning and we had a long talk over the position ... The Constituent Assembly has had a short reign. Chernov was arrested this morning and the Duma closed. These people are weak and not man enough to stand up for their own rights. Therefore, they are not fit to govern'.[3] Early that morning, at 4 a.m., the Bolsheviks had used force to suppress the Constituent Assembly, which had been democratically elected to determine the future government of Russia and had only finally met the day before. They arrested its chairman, Chernov, and closed the Duma, which had been reduced to insignificance after the rebirth of the Petrograd Soviet in March. The Bolshevik policy on the banks, which had been on strike since the overthrow of the Provisional Government, was one of confiscation without compensation. In the circumstances Keyes would be taking a grave risk advancing a very large sum to buy the banks.

On Tuesday 22 January there was an extraordinary change in the weather, 'A violent thaw all day, the streets simply running with water. If this continues the Neva will break up. When that occurs, it foretells a great disaster for the country. Poor devils they will have the disaster anyhow, I fear'.[4] Comte Louis de Robien, a French diplomat, noted in his memoirs, 'The temperature suddenly rose to two degrees below zero'.[5] That was the beginning of a thaw which continued for eight days with such intensity that the snow melted. Even the General's habitual optimism briefly deserted him and he was reduced to writing, 'Things looking very bad and black'.[6]

Germany could have made short work of the Bolsheviks rather than entering into peace negotiations with them. In Poole's view, 'It would pay the Hun to come to Petrograd: first to crush the Bolshevik, which is a very dangerous poison for his people; and secondly because of his great interests in the country, which are endangered by Bolshevik propaganda. The "pros" outweigh the very obvious "cons". I hear the bankers are certain he will come'.[7] In the event, however, Germany decided to continue the peace talks.

Keyes changed his mind about dealing with Jaroszynski, despite

---

3   Poole, Diary, 19 January 1918.
4   Poole, Diary, 22 January 1918.
5   Louis de Robien, *The Diary of a Diplomat in Russia, 1917-1918* (London, 1969).
6   Poole, Diary, 29 January 1918.
7   Poole, Diary, 25 January 1918.

receiving official instructions from London on 24 January.[8] He decided to follow the General's advice and go instead through Poliakov. Poole noted, 'Dined with Poliakoffs at night',[9] and two days later the deal seemed to be reaching a conclusion when he and Poliakov 'had an interesting interview' with Keyes 'and practically squared matters up'.[10]

On 1 February the General had a nervous moment. He had prudently insisted that the British armoured car personnel being transported by railway to Murmansk for their sea passage home should wait in the sidings outside the capital, rather than entering Petrograd before the next stage of their journey. Unfortunately, Lieutenant Commander Dye and Lieutenant Smith, who were not with the main party, were arrested after two bombs, retained as souvenirs, were found in their hotel. The General now reaped the benefit of his unofficial line of communication with Trotsky, 'Report in morning that Smith and Dye of armoured cars were arrested in Astoria this morning. Bobby went down, and the matter was all arranged. It was entirely their own fault and the Bolshevik attitude was quite correct'.[11]

With this matter resolved, the day ended on a good note, 'Long meeting Keyes, Poliakov at night – we are getting things fixed a bit now'.[12] The following day was inconclusive, 'Went down to Keyes' office in afternoon to discuss this business with him'.[13] Then there was a setback, 'Keyes telephones to say the deal is off'.[14] Poole himself was unperturbed, but worried lest pressure was brought to bear on Keyes to proceed in line with the official instructions received on 24 January and agree to Jaroszynski's terms. So he went on to the British Embassy and 'Had a long interview with Lindley over the Poliakov business and frightened him badly'.[15] After Buchanan had left Petrograd for home on 7 January, Francis Lindley became the British Chargé d'Affaires.

The Bolsheviks had by this point already demonstrated their complete lack of respect for the norms of diplomatic behaviour by arresting, in the Romanian Legation, Count Diamandi and incarcerating him in the fortress of St Peter and St Paul. When the entire diplomatic community protested,

---

8   Kettle, *The Allies and the Russian Collapse*, i, p. 206.
9   Poole, Diary, 28 January 1918.
10 Poole, Diary, 30 January 1918.
11 Poole, Diary, 1 February 1918.
12 Poole, Diary, 1 February 1918. Poliakov written as 'Poli' or 'P' in the original, here and below.
13 Poole, Diary, 2 February 1918.
14 Poole, Diary, 3 February 1918.
15 Poole, Diary, 4 February 1918.

led by the American David Francis, who had become the senior ambassador after the departure for home of Sir George Buchanan, they were made to look foolish. Lenin cut short Francis to remind him that French was the language of diplomacy, which left him unable to continue and caused the hot-headed Serbian Ambassador to lose his temper, much to the derision of the Bolsheviks. The Bolsheviks had proved yet again that they were the power that mattered. Poole described the impact on the diplomatic community, 'Great "wind up" re Diamandi. He was let out, but all the embassies are now very jumpy and don't know what will happen next. The Italian Embassy was looted yesterday by a band of a hundred armed hooligans and that has put the lid on'.[16]

Although Lindley backed off, it was an anxious day for the General, 'Poliakov tells me that the rumour is that peace has already been signed'.[17] The rumour proved premature. It was Jaroszynski who capitulated: the prospect of ready cash, albeit far less than he had negotiated for, was far too tempting to resist given the circumstances.

Two days later the General wrote a remarkable letter to Alice. This encapsulates the collapse of civilised life in Petrograd and explains why Jaroszynski had decided to capitulate:

> We shall get a mail in today and hear all your news. We are also expecting Lessing and I daresay you will have seen him before he sailed, so I shall hear all about you. The mail has been unduly stuck up, because they have had a little civil war in Finland. This has resulted in stoppage of all trains. However, things are more or less clear again and the train got in last night. Things are in a pretty desperate state here. We are drifting on pretty quickly to anarchy and perhaps one of the most colossal tragedies the world has ever heard of. There are some two and a half millions of people here. Food is practically stopped and the railways are getting worse and worse. Ninety per cent of the workmen are already out of employment. Typhus from bad food has started. The anarchist party is gaining ground every day. So, if one is a pessimist by nature, there is plenty of scope for thought.

---

16 Poole, Diary, 15 January 1918.
17 Poole, Diary, 4 February 1918.

Personally, I hope for the best. If we are not raided, I have enough food for all my people. We have enough arms to defend ourselves against hooligans, so our situation is not too bad. Then there is the peace question. Trotsky has gone off to Brest-Litovsk and I think he will sign peace. If he refuses, then there is nothing to stop the Hun from being here (he can come through by train and take the place in ten minutes) in three or four days. If he were to come, at least 60 per cent of the people would welcome him and decorate the streets. Naturally all the educated people would welcome him as the only possible way of saving them.

I hope we should be able to get away all right. The whole life here is most extraordinary. Highway robbery in daylight in the main streets. If I go out to dinner at night, I carry a revolver loose in my coat pocket and never take my hand off it! Fancy in London if you walked from Hyde Park Hotel to Belgrave Square and were ready to shoot without a word anyone who approached you. It's all so comic that it makes one laugh, only it's all so sad to see a great nation brought to such a state.

They are now taking over all houses. The state gets half the rent, the city council the other half (that's if anyone can be made to pay rent!) and the owner as compensation gets a flat free for his life. All the money to one's credit in the bank over 25,000 roubles is forfeited. All shares in companies are taken. In fact, there is nothing you can imagine that can't or won't happen. The funny part is, as far as I am concerned, that I never felt better or in better spirits in my life. We are all very fit and very cheerful. I suppose it is that our imagination is not strong enough to cope with possibilities!! I had my photograph taken the other day, which I will send when I get. So you will see from that how young I feel.

I wonder if you saw General Judson, US Army. I asked him to look in to see you to say I keep quite fit. I don't think now it will be very long before I leave this delightful country. Don't be frightened or fussed by all these accounts of horrors I have told you. There is nothing to be afraid of, sweetheart. We are all in God's hands. Goodbye sweetheart. All my love to you and the little sons.[18]

---

18   Frederick Poole to Alice Poole, 31 January 1918.

Poole began to sense victory 'Went in morning to Keyes and thrashed out the whole Y [sic] deal. I think now we have got things on a workable basis and it may possibly go through'.[19] The following day he informed Alice, 'Our work here is practically done now and I expect to get orders to come away any day now. Indeed, it is important that I should come, as there is so much at home which wants to be put right. So, I hope now it won't be long. I shall be so glad. It's been very dull and lonely without you'.[20]

Poole felt a successful conclusion was imminent, 'Had a meeting at Poliakov's house at 9 a.m. to see X and Keyes. We had a long talk and made a proposition, which he accepted. So, we meet tomorrow to discuss the final details'.[21] The General's papers do not identify the mysterious X who attended this crucial meeting at Poliakov's. The only specific reference to meeting a Russian financier other than Poliakov during the negotiations and the aftermath is candid, 'Had lunch at Poliakov's to meet Pokrovski, who is the great Russian expert re finance. He paints a very gloomy picture of the situation, but like us all hopes things may improve'.[22]

The deal was done over the weekend. On the Saturday, Keyes and Poole had a successful meeting at Poliakov's house and then went to brief Lindley, 'Meeting at P's house 9 a.m. Things went on well and all details fixed up. Keyes and I then went on to embassy and had long talk to Lindley'.[23] When Poole returned on the Sunday to Poliakov's house, the negotiations were completed, 'Meeting at Poliakov's house 9 a.m., which now settles off everything. I hope the results will be really good. In any case it's worth the risk'.[24] The deal was done at 10 per cent of the price approved by the British Government, which resulted in a saving of £4,500,000.

The moral Poole drew from witnessing life under Bolshevik rule was practical and prophetic:

The whole show is disintegrating and falling to pieces and the most terrible tragedies [are] in store for these unfortunate people. It will result in time in the extinction of the 'bourgeois' class, i.e. all

---

19   Poole, Diary, 5 February 1918.
20   Frederick Poole to Alice Poole, 6 February 1918.
21   Poole, Diary, 8 February 1918.
22   Poole, Diary, 17 February. Kettle has identified Pokrovski as Chairman of the Siberian Bank.
23   Poole, Diary, 9 February 1918.
24   Poole, Diary, 10 February 1918.

above working men. The great lesson it drives home to me is the vital necessity of teaching our boys a trade. Anyone with a trade can never be hurt. It is the professional classes that will go under; but if you are an engineer or something like that you can always keep yourself.[25]

While these great events were happening, the General continued to enjoy the society of his next-door neighbours. They celebrated the Russian Christmas together: 'This is Russian Xmas Eve and a great festival. Helped to decorate Accurtis' Christmas tree in afternoon';[26] and 'Went to the Accurtis' Xmas tree in afternoon. The children did some tableaux';[27] On Russian New Year's Eve 'Supper at midnight with Accurtis but got away early'.[28] Even now the Russians did not allow their hideous predicament to suppress their love of the arts, 'Went to ballet at night with Accurtis'.[29]

---

25 Frederick Poole to Alice Poole, 17 January 1918.
26 Poole, Diary, 6 January 1918.
27 Poole, Diary, 7 January 1918.
28 Poole, Diary, 13 January 1918.
29 Poole, Diary, 10 February 1918.

17

Finland

In February 1918 the General received new instructions, 'I am made head of a new venture and am to go home at once to discuss matters'.[1] He was already prepared, 'We are all very well here, gradually reducing our staff. In fact, by the end of this month, I shall have got rid of practically all but the last lot, which includes myself, so then there will only be us to arrange for'.[2] He planned to travel by train to Helsinki and thence by ship to Stockholm, an arrangement confirmed when Major McAlpine returned from Helsinki, 'The Swedes say they will let us through on their ship'.[3]

There was no safe way home. It was a choice of either risking interception by the Germans on a neutral ship or travelling by railway northwards to the head of the Gulf of Bothnia and crossing into Sweden. The latter depended on securing safe passage between the Red and White forces in the Finnish Civil War. 'In Finland the situation is that the Red Guard hold Helsingfors and Viborg and the White Guard most of the rest of the country. The Senate has moved to Vasa and is probably receiving Swedish help.'[4] The Front Line ran east from close to Pori on the Gulf of Bothnia to Lake Ladoga north of Petrograd.

The General's party left Petrograd by the overnight train from Finland Station on Sunday 24 February. It included Countess Zamoiska, who wanted to join her husband. Poole had met the Zamoiskis in Kiev on 19

---
1   Poole, Diary, 15 February 1918.
2   Frederick Poole to Alice Poole, 22 January 1918.
3   Poole, Diary, 19 February 1918.
4   Poole, Diary, 29 January 29 1918. Helsingfors was Helsinki.

General Sir Frederick Poole

October 1917, and on 25 October he and Finlayson had dined with Adam Zamoiski at Privato, a fashionable restaurant still operating in Petrograd. This was the night before Finlayson's return to the Western Front and Zamoiski's departure for his new job in Paris, representing the government of independent Poland.[5] Zamoiski asked the General to protect his wife, which he duly did after her arrival in Petrograd from Kiev. The General now connived at Countess Zamoiska's escape from Russia without proper papers.

> Busy packing all day and making final arrangements. Had splitting headache and was seeing some different person all the time. Started off at 6 p.m. It was quite exciting to see if we should get Countess Zamoiska through the frontier, as she had no passport, but Bobby and my 'pink' passport worked it all right. All quiet and quite comfortable travelling.[6]

The railway journey may have been slightly more eventful than the General let on in his diary. This is the incident described by his great niece Bridget:

> As far as I remember the story about Uncle Fred using his fists on the train in Russia went something like this ... he was travelling with a lady he knew and at some point, when the train stopped, a drunken bear of a man clambered onto the train and made himself known in an extremely aggressive and unpleasant manner. Uncle Fred obviously thought that he was very dangerous, as he staggered at them, and so punched him on the nose (hard) at which point said drunken 'bear' lost his balance and fell from the train! ... it was a real 'Take that sir, for your drunken impudence' moment. I am sure it was *anything* but funny at the time.[7]

The journey was slow, taking eighteen hours to cover the 442 kilometres. The train was delayed by the damage inflicted on the line in the fighting between Red and White Finns and by Customs formalities.

Poole was greeted on his arrival at Helsinki Station at midday on Monday

---

5   Poole, Diary, 25 October 1918. 'They were both jubilant at going away.'
6   Poole, Diary, 24 February 1918.
7   Private information from Bridget Graham-Cloete.

Finland

25 February by Montgomery Grove, the British Consul, with the news that he had just missed the boat to Stockholm – the *Arcturus*. Opposite the station was the Societetshus Hotel in a modern building completed shortly before the outbreak of the war in 1914. The General moved into a luxurious room, complete with a telephone and a private bathroom, and felt an immediate sense of relief: 'This is quite a civilized place, as different as possible from Petrograd – quite European. A very clean and comfortable hotel: good food except that there is no bread'.[8] Although Finland was embroiled in civil war and bread was not to be had, standards long since forgotten in Petrograd were still maintained.

The General had an extraordinary encounter with a terrified member of the Romanov family staying in the same hotel, 'Was introduced to the Grand Duke George in evening. He is very anxious for me to take him home, but of course I can't', as the Romanovs were not welcome in England.[9] On his last night at the hotel, Poole's routine of going to bed early was disturbed, 'Grand Duke George came in to me about midnight – very anxious for me to take him out. He is a poorish specimen, but I'm very sorry for him'.[10] The Grand Duke was later arrested by the Finnish Reds, sent back to the Bolsheviks and shot in 1919.

The following day, Poole learned that the British diplomatic community had decided to leave Petrograd via Finland. Montgomery Grove organised hotel accommodation for the incoming diplomatic community from Petrograd, whose numbers had been swelled by contingents from other countries deciding to accompany the British. Lars Krogius, the owner of the Finska Steamship Company, was sent round to the sailors' Soviet, Centroflot, which controlled the Russian fleet in Helsinki. Krogius was to ask for the use of one of the ships they had seized from him. The sailors had earlier started a reign of terror by brutally murdering their admiral and other officers when Nicholas II was overthrown. They had such a fearsome reputation that the visiting naval section of Senator Root's mission left within the day without inspecting the fleet.

Naturally enough, Centroflot did not want any vessels to leave Helsinki because of the risk that they would be diverted and used to bring reinforcements to the White Finnish forces. The Germans were also

---

8   Poole, Diary, 25 February 1918.
9   Poole, Diary, 26 February 1918.
10 Poole, Diary, 1 March 1918.

advancing to the south of the Baltic at this time and were facilitating the return of the Jaeger platoon, formed from Finnish nationalists in exile, to reinforce the Whites. When Krogius returned empty-handed, the General prevailed on Fawcett, the vice consul who had been in Helsinki much longer than Grove and was well connected, to see whether a member of the government could help. The result was predictable; without the sanction of the sailors nothing could be done. So a cable was sent to Sweden to see whether the *Arcturus* could be sent back to Helsinki.

The following day Poole sent new instructions to Sweden, asking for the *Arcturus* to be sent to Åbo instead of Helsinki. He had learned that, far from being a Swedish ship, the *Arcturus* belonged to the Finska Steamship Company and stood the risk of being confiscated by Centroflot, which explained why the *Arcturus* had sailed from Helsinki before the General's arrival. Remarkably, despite civil war in Finland and the anarchy prevailing across the border in Russia, the long-distance telephone line between Helsinki and Petrograd, installed in 1916, was still working and Poole was able to telephone the British Embassy there to discuss arrangements.

In the event, the number of the party travelling was inflated to around 150 by the Belgian, French and Serbian embassies accompanying the British. Their train reached Helsinki at 8 p.m. on 1 March. The General ordered a special train for onward travel to Åbo and laid in rations for the sea voyage in the *Arcturus*. These rations were obtained unconventionally from a number of British submarines operating in the Baltic and based in Helsinki. These submarines were later blown up to prevent their capture by the Germans.

The train carrying Poole and the diplomats left Helsinki early on 2 March and reached Åbo the same afternoon. By now those who had travelled from Petrograd were exhausted. They had endured a long wait before their train had been allowed to leave Petrograd; then a twenty-four journey to Helsinki, followed by an early start and another six and a half hours in the train.[11] Sunday brought bad news: the *Arcturus* was unavailable and there was no prospect of chartering another ship. All the available shipping had been commandeered to bring reinforcements to the White forces and there was no point in sledging over the ice to the

---

11 Poole, Diary, 2 March. 'Went to Bourse, a very comfortable hotel – but no bathroom! Long afternoon, fixing up all the people into their rooms. Poor women many of them very tired'. The Hamburger Börs was not quite up to the standard of the Societetshus, but it did provide a comfortable and sorely needed night's rest.

Finland

Åland Islands, from which boats plied regularly to and from the Swedish mainland. The Germans were said to have occupied them and indeed did so on 5 March. The only remaining hope of reaching Sweden lay in crossing the civil war Front Line which divided the Red and White Finnish forces.

On the Monday, the General and his party left Åbo at 9 a.m. by special train and at 2 p.m. arrived at Tammerfors, the town and railway junction closest to the Front Line. Lindley and his immediate team from the British Embassy, who had gone there direct from Helsinki, were attempting to negotiate a crossing into the territory held by the White Finns, but Poole was unsure whether any agreement Lindley reached would include all of his party:

> They have interviewed the Reds and, after great opposition, have got leave to try to see if the Whites will let them through – and I hope us also. An aeroplane flew over their lines and dropped letters saying that we would send a representative tomorrow morning early to arrange details. The Reds are very averse to the whole thing, but I hope we shall manage it. The Red troops one sees here are a tough-looking lot and no mean fighters as far as the raw material goes. Tammerfors is a well-built town – 40,000 inhabitants – and quite civilized.[12]

Poole concentrated on establishing a rapport with August Wesley, the commander of the Red forces:

> Heard in morning all goes well. The Whites are going to let us through and we start tomorrow morning. They had never got our message from the aeroplane and fired on our party while going across – but no damage done. Had a long talk to Red C-in-C. He is a very intelligent man and speaks perfect English after many years in States. If all have his views, then the cause for which they are fighting is not unreasonable, simply more advanced than our democratic ideas.[13]

It was the first time that Poole had ever had direct dealings with a Communist. Previously he had relied on intermediaries, using Victor

---

12 Poole, Diary, 4 March 1918.
13 Poole, Diary, 6 March 1918. August Wesley, anglicised from Wesslin, was a local man, born in Tammerfors in 1887, who had emigrated to the USA in 1904 and returned home in 1917.

Warrender to contact Lenin in June 1917 and Bobby to deal with Trotsky and his colleagues in December 1917. Wesley's goodwill proved enough to produce a train on the following day to take the British contingent from Tammerfors to the Front Line, though even then their progress was challenged by two Communist commissars.

> Started at 8.00 a.m. for the front after great opposition – probably fostered by Hun agents – from two Red commissars. Indeed, at Lyly, just before we crossed, they definitely stopped the whole thing and put Wesley, the Red C-in-C, in arrest as a traitor! However, we forced their hands and were allowed to go. We detrained under a strong escort of Reds and, when the train had gone, the White sledges came up and we loaded our kit and went across. It was about four miles from railhead to railhead. The Whites did us very well on arrival – had food ready for us and a train waiting. Started off at 4.00 p.m. At Seinäjoki, 9.00 p.m., we were met by General Mannerheim, C-in-C Whites. I had known him before. He is capable, but I think his staff is bad. They make the great mistake of underestimating their opponents. Of what I saw of the two forces I consider the Red are the best. They suffer through lack of discipline and so will lose, but it will be a desperate struggle and if the Huns and Swedes didn't interfere, they would win.[14]

Finland had declared its independence from Russia on 6 December 1917 and Mannerheim wanted access to the Allied military stores sent to Russia but delayed in transit. There was little Poole could do to help him, as the White Finnish government was on the point of entering an alliance with Germany, now about to launch its final offensive on the Western Front. With Mannerheim's help, however, the British reached Tornea on Friday 8 March, where they crossed into Sweden and boarded the night train from Haparanda to Stockholm: 'Travelling all day – very comfortable. By papers we see that Finland has made a treaty with Germany. She is now delivered into Germany's hands body and soul. This is, of course, bad for us but far worse for Sweden.'[15]

The entire staff of the British Legation turned out to welcome the train

---

14 Poole, Diary, 7 March 1918.
15 Poole, Diary, 9 March 1918. Marshal Mannerheim formed a high opinion of General Poole, whom he described in his memoirs in fulsome terms.

on its arrival in Stockholm. Sir Esmé Howard, the British Minister, later wrote in his memoirs, 'They arrived in Stockholm like people who had seen Hell and at last been allowed to enter the gates of Paradise'.[16] The General had intended to be on his way home immediately to begin his next assignment but was dissuaded by Howard, who wanted to hold discussions about the Allied economic blockade, since its effectiveness had become a topic of vital significance as Germany prepared to unleash its final attack on the Western Front. The following day the General lunched at the legation and afterwards was presented to the Crown Princess of Sweden, 'who was very anxious to see us. She is a nice simple woman – very like her grandmother. She must have had a bad time living in this pro-German court'.[17]

After boarding the night train to Oslo, Poole decided Howard was, 'a good man with good ideas, but spoilt by his association with that sink of incompetence, the Foreign Office'.[18] Although the General had come to loathe the Foreign Office for its failure to reach an accommodation with the Bolsheviks, he was wise enough to recognise Howard's abilities, which subsequently resulted in him becoming British Ambassador to Washington and receiving a peerage.

Poole, who was being summoned home to head a new venture, did not yet know that he was to become Commander-in-Chief of Allied Forces in North Russia with dictatorial powers and that this would be his opportunity to see whether he could do better than the Foreign Office.

---

16 Sir Esmé Howard, *Theatre of Life* (London, 1936).
17 Poole, Diary, 11 and 13 March 1918. Princess Margaret was the eldest child of the Duke of Connaught, the seventh of Queen Victoria's nine offspring. Born in 1882, she died in 1920.
18 Poole, Diary, 13 March 1918.

18

North Russia

Major General Frederick Poole set off on the first stage of his journey to North Russia by a special train at 6 p.m. from Euston Station on Saturday 18 May 1918, accompanied by Major Banting, his new ADC Macpherson, two other officers and two personal servants, Cox, and his father-in-law's butler, Humphries. As Lord Mayor of London Charles Hanson did not need a butler as he had given up the lease on Wilton Place and moved into the Mansion House, where the General was living with his wife and sons before he set out for Russia. Alice Poole, owing to her mother's ill heath, was acting as hostess for her father. For the first time in his life Frederick Poole was financially secure.[1]

Before his departure, however, the General had been not been feeling his usual confident self. Alice with her calm and supportive presence had brought him reassurance. As he travelled north on the special train, he acknowledged his debt to her: 'You have been a great help to me. I'm settled down now'.[2] On board ship travelling to Murmansk he did so again, 'Well sweetheart it was a very happy time wasn't it – a nice break in the drudgery of war. I am so glad you are not a little-minded small-hearted woman – always scheming for your own man to be safe at home and not caring a cuss about other people's men. Your way is the big and right way, darling, even if it is the hardest at the time'.[3]

Consistent with the views he had formed in Petrograd, the General now

---

1   Beryl Nicholson's estate had a probate value of £34,803. *Coventry Evening Standard*, 7 June 1918.
2   Frederick Poole to Alice Poole, 18 May 1918.
3   Frederick Poole to Alice Poole, 24 May 1918.

tried hard to achieve an accommodation with the Bolsheviks to frustrate Germany gaining control of the Russian economy. Although he later changed his mind about the Bolsheviks, he never deviated from his view about the larger question of who controlled the Russian economy. Even in the final weeks before the Armistice on 11 November 1918, he observed, 'The one way we can lose this war is by allowing Germany to get hold of Russia and use her as a supply depôt for men and material. The one way that she will be able to attain that objective is by limiting our very small presence everywhere'.[4]

Poole was fully aware of how the Allied economic blockade was undermining Germany's capacity to make war. With the perspective gained from meetings in Stockholm and Oslo, he concluded 'The impression here is that the internal state of Germany is very bad – worse than is generally expected'.[5] There was, in fact, common ground between the Allies and the Bolsheviks about denying German ambitions in north Russia. When the Bolsheviks started the peace negotiations with Germany, which were concluded by the Treaty of Brest-Litovsk, Poole had noted, 'No news. I hear the Germans have made proposals re the White Sea, which practically involve turning us out of Murmansk. The Russians have refused them'.[6] Notwithstanding German pressure, the Bolshevik position had remained unchanged, so much so that on 2 March, the day before the conclusion of the treaty, Trotsky sent an explicit signal to the Murmansk Soviet instructing them to collaborate with the Allies: 'You are ordered to cooperate with Allied Missions in everything and to put all obstacles in the way of advancing Germans. The robbers are attacking us. We are obliged to save the country and the revolution'.[7]

Rear Admiral Thomas Kemp, the Senior Naval Officer in the White Sea, who had withdrawn from Archangel with his flotilla at the close of the navigation season to spend the winter of 1917-18 in the ice-free port of Murmansk, responded by landing a small party of marines and requesting additional support from London. HMS *Cochrane*, an armoured cruiser, arrived on 9 March with five hundred Royal Marines.

---

4   Poole, Diary, 2 October 1918.
5   Poole, Diary, 14 March 1918. The subject had been his special concern after his arrival in England, when his office had been at the 'Restriction of Enemy Supplies Department, 6 Waterloo Place, SW1'.
6   Poole, Diary, 29 December 1918.
7   Henry Newbolt, Official History of the War, *Naval Operations*, v (London, 1931).

North Russia

Poole's ship approached the Russian coastline at full speed and at action stations, 'We were lucky to get in without being fired at, as there are two submarines operating outside which have lately sunk several steamers and fishing boats'.[8] He established his headquarters on Kemp's flagship HMS *Glory*, as the town, which had barely existed before the opening of the railway to Petrograd in 1916, had no suitable accommodation and few comforts to offer. The only entertainment the General enjoyed in Murmansk was watching a boxing competition organised for the men under his command. The landscape was devoid of trees, and even the simple pleasure of walking was made hideous by the bogs and streams which emerged when the coming of summer melted the top layer of the tundra.

After interviews with Admiral Kemp, French officers and the Murmansk Soviet, the General concluded that, 'It doesn't look too cheerful, but there are possibilities. As we walked home, someone fired from a distance – bullet passed just over our heads. I hope it was only accidental'.[9] It was, however, a potentially dire situation. Germany now controlled Finland, with 55,000 troops stationed there and with the support of a similar number of White Finns. The line linking the Russian railway system with Murmansk was expected to be overrun by twenty thousand men attacking its key points at Kandalashka, Kem and Petrozavodsk. This would mean Germany securing the ice-free port of Murmansk and establishing a submarine base there to mount systematic attacks on Allied shipping. Archangel, where there was a vast accumulation of undelivered Allied aid, lay similarly exposed.

General Poole later wrote in his Despatch No. 1, published in the *London Gazette* in July 1920:

> According to orders received from the War Office, I proceeded to Murman, where I disembarked on 24 May 1918, to assume command of the Allied Forces in North Russia. My instructions were to organise the Czecho-Slovaks, of whom there were said to be some twenty thousand en route to Archangel and Murman, and these troops, together with any local troops I might be able to raise, were to form the bulk of my force, stiffened with a few Allied troops of whom I might ultimately hope to obtain about five thousand.[10]

---

8 Poole, Diary, 24 May 1918.
9 Poole, Diary, 25 May 1918.
10 *London Gazette*, 6 April 1920.

Archangel and Northern Russia

Since the ferocity of the German Spring Offensive on the Western Front ruled out the possibility of sending more than token military reinforcements, 'My Czechs', as the General called them, were needed if a credible Allied military presence was to be established in North Russia. This force had come into being in 1916 from Czech and Slovak prisoners of war volunteering to help liberate their country from the Austrian Empire. Following the decision of the Bolsheviks to make peace, they were being transported on the Trans-Siberian Railway to Vladivostok, Russia's ice-free port on the Pacific Ocean, with the intention that they should be shipped back to fight on the Western Front. The idea now was to divert those who were still at the initial stages of their journey eastwards to north Russia.

North Russia

On the Sunday the General was 'busy all morning' and 'inspected marine barracks ashore in afternoon', where the token force of British marines was quartered.[11] Poole also saw Commander Malcolm Maclaren, a British secret agent, and Nyman, a delegate from the Finnish Red Guard who spoke English perfectly. Nyman was confident of finding recruits to fight the White Finns and their German allies, so Poole engaged him as a 'sergeant to be attached to my staff'.[12] A telegram came from the Admiralty giving Poole command of all naval ranks when ashore and announcing the dispatch of Major General Maynard with six hundred men to be his deputy in Murmansk.

In a private meeting Vesselago of the Murmansk Soviet informed Poole that 'the commissar sent up from Moscow, Natzaremus, has come with full powers from Lenin and Trotsky to deal with the Allies if possible and they wanted to know if I had full powers from my government to treat'.[13] Poole replied that he had 'full military powers, but no authority to make any treaties, which were of course solely a matter for the government to carry out'. In answer to Vesselago's question as to his intentions, 'I explained we were not willing to show our hand until we know definitely what they were prepared to do, as otherwise we stood the chance of all our dispositions being given away to the Hun'.[14]

Their conversation then took a better turn, 'He said we are raising an army and we have also 50,000 Czechs at Vologda. I said, "Well now that's a solid proposition". I will reply at once that I am prepared as a basis to arm and equip these Czechs and find officers and NCOs to assist in training and feed them'. Vesselago said he 'would put it all before the commissar tonight' and added, 'if the commissar was not willing to go on, he said he could answer that Murmansk province would declare itself a republic and ask for Allied help'.

Vesselago then reported back to Natzaremus, who had nothing but contempt for him as a former ADC to Admiral Kyetlinski, who had been the senior Russian naval officer at Murmansk until he was murdered by his own sailors on 10 February 1918. Vesselago returned with the response from Natzaremus. Poole wrote 'The commissar writes that he wants to

---

11 Poole, Diary, 26 May 1918.
12 Poole, Diary, 26 May 1918.
13 Poole, Diary, 26 May 1918.
14 Poole, Diary, 26 May 1918.

General Sir Frederick Poole

see me before he goes to Moscow to discuss the situation'.[15] At this point *Porto* arrived in evening, bringing a letter for me and reinforcements – four hundred marines. Had quite a good effect on local opinion'.[16] Then Natzaremus himself came to see the General:

> Kemp and I had a long interview with Natzaremus. He is a clever, energetic man, who takes himself seriously. He has created much ill-will for himself by his forceful methods of speaking to the Russians here, who don't like to be told they are lazy and foolish. We asked him to tell us clearly how he stood with us and what his instructions were as regards defending the place and the line. He said that unless and until we were prepared to recognise the Bolshevik Government, he would say nothing officially. We said that as this is outside the scope of our instructions we could not talk on that basis.
>
> Speaking unofficially, he said that they firmly intended to fight and were sending up here at once the Czechs – two divisions of the new army, guns, aeroplanes and all necessaries. I said I would be responsible for the Czechs, if he would produce them, and also help to train any other heroes he might bring along. We had long talk about recognition, about which they are very anxious and upon which they lay very great stress. We parted on very friendly terms with a good understanding of mutual cooperation unofficially. I personally think there is no doubt we are foolish not to recognise them. I have always thought so.

The only sour note in Poole's account of the day is the reference to a telegram received after the meeting. This cast doubt on whether the Bolsheviks could provide safe passage for the Czechs to North Russia. The telegram – sent from Moscow by Lieutenant Colonel Lavergne, the senior French officer remaining in Russia – referred to an incident at Penza on the western end of the Trans-Siberian line caused by the Czechs.[17] Discontented about the long delay in their passage eastwards, and apprehensive about their security, the Czechs had refused to hand over their weapons. The Bolsheviks,

---

15 Poole, Diary, 28 May 1918.
16 Poole, Diary, 29 May 1918.
17 Poole, Diary, 31 May 1918.

however, did not want any trouble. Trains were going in the other direction repatriating prisoners of war to Austria, Hungary and Germany; they were the enemies of the Czechs and Slovaks, who wanted independence from the Austro-Hungarian Empire and therefore sided with the Allies. The whole railway system was anyway barely functioning, having been reduced to a parlous state by the demands of the war and then overwhelmed by the chaos that had ensued since the Revolution. For lack of transport to carry food, there was starvation in Petrograd and Moscow.

The General gained the support of his French and American colleagues for his recommendation of recognition of the Bolsheviks as the legitimate government of Russia: 'French agreed as to necessity for recognition of government and wired their government accordingly. The Yank would not wire to his government as he says he isn't allowed to but wired his admiral in London instead!'[18] The following day, Sunday 2 June, Natzeremus 'left Murmansk for Petrograd and Moscow, to confer with Lenin'.[19]

Poole was already beginning to have doubts, rightly recognising that the Bolsheviks might be powerless to resist German demands. Having defeated Russia and being engaged in a final offensive to crush the Allies on the Western Front, he realised that the Germans would under no circumstances allow the Czechs free passage to Murmansk to be reconstituted as a hostile force under British control.

> My Czechs have not turned up yet and the news I get from the French tells me that it is not by any means certain that they will, but it's all in the lap of the Gods and we shall see. Anyhow I am still optimistic and that is the main point after all. The Hun seems to be pretty powerful in Russia generally, so it makes it a little difficult for us as he is always bringing pressure to bear on the government to block us – but on the whole we keep our end up pretty well.[20]

Poole's doubts increased when Lieutenant Colonel Cudbert Thornhill returned from an Intelligence gathering trip with the conclusion that there was 'very little chance of getting Czechs'.[21] On 8 June Poole was invited to

---

18 Poole, Diary, 1 June 1918.
19 Strakhovsky, *Origins of American Intervention in North Russia* (Princeton, 1937).
20 Frederick Poole to Alice Poole, 1 June 1918.
21 Poole, Diary, 7 June 1918.

attend a meeting of the Murmansk Soviet. 'They read us – unofficially – a telegram sent to them signed by Lenin and Chicherin saying that Russian ships will be torpedoed as long as the Allies remain here. Secondly, that Allied presence in Murmansk is a breach of the Brest-Litovsk treaty.'[22]

Other news arrived. 'I hear Natzaremus is not coming back here. He is sent to Samara instead to quell the rebellion. The latter appears to be making headway and may probably mean the overthrow of the government.'[23] After the Czechs had occupied Samara, a new government had been formed to oppose the Bolsheviks. Its legitimacy came from the mandate its members derived from having been elected to serve in the Constituent Assembly, hence its name 'The Committee of Members of the Constituent Assembly'. Samara was a key strategic location, being on both the Volga River and the Trans-Siberian Railway.

The following day the General received a 'very urgent and alarming wire from Lockhart saying it's most important in view of the developments of the Czech rising that I go at once to Vologda to have a conference with the Allied ambassadors, as it is pressing to make our decisions.'[24] Bruce-Lockhart was still acting in Petrograd as the unofficial representative of the British Government, but the Bolsheviks had become increasingly distrustful of his activities. The other Allied embassies had returned to Russia in February 1918, after being prevented from following the British across the Front Line in the Finnish Civil War, and had settled at Vologda. Any accommodation with the Bolsheviks now begged the question of whether they could still be regarded as the de facto government of Russia. Poole set off by ship to Archangel, intending to travel by the railway southwards to where it joined the main Russian railway system at Vologda, but thick ice forced his return to Murmansk.

On his return Poole received a cable informing him that Sir Eric Geddes, who was both the First Sea Lord and a member of Lloyd George's War Cabinet, would arrive in Murmansk on Sunday. 'This is great news as it shows they are really taking some considerable interest in us.'[25] That evening two ships arrived from home with stores as well as Francis Lindley, who was returning to Russia as the British Chargé d'Affaires, and an economic

---

22 Poole, Diary, 8 June 1918.
23 Poole, Diary, 16 June 1918.
24 Poole, Diary, 17 June 1918.
25 Poole, Diary, 20 June 1918.

mission led by Sir William Clark to investigate the possibilities of trade with the Bolsheviks. Clark was a career civil servant who had started in the Board of Trade and specialised in trade matters in a distinguished career. In 1917, he had been appointed Comptroller General of Overseas Trade Department by Lloyd George, under whom he had served at both the Board of Trade and the Exchequer. This was the government's belated response to Poole's request for the dispatch of an expert on trade.

On 23 June Major General Maynard and Brigadier General Finlayson arrived. Poole had requested Finlayson's return to Russia as a man he could trust to take operational control if there were to be an Allied military intervention in Archangel. The War Office had chosen Maynard to manage the Murmansk theatre under Poole's overall command. Poole 'Found them all very happy and full of war'.[26] Maynard also found Poole 'full of war'. Maynard describes how after disembarking he went in search of the General. He discovered him in an animated discussion with Rear Admiral Kemp on HMS *Glory* about the practicalities of making the sea passage to Archangel in the light of the unseasonal delay in the ice melting.[27] Maynard remembered being briefed by Poole that 'there was officially no state of war between the Bolsheviks and ourselves'. This indicates that the General's thinking had now veered away from an accommodation with the Bolsheviks. Now, after his discussion with Kemp, he wanted to secure Archangel before either the Germans arrived or the Bolsheviks, acting on their behalf, became entrenched there.

'In evening HMS *Southampton* arrived having Sir Eric Geddes on board – incognito as General Campbell. He sent for us at once and we were kept talking till 2 a.m. News from France more cheerful especially as the Americans are coming in very fast.'[28] Lloyd George had discovered Geddes in the Ministry of Munitions and been so impressed by his abilities that he had him sent to resolve the transport difficulties of the British Expeditionary Force, which Geddes did by the construction of a large network of light railways that could take the huge volume of supplies needed to maintain a force of a million and a half men, winning the approval of Sir Douglas Haig. In 1917, as Prime Minister, Lloyd George cajoled a reluctant Admiralty into introducing the convoy system as a defence against German submarines

---

26 Poole, Diary, 23 June 2018.
27 Sir Charles Maynard, *Murmansk Venture* (London, 1928).
28 Poole, Diary, 23 June 2018.

with a mandate for unrestricted sinking of all ships whether naval or civilian. Lloyd George then followed up this initiative by appointing Geddes First Sea Lord.

Poole took an immediate liking to Geddes, an approachable, energetic and practical man, who, still only forty-one, had made a major contribution to the war effort. The following day the *Southampton* headed westwards to inspect the small port of Petsamo, where there was an Allied garrison stationed to counter the possibility of hostile action by the Germans. Poole made the most of his opportunity, 'Spent the voyage having a heart-to-heart talk to Geddes. I like him. He is the regular buccaneer type and is all out to help if we can show him the value which we can get out of this country if we make headway'.[29] Geddes had already made his presence felt in Murmansk that morning, even trying to persuade Maynard to take him on a reconnaissance southward by rail. Poole accompanied Geddes on a full inspection of Petsamo and its hinterland, and the day ended on a convivial note before Poole returned separately to Murmansk: 'Dined on *Southampton* and started back at 10.30pm'.[30] By contrast with Murmansk, Poole found Petsamo congenial, 'It is rather a clean civilized-looking little hamlet. A big monastery has exercised a civilizing influence'. There was only one discordant note: 'Mosquitos very bad; was bitten to pieces'.

Back on HMS *Glory* in Murmansk the General received telegrams from Young and McGrath 'which leave it pretty certain we shall be opposed strongly at Archangel'.[31] Poole had sent Captain McGrath, one of the four British officers who had accompanied him from London to Murmansk, to gather Intelligence in Archangel. Poole accordingly decided against an immediate assault on Archangel, 'Discussed the situation with Finlayson and we agree that we shall be better to wait and not precipitate a crisis. We could certainly get into Archangel with our present force, but it is equally certain the Hun can push us out again if he likes'.[32] That evening, after a farewell dinner with Poole, Geddes left for home on HMS *Southampton*.

Poole had been too busy to send a letter to Alice by the returning HMS

---

29 Poole, Diary, 24 June 1918. As HMS *Southampton* left Murmansk at 1 p.m. and arrived at Petsamo at 9 p.m. there was certainly the time for a full discussion.
30 Poole, Diary, 25 June 1918.
31 Poole, Diary, 26 June 1918. The General had been warmly received by Douglas Young when visiting Archangel in March 1917, just before the abdication of Nicholas II. Young was still there as the British Consul, despite all the subsequent upheaval.
32 Poole, Diary, 26 June 1918.

Southampton and the pressure of events did not let up. He barely found the time when the next vessel was going home to write:

> We have a ship going home tonight so I will get a line off to you to say all well. Things are moving along now. I think Russia has declared war on the Allies!! She certainly has on us! And I am expecting one of my detachments down the line to be scrapping any time. I'm not very frightened – the lot they can put against us don't amount to much – but it's annoying that the Bolshevik Government has gone absolutely pro-Hun. Of course, it is under Hun pressure. Here we are quite top dog and the local government is committed up to the neck and can't get out of it even if they want to.
>
> No other news and I'm very busy so can't write much, darling. It's been beastly hot the last few days and the mosquitoes very bad.[33]

Three days later Poole received welcome news from home, 'Good telegram from Geddes at night. He has fixed up my five thousand men for me', which meant that he would now have the means to risk a move on Archangel.[34] Then he learned that the German Ambassador to the Bolshevik government had been murdered, 'This will change the situation considerably'.[35] The murder was intended to create a rupture between the Bolsheviks and the Germans and to provide a clear signal that there was now serious opposition to the Bolsheviks. This was from the less extreme Social Revolutionaries who had won a majority in the Constituent Assembly elected by democratic franchise to determine the future government of Russia. That impression was soon reinforced, 'All sorts of rumours about due to Mirbach's death – e.g. Lenin and Trotsky have fled. Germany has declared war on Russia. Whatever happens, it seems it must be good for us'.[36] He added 'Apparently the Social Revolutionaries have started a revolution at Moscow. It was they who killed Mirbach. There seems to be fighting going on there'.[37]

A counter-revolution against the Bolsheviks was happening but Poole was hamstrung, 'Had urgent wire from Noulens saying that counter-

---

33 Frederick Poole to Alice Poole, 3 July 1918.
34 Poole, Diary, 6 July 1918.
35 Poole, Diary, 7 July 1918.
36 Poole, Diary, 8 July 1918.
37 Poole, Diary, 10 July 1918.

revolutionary troops had seized Yaroslav and urging me to act at once from Archangel. So I would, if I had anything to act with!! Sent message to urge the Czechs to occupy Vologda and come to Archangel'.[38] He heard again from Vologda, 'A very jumpy wire from the Allied embassies at Vologda asking me to come at once' and added 'I wish I could'.[39]

Pending the arrival of the promised reinforcements from home, the General took final measures to secure his position at Murmansk. Although he had persuaded the Murmansk Soviet to break with the Bolsheviks, there were three hundred Russian sailors in two ships, the *Askold* and the *Chesma*, who were out of control. Their latest outrage, on 12 July, was to throw bombs into Vesselago's house in an attempt to kill him. The General acted swiftly and decisively. He seized both vessels and dispatched the sailors by train down the railway to the limit of the territory under his control, where they were left to continue their journey on foot with three days of rations. The *Askold* was taken into service by the Royal Navy, renamed *Glory IV* and brought to the England in 1919; the *Chesma*, which had been grounded, could not be reused.

Poole tried to be upbeat in a congratulatory letter to his father-in-law on being made a baronet, which, until the abolition of hereditary honours, was given by long tradition to Lord Mayors of London. Even so, he was nervous about the challenge presented in taking Archangel.

> My dear Pa, It makes me very pleased and proud to see that you are made a Bart! Many congratulations on your well-deserved honour and may you live long to enjoy it.
>
> I'm keeping very fit and quite pleased with my progress out here. We have brought off a successful revolution against Lenin and Trotsky's government and here in this district are declared pro-Allies, which is no small achievement. We have a government here but in point of fact I find myself a complete autocrat and it's very hard work – apart from all military work. I am up in to the neck with all the local politics and have to keep a strong hand on the administration of the whole of this district. In a very short time if all goes well I shall be more involved still, as I am going into Archangel

---

38 Poole, Diary, 8 July 1918. Noulens was the French Ambassador.
39 Poole, Diary, 16 July 1918.

and, if we get it, it will mean we take over a country in a few months which is nearly as large as the rest of Europe! My 'civil advisers' here have decided that this new possession (when we get it!) is to be run by a council of five. The headquarters of the government are to be 'wherever General Poole is'!!!! As a matter of fact, if the Bolsheviks and Huns oppose us at all, it will be the maddest military venture on record, as I have only a handful of men and it's a considerably harder proposition than Gallipoli.[40] But all the same I trust in the psychology of the Slav and I think it's worth the gamble. Anyhow it will all be settled one way or the other by the time you get this.[41]

Charles Orr, who understood how official circles worked, wrote to Alice asking for news of his old friend. The tone of his letter suggests that the General's actions were well received in London:

Have you any news of your husband and is there any means of sending him a letter? The papers of course tell one nothing, and you must be having a very anxious time. I met a man the other day in the Naval Intelligence who told me that the War Cabinet had the very highest opinion of your husband and have practically left in his hands the whole of our diplomacy in Russia, so I fancy he has got his chance and I can imagine no one more likely to pull the fat out of the fire in Russia and restore our somewhat damaged prestige there. One feels that anything may happen at any moment, and this Murman business may develop into something big. Of course, it is a thousand times better for your husband than being out in France where, however big his appointment, he would not be on his own but would be one of a hundred or a score of other men acting under Foch or Haig …[42]

Yet Poole knew that, if he failed to take Archangel, at best the credit he

---

40 This was the failed British attempt in 1915 to force the passage of the Dardanelles and reopen communications with Russia via the Black Sea. Shore batteries and mines had defeated the Navy's attempt to force the passage. The Turkish army entrenched on the commanding heights above had defeated the Allied troops landed to dislodge them.
41 Frederick Poole to Sir Charles Hanson, 23 July 1918.
42 Charles Orr to Alice Poole, 30 July 1918.

had built up in London would vanish and at worst he would be disgraced. On the same day he was writing to congratulate his father-in-law he revealed to Alice his anxieties about the risks involved. What he said about a massive explosion was far from fanciful. When he had visited Archangel before the abdication of Nicholas II, he had seen the damage caused by German agents, who in the previous month had blown up some five thousand tonnes of munitions and equipment on Solombola Island, causing five hundred deaths.[43]

> If it comes off it will be a big thing, but of course it's an awful gamble. They have such opportunities and so many horrors opposed to us that it makes one's brain reek! Including one little stunt for 'putting up' all the thousands of tons of explosives which are there. This would blow the whole place and thousands of people to kingdom come! However, I have great hopes it will all go well and I am quite prepared to take the risk of a bad failure.[44]

In the end, on 27 July 1918 Poole went ahead with his small force, augmented by a contingent from France, but without the five thousand troops promised in the telegram from Geddes.[45] He felt the risk was worthwhile because he knew, thanks to his Intelligence network, that he could count on an uprising in the town against the Bolsheviks. He also had the imagination to see how the impact of that uprising would be magnified by mounting a diversionary attack in the rear to threaten the Bolshevik line of communications down the railway to Vologda.

The bravery of Captain Altham in HMS *Attentive* and the use of aircraft launched from the seaborne carrier *Nairana* unnerved the Bolsheviks. They weakly surrendered their strong natural position on Modyuski Island, which commands the sea approaches to Archangel. They then lost their nerve completely and abandoned the town when confronted by the well-planned rising led by a former Russian naval officer, Georgi Chaplin, together with

---

43 Samuel Hoare, *The Fourth Seal* (London, 1930).
44 Frederick Poole to Alice Poole, 23 July 1918.
45 Alice Poole was moved to add when later transcribing the General's letters, 'Note. I met Lord Milner about this time and he told me I would probably see next day that Archangel had fallen – that Dad was going to take it. He also said, "It seems such a little force, doesn't it". They were all or mostly (the English soldiers (I don't know whether Dad's Russians were in it) – C3 men. A.P. (Alice Poole)'. Note in the author's possession.

reports that their retreat was being cut off by the diversionary attack in the rear led by Lieutenant Colonel Thornhill.

A combined operation between air, military and naval forces was indeed pioneering, but an awareness of the three came naturally to Poole. A keen sailor with an understanding of the sea, he had learned, in evolving counter-battery techniques, the art of using air power to support the men on the ground. Prudently, the General insisted on a rehearsal on 29 July, before going into action, to establish a proper framework of cooperation and avoid service rivalries. 'There has been a little friction owing to dual control between sailors and RA. I hope I have settled it up all right.'[46] Maynard was generous enough to record in *The Murmansk Venture* that the General had evolved from an 'expert gunner' into a 'fine all-round soldier'. Poole's verdict on Maynard, in turn, was not ungenerous, 'He is too hide-bound to really be a success at this sort of work, but he is a good soldier and that makes up for a lot.'[47] Poole, who bore overall responsibility, was generous in his praise for those involved in capturing Modyuski Island.

> *Aube* went ashore in the fog but got off again without damage about 5.00 a.m. Meanwhile *Attentive* and *Nairana* got safely to the rendezvous and seized the lightship and demanded instant surrender of the island of Modyuski. At first they agreed to surrender but afterwards they decided to put up a fight. We bombarded the batteries which replied and made fairly effective shooting until the aeroplanes got busy and bombed them. This quickly finished the whole thing. They left rear guards to hamper us – fled to the south of the island and escaped. We had no casualties. The *Attentive* had one shell through her funnel but no damage done.
>
> We arrived about 4 p.m. when all the scrap had finished, so saw none of it. About 8.45 p.m. we had finished cleaning up the island – we took a few prisoners about thirty – a thousand rifles, a few machine-guns etc. The guns were 6-inch and a battery of 6-inch howitzers. They were working hard at their preparations and in a short time would have made the whole island so strong that its capture would have constituted a formidable operation. Indeed, if

---

46 Poole, Diary, 28 July 1918.
47 Poole, Diary, 16 July 1918.

they had had any heart, we should never have been able to take on the job with the three hundred men we landed. Kemp did well to decide to go in with the forces at his disposal.[48]

Even after capturing Modyuski Island, victory was far from assured. Passage had to be negotiated past the ice-breakers that had been scuppered to block the Maimaxa channel which leads from Modyuski Island to the port of Archangel. Fortunately, Altham found a way through and the force was able to continue to Ekonomiya on the northern end of Solombala Island, connected in summer by a bridge of boats to Archangel, and learned that the rising in the town had been successful.

It was a close-run affair as Bolshevik reinforcements, stiffened by German troops, had reached Isakogorka, nine kilometres from the terminus of the railway line at Bakharitsa on the opposite side of the River Dvina to the town of Archangel. Altham was therefore sent upriver to stall their advance.

At 6.00 a.m. loaded up landing parties on to the trawlers and they with *Attentive* started on up the channel and about four miles up *Attentive* reported ice-breakers sunk across channel thus blocking us. Kemp and I decided to go up in the yacht to investigate. French officer arrived and reports the Bolshevik government has fled. Archangel quiet and hoping for our arrival.

When we reached the block we found that the *Attentive* had investigated and that the channel was still passable with difficulty, so we decided to push on up and make Ekonomiya. Just as we started we got a wireless that the rising was going well and that they were masters of Solombala. We therefore sent on the *Attentive* and two trawlers to help them while we rounded up Ekonomiya. Everything most quiet, white flags everywhere, people waving hands and glad to see us. Then we pushed along in a triumphal procession – quiet enthusiasm everywhere and when we dropped anchor off Archangel it was wonderful. Thousands of people cheering themselves hoarse, sirens of steamers hooting, church bells ringing, bands playing, etc.

The members of the new government (one hour old) came off

---

48 Poole, Diary, 1 August 1918.

to welcome me and made long speeches. Then I went ashore and inspected the guard of honour – enormous enthusiasm! Then, as the people all wished to see me, we formed a triumphal procession and walked up to the town hall. Streets absolutely packed, people screaming with joy and pelting me with flowers. I never saw anything like it. The rising has been organised here by one Chaplin, who is a Russian naval officer, and McGrath. The situation is that here the people are sick to death of the Bolsheviks and have gone solid for us. In Bakharitsa the Bolsheviks are still holding the town, but the main bulk of them have fallen back south to meet Kedroff, the Bolshevik C-in-C, who is coming up the line to oppose us. Our new supporters are enthusiastic but timid and don't know quite what to do.

We had no sleep at all at night as we got constant reports of Kedroff's advance. He has got as far as Isakogorka. We sent *Attentive* upriver as far as she can go to get her jaws in his advance.[49]

The victory was made all the sweeter by it coinciding with the General's forty-ninth birthday on 3 August:

In morning we had a little scrap at Isakogorka with Kedroff's advanced troops. The *Attentive* shelled them off the ridge, which is a very strong position and we got them just in time. Then they cleared out of the station which we occupied and fell back along the line about six versts to the next station. Here we gave them hell. We had aeroplanes over them all day with bombs and machine-guns and in the evening a combined bombing by four planes. All this will shake their nerve. The *Stephen* and *Asturian* got up in the afternoon, so now we are well off for troops. We got off a party at once under Colonel Guard with orders to shove along as far as possible tonight. My birthday! Forty-nine years old.[50]

On 7 August Sir Henry Wilson, now Chief of the Imperial General Staff, sent a telegram of congratulation on this 'vigorous and well-timed action'.

---

49 Poole, Diary, 2 August 1918.
50 Poole, Diary, 3 August 1918.

Well done Elope. The results of your vigorous and well-timed action give us every confidence for the future and have more than justified our expectations.[51]

---

51   Telegram in the author's possession. Elope was the name of the operation.

19

Recall

The General was in high spirits after he landed at Archangel. The finest house in the town had been requisitioned for his use, a welcome change after living on board ship since his departure from England ten weeks previously. The house had electric lighting, plumbing, large rooms and magnificent furnishings. It was on Troitsky Street, the main thoroughfare of the city. After the arrival of Richard Chancellor's expedition from England in 1553, Archangel had become the point of entry into North Russia and had grown wealthy thanks to the abundance of the surrounding forest. More recently it had been the key port handling the inflow of armaments and supplies for Russia's war needs. Its many sawmills, its harbour crowded with shipping, its trams and street lighting, and its magnificent cathedral, were a world away from the comfortless conditions of Murmansk.

A highly decorated Cossack warrior attached himself to the General as his personal bodyguard, standing outside his house and accompanying him when he went out. The historical museum at Archangel has a photograph of him holding a drawn scimitar and standing behind the General, who is holding a huge swagger stick. Together they reduce the Russian Governor-General and his ADC to shadowy-looking figures. After the rigours of Bolshevik government the arrival of the Allies brought a sense of relief and calm to a city swollen by refugees from Moscow and Petrograd.

Politically, the challenges facing Poole were complex. When the Bolshevik regime in Archangel had been overthrown, a civilian government headed by a returned Socialist exile called Tchaikovsky had been put into office and Allied diplomatic representatives had made their headquarters in the town. Poole found it impossible to work with Tchaikovsky because the latter refused to accept that the political agenda in Russia was being dictated by the Bolsheviks employing force and terror. This was despite Tchaikovsky having been an elected representative of the Constituent Assembly which had been suppressed immediately it had attempted to act democratically. He was a theoretician rather than a man of action, keen at all costs to appease and placate opposition rather than exercise any degree of firmness and force. Unfortunately for Poole, Tchaikovsky's government was taken seriously by the American diplomatic representatives in Archangel. The position had not changed since Senator Root's mission to the Provisional Government, which had been keen to develop opportunities for trade but was implacably opposed to any interference in Russian politics. Poole found what he had never experienced in Murmansk: serious constraints on his power as Commander-in-Chief in North Russia.

Militarily, Poole's objective was clear: he had to link up with the Czechs on the Trans-Siberian Railway, the only coherent military force available to the Allies in Russia. That meant advancing from Archangel southwards along the railway line to Vologda and south east up the River Dvina towards Kotlas. There was a three-pronged advance: A Force on the railway; C Force – also known as the 'Kotlas Expedition' and as the 'Dvina River Force' – on the river; and B Force, moving across challenging country, between these two lines of advance. A small contingent of aircraft provided aerial reconnaissance and additional firepower.

Vologda is a railway junction on the route eastwards from Petrograd to Siberia. To the south it provides access to Moscow, which the Bolsheviks had made the capital of Russia, as Petrograd was too exposed to the German army. It is also linked by the River Sukohna with the northern Dvina, which it joins near Kotlas. Kotlas itself is connected by a branch line to Viatka, some 600 kilometres east of Vologda on the main railway line linking Petrograd with the Trans-Siberian Railway, which it joins at Chelyabinsk and further eastwards at Omsk. The through trains between Petrograd and Vladivostok had only begun taking the route via Ekaterinburg to Omsk instead of going via Chelyabinsk in 1914.

Although Poole had captured Archangel, he had not achieved a decisive victory. The best of the river steamers had made their escape up the Dvina. With less than a hundred men against an enemy two thousand strong, Thornhill also did not have the force to cut off the Bolshevik retreat down the railway line to Vologda. The initial advantage of throwing the Bolsheviks onto the defensive was then frittered away by the delay in sending the five thousand troops promised by Geddes in his telegram of 6 July. On 29 July Poole was informed that five thousand Americans without fighting experience would be sent, a different proposition to the battle-hardened soldiers he had expected. Even so, the timing of their arrival remained uncertain. Further bad news came, 'A cable from home shows that they let us down again. The British battalion which was promised for middle August is not likely to come before 28th and the Americans before middle September. It is a most awful pity as every day is such vital importance'.[1] Geddes was unable to make good his promise because fighting on the Western Front had reached a critical stage; the German advance had been checked and a successful counter-attack had been launched on 8 August. All available troops were needed to press this home.

Poole felt no better the following day after a meeting in the morning with the US Ambassador Francis and dinner with him, followed by a bridge party with other Allied diplomats, 'News from England re the arrival of reinforcements is not good. They are all much later than I hoped and expected'.[2]

The General's dissatisfaction was increased by competing demands from the Murmansk theatre. A more cautious soldier, Maynard did not want to risk his own position to make more troops available for the advance from Archangel:

Cable from home suggesting alterations in my proposed disposition of troops for the winter on the grounds that Murman is left too weak. Of course, it is too weak, but they are not going to put it right by taking away five hundred men from here, which is also much too weak, and putting them there. If they want security, they must provide men. Cabled them in this sense.[3]

There was also worrying news about the Bolsheviks being assisted by the Germans, who 'have sent out instructions all round and are helping the Bolsheviks to organize'.[4] Three days later Poole noted, 'The opposition seems

---

1 Poole, Diary, 13 August 1918.
2 Poole, Diary, 14 August 1918.
3 Poole, Diary, 23 August 1918.
4 Poole, Diary, 15 August 1918.

to be stiffening against us and we shall have very heavy fighting before we make good'.[5]

It was not until 26 August that the promised British battalion, the 2/10th Royal Scots, disembarked; they were a thousand strong, but 'They are not a very inspiring lot of warriors as they are all B2 men – small and bad physique'. The promised American troops did not arrive until 4 September. This delay in sending reinforcements allowed the initiative to pass back to the Bolsheviks, stiffened with German help. The chance of reaching Kotlas and linking up with the Czechs had faded. 'In afternoon a Polish officer who had come from the Czecho-Slovaks came up with a message. He had been to Vologda thence to Kotlas and so down the river. He reports reinforcements going up to Kotlas including a Hun officer to organize a new division.'[6]

The General's frustrations were coming to a head. Winter was approaching and the enemy was growing stronger. The Russian civil government, however, was proving at best a distraction and an annoyance and, at worst, a malevolent influence, doing nothing to check press articles hostile to the Allied cause or to prevent agitators stirring up strikes:

> Feeling much better and went out for an hour or two in the afternoon. Troubles with the government. That damned old fool Chaikovsky is on the rampage again. If only I could find a strong reliable Russian, I would cut this crowd – like Cromwell! And put him in – but alas there isn't such a man. German concentration six thousand strong reported at Vyatka. Personally, I don't believe it.[7]

Help came from an unexpected quarter in the form of an endorsement from the Russian Orthodox Church, but its days of influence were over and the impact was nugatory. General Poole was publicly prayed for in the Nikolski monastery. He also was given a wooden icon with an inscription on the back describing him as the Saviour of Russia. This was, however, highly optimistic given the paucity in numbers and quality of the Allied troops under his command and the disinclination of the Russian people to fight for their own liberty.

---

5   Poole, Diary, 18 August 1918.
6   Poole, Diary, 24 August 1918.
7   Poole, Diary, 1 September 1918.

Recall

At 9.00 a.m. started forth to undergo the experience probably unique for any Englishman of being publicly prayed for and blessed by the Russian Church!! It was done by the monks of the Nikolski monastery. Macpherson and I got up to the church and were greeted with a peel of bells. Then we were conducted by a priest, who kissed my hands, onto a special carpet in the middle of the church facing the altar while all the congregation stood round. The first part of the service was a kind of litany and Holy Communion – the bread and wine were also given to us. Then there were prayers for the English General 'Frederick the son of Robert' and for the success of the Allied and Russian armies generally. Then we were given the Bible to kiss; then we were conducted up to the altar and had to kiss the figures of the saints at each side of it – in all these cases having to cross ourselves before doing so. All this time the choir was singing a hymn of which the refrain was 'Long life to Frederick the son of Robert'. Then we went back into the middle of the church again and were blessed by the abbot and presented with a loaf of bread and an icon and made to kiss the cross. Then a procession was formed and we marched out of the church into the refectory where we had a sort of breakfast. There were prayers and hymns for me both before and after the meal. Our own padre took part in the service but did not officiate. It was all very thrilling and, although we were not of the same creeds, yet sincerity and devotion such as they showed can do no harm and must do good.[8]

A month after his triumphal arrival in Archangel Poole, unusually for him, was feeling ill and exhausted:

I'm most awfully busy, so I can't write properly. Things are going on very well on the whole, but one has to face difficulty upon difficulty – so the only possible asset for success is to have boundless optimism! My great trouble is that we shall soon have winter down upon us. If only I could put back the calendar for three months, it would make all the difference! The news from France is splendid. It really looks as though we had got the measure of the Hun this time. You will be back in town when you get this I expect, as the boys will be due to

---

8   Poole, Diary, 28 August 1918.

return to school. I hope they have had a really nice holiday. I expect they did. I do so wish I could have been back with you, sweetheart. I often wonder what you are doing and all about home. I was quite seedy last week – flu – two days in bed but I'm OK again now. Only I'm tired. My God I daren't let myself begin to think how tired I am. When the war is over I shall go to bed for two months!! Goodbye, sweetheart, all my love to you and the boys. Fred.[9]

At this point, and under very considerable pressure, Poole miscalculated badly. He allowed a coup to be made against the Russian civil government. This resulted in the arrest of Tchaikovksy and his ministers and their removal from Archangel to the monastery on Solovetsky Island in the White Sea. The coup was organised by Chaplin, the naval officer who had led the uprising against the Bolsheviks. He had subsequently given valuable information to C Force advancing up the Dvina on how to negotiate a passage through shallows, sandbanks and currents, as well as the hazards left by the retreating Bolsheviks. The General approved of Chaplin and understood his impatience with the Russian civil government, which had cold-shouldered Chaplin, despite his critical role in organising the coup that overthrew the Bolsheviks. There is an uncharacteristically blunt reference in the General's diary, 'I have decided to make Chaplin hold his hand in the kidnapping scheme and allow the government to exist. If they bother me, I'll have them put away'.[10] A further diary reference, however, just two days before the coup, indicates the closeness of the General's relationship with Chaplin and their joint dissatisfaction with the Russian civil government, 'Chaplin very anxious to take extreme measures and, as all their legislation is directed against us, I am not disinclined to agree with him!'[11] The coup took place during the night of 5 September 1918.

Poole hoped that Chaplin's coup would both remove those openly hostile, or at best indifferent, in their attitude to the Allied cause and replace them with others who were committed to supporting the Allies. Had it not been for the objections of the Allied diplomats, Poole would have allowed Chaplin to initiate an entirely new government instead of purging the existing one:

---

9   Frederick Poole to Alice Poole, 4 September 1918.
10 Poole, Diary, 10 August 1918.
11 Poole, Diary, 4 September 1918.

Recall

I attended a conference of ambassadors and it was decided we must bring back the government and reinstate them after having arranged that the most pernicious elements should be eliminated. The net result of it all ought to be that that we are much stronger, as we shall be pulling strings and they will have to dance to our tune. But I mistrust our ambassadors. They are so afraid of possible results that they alienate people who are really devoted to our cause. All my sympathies are with Chaplin and Co. The position was getting bad and the attitude of the government towards the military element was more and more provocative. Chaplin and Startsev came round at night and wanted to defy the ambassadors and start a new government but I persuaded them to hold their hand. A very tiring and anxious day.[12]

The American Ambassador, David Francis, and the American Consul both protested to their government. Repercussions from the highest level were not slow in coming both from the War Office and, via Francis Lindley, the British Chargé d'Affaires, from the Foreign Office. Poole was warned to stay clear of local politics and threatened with the withdrawal of the recently arrived American troops. He concluded that his usefulness at Archangel had ceased.

In the afternoon my troubles began. First a cable – a very kind one – from War Office telling me in effect to keep quite clear of meddling in politics and saying I must be careful to avoid offending the susceptibilities of our Allies!

Then a letter from Lindley enclosing a Foreign Office cable which explained the whole matter. Francis has wired to States saying that the military governor I have appointed is taking strict measures to suppress Bolshevism. President Wilson takes the view that no interference in internal affairs is to be tolerated as far as America is concerned, that he views my dealings with apprehension, and that if I continue, he will withdraw the American troops from here ... I expect it would be better for the cause if our people offer me as a sacrifice to appease American susceptibilities. ... .[13]

---
12 Poole, Diary, 6 September 1918. Startsev was the vice president of the Archangel Duma.
13 Poole, Diary, 14 September 1918.

Poole was right to view himself as a sacrifice. Whilst he could count on the support of the War Office and of Sir Henry Wilson as Chief of the Imperial General Staff, he had no friends at the Foreign Office to deflect the criticism coming from President Wilson. Nor was Francis Lindley willing to stand up for him. Lindley lacked Sir George Buchanan's stature and may have thought Poole unorthodox. At Archangel Poole had had neither the time nor the patience to accord Lindley the respect the latter no doubt felt was his due:

> Got a very nice wire from Henry Wilson giving me the tip that the Foreign Office have got their knife into me and warning me to go slow. I fear it really means the end! The Foreign Office are bound to beat the War Office, as nobody understands the real situation. I don't mind as I know I have acted rightly, and the military performance out here will compare very favourably to the diplomatic record.[14]

Poole had nothing to reproach himself for militarily. His style of leadership was in stark contrast to the orthodox and cautious Maynard in the Murmansk sector.[15] Poole's methods had paid off well both in capturing Archangel and in the subsequent advance inland. C Force briefly reached Troitsa about 380 kilometres from Archangel and 223 kilometres short of Kotlas on 19 August, but the Bolsheviks counter-attacked and pushed the Allies back 60 kilometres to Bereznik. On 5 September A Force occupied Obozerskaya, which was 121 kilometres down the railway from Archangel. It was too weak, however, to prevent the Bolsheviks evacuating their armoured trains, leaving just the shell of the town to be occupied.

The War Office now professed dissatisfaction with the General's staff work, but this was merely a pretext to send out a successor. A small polyglot force such as Poole's did not so much require good staff work as bold officers with plenty of initiative and imagination who were prepared to take responsibility and to improvise in testing and unpredictable conditions.

This point was illustrated by C Force, which consisted of 150 French, 50 British, 160 Russians and 40 Poles, led by a French officer, Commandant

---

14 Poole, Diary, 22 September 1918. Poole also thought little of Captain Charles Wills, who had become the Senior Naval Officer at Archangel: 'He is not the right man for the job. Too pedantic and afraid of his own shadow'.
15 Poole, Diary, 21 August 1918.

Ringue, who had been in the thick of fighting on the Western Front. His force set out on 6 August and reached Bereznik 320 kilometres upriver from Archangel on 11 August. It was an impressive achievement given the damage done by the retreating Bolsheviks, who had removed buoys and beacons, sunk obstructions in the channel, laid mines and departed not only with the best vessels but also all the skilled pilots. Ringue was wounded in a Bolshevik counter-attack on 11 August. This could have led to a reverse but did not happen because Poole had other officers of similar calibre in his small team. In this instance Commander Cowan made the difference. He had distinguished himself already in the seaborne assault on Archangel in command of the *Nairana*, a converted ferry that acted as a primitive form of aircraft carrier. Poole's own account is laconic:

> Saw Cowan in morning who has just come back from Bereznik. Things are not too good there as, after Ringue was wounded, the Bolshi 'fleet' came down and attacked in force. They were driven off but the French captain left in charge was wounded and seems to have got a bit rattled! However, Cowan squared up the situation and they are now quite happy. We shan't be able to push on much though until we get more reinforcements.[16]

The following day Poole noted, 'Josselyn has taken over command of the Kotlas Force (C Force) and is quite happy. Things are not really bad at all'. Josselyn, who had done well on the Western Front in a territorial regiment and had become a lieutenant colonel, rose to the challenge.

A Force was commanded by Lieutenant Colonel Frederick Guard. It was a remarkable level of responsibility for a young man still only in his thirtieth year, but well deserved after a meteoric rise on the Western Front from being commissioned as a second lieutenant in February 1915 to commanding the 15th Battalion, Royal Scots, in July 1917. For his services in North Russia, he won the CMG and the Croix de Guerre, richly deserved given the difficulty of advancing along the railway line, where the viaducts destroyed by the Bolsheviks had to be painstakingly replaced and where there was little scope for flanking operations because of the tundra which had been made wet and muddy on the surface by the brief heat of summer.

---

16 Poole, Diary, 13 August.

General Sir Frederick Poole

Among the many brave officers in Poole's command was Captain Denys Garstin in B Force. He came to the General's attention when the Russian fleet had steamed into Helsinki after a narrow escape from the German Navy on the Baltic coastline. Later, Garstin managed to make his escape from Petrograd to Archangel in a hazardous and exhausting journey, as he was without the proper papers and so unable to use the railway line. Garstin was twice decorated – DSO and MC – before his untimely death on 15 August aged only twenty-eight. Poole informed Alice, 'Mail goes in five minutes so have no time to write. All well. We had a fight about a hundred miles from here two days ago and knocked them rather badly. We captured an armoured car which is useful. I'm sorry to say I had one of my best officers killed, a Captain Garstin. His people I find live at Penzance. I must write to his mother'.[17]

On the political front, the French Ambassador supported Poole, 'I lunched with Noulens – very good lunch. He is much in my favour. He has sent a wire to Versailles saying that on no account am I to be allowed to resign!!'[18] Noulens had respected Poole since their first meeting at the Swedish frontier in July 1917. He preferred the determined Poole to the ill-at-ease Henderson, who had just turned down the opportunity to succeed Sir George Buchanan. In Petrograd he had seen how Poole's methods in dealing with the Bolsheviks had worked. He had also observed Poole minutely taking the action that enabled the British contingent to make their way across the lines in the Finnish Civil War in February 1918. Noulens' support, however, bore little weight against the combined force of President Wilson's displeasure and the hostility of the Foreign Office.

On 26 September Poole received a cable from Sir Henry Wilson 'saying I can come home and discuss the situation when I am ready', a polite intimation that his tenure at Archangel was coming to an end. Four days later Brigadier General Edmund Ironside arrived, ostensibly to strengthen the General's team but in fact to succeed him.

The General parted company on friendly terms with the American Ambassador, 'Francis gave a farewell party to me at night – a very good dinner. I really like the old man – if he would only learn not to talk!'[19] Although Francis had undermined Poole's position, neither man let this sour their

---

17 Frederick Poole to Alice Poole, 19 August 1918.
18 Poole, Diary, 24 September 1918.
19 Poole, Diary, 9 October 1918.

personal relationship. On 14 October Poole left for home on HMS *Attentive* under the command of Captain Altham, who was charmed and delighted at having the General on board and regretful when the journey ended:

> Wireless, of course, had announced our approach and we had requested cars and sleepers on the night train south for our distinguished military passengers. Would they catch it? At one time it looked as if it might be almost a matter of minutes and the General came up on the bridge, as ever a cheery and welcome visitor. 'We will do it,' he was told, 'and you will have time for dinner first, sir.' The little *Attentive* was putting her best foot forward now and with eyes rigged out like hat pegs we slipped through the darkness and past dimmed guiding lights and gate-marking vessels which showed the one gap in the boom open for us, as the gates of a level-crossing for an express train.
>
> A friendly little torpedo boat helped us by giving a lead for the last part of the way but had much ado to keep ahead of us. As we neared Leith he signalled: 'I want to reduce now', so the *Attentive* eased up and our small friend slipped off like a hare escaping from a greyhound. At half-past seven, as the bell struck, we dropped anchor. At dinner a signal came that the night mail started half an hour sooner than we expected and the cars were waiting. With many regrets we saw our cheery passengers over the side and off for the shore in a tug. They caught the train and arrived in London just under a week from the time of leaving Archangel.[20]

Back in England Poole received a letter from Macpherson, his ADC. The first paragraph was dated 15 October and the rest 18 October. It concerned the General's personal life in Archangel rather than his military experiences. Not only had the General made himself comfortable in Archangel, but he had become reasonably fluent in Russian and more than comfortable with the lifestyle of a Commander-in-Chief. Baroness Accurti, who had arrived penniless with Tamara from Petrograd, had used her access to the General well: she had a house and was receiving well-connected British officers, including Major Sir George Prescott, who had succeeded to a baronetcy. She

---

20 Edward Altham, 'Some Naval Work in North Russia, 1918-1919', *Naval Review*, 9 (1921).

was also securing visas that would soon enable her to travel with Tamara to Paris, where she would prove to be one of the few exiles to prosper. She was a remarkable woman.

> Dear General, Archangel seems quite empty since you left, and many people are enquiring after you. We all felt very sorry to see you leave and hope that we won't have to wait long for your return. Last night I dined at the Baroness's house with Sir George Prescott. We left early which suited us very well as I was feeling rather tired. During dinner we spoke about the jolly times when you dined at the Baroness's talking Russian most of the time.
>
> ...
>
> The other day we had quite a jolly time at the Baroness's. General Needham, Colonel Skene and a few other officers dined with Captain Prince, the American censor. After dinner I went to see the Admiral [Kemp] and learned he was leaving Archangel. I am rather sorry, as he was very nice to you when you were having hard and worried times. I suppose the news from the Western Front is causing great joy and excitement at home … I suppose Mrs Poole was very glad to see you and I hope your boys will get a few days leave to come up to town to see you … Last time I spoke to the Baroness she said now that you are not there, she sees how much better you are than the whole crowd put together. Everything seems so vacant. Hope to see you real soon back in your little kingdom. With best regards to you and Mrs Poole, Yours sincerely, Mac.[21]

Macpherson's letter included a note from Tamara to her friend and protector,

> Dear General, I was very sorry to see you go away, but I hope to see you very soon back in Archangel. It is very sad to work in the Intelligence [department] without Colonel Thornhill. Everybody seems to be going away. Mac is in a bad humour and sad. Please if you can ask Lolla [unidentified] to send me films for my little camera. Best love to you and your sons. Yours Tamara Accurti.

---

21 Letter in the author's possession.

20

South Russia

The Armistice on 11 November 1918, which stopped the fighting on the Western Front, did not bring an end to General Poole's war. Sir Henry Wilson next sent him on a mission to General Denikin to report on the White forces in South Russia fighting the Bolsheviks, so that the War Cabinet could decide on whether to help them. Poole was the obvious choice. He had been at the centre of events in Russia from the final months of Nicholas II's reign, through the Revolution, the Provisional Government, the Bolshevik seizure of power, the descent into civil war and the Allied intervention. He had travelled widely in the country and been involved in all aspects of Russian affairs. His original brief had widened from the purely military to embrace both diplomacy and politics; in doing so it had involved him in banking, commerce, finance, and trade and even espionage. He knew many of the key people and had made many relevant contacts. He was to be accompanied by Lieutenant Colonel Keyes, with whom he had collaborated on the purchase of the Russian banks.

Mission Orders

In order to enable the War Cabinet to form an opinion as to the extent of support, if any, it would be necessary or advisable to extend to General Denikin and other movements in the North Caucasus and Don territories, it was decided to send a mission under my command to proceed to Denikin's headquarters and ascertain the political, military and economic situation in these territories.

I am debarred from promising any help. I can only see the situation and forward to the War Cabinet Denikin's demands, criticising as I find necessary.

When I have seen all necessary, I am to return to report in London.[1]

Although the land route to south Russia was closed by the Bolsheviks, the surrender of Turkey made it possible to reach it via the Dardanelles and the Bosphorus. Poole set out from Charing Cross Station on 23 November 1918. His party of eight, including his servant Cox, crossed the Channel to Boulogne, and travelled by train via Paris and Rome to the naval base of Taranto on the southern tip of Italy. A British naval ship them took them through the Corinth Canal to Athens and on to Constantinople.

Poole spent three days in Constantinople. Although he met the British authorities there, they were too busy dealing with the situation in Turkey after its defeat to devote any attention to Russia. He also met three White officers just returned from Odessa. They reported that Denikin's army was in good spirits but short of every kind of supply. This was confirmed by Colonel A.P. Blackwood, who had recently been in South Russia and who gave him a list of General Denikin's demands.

The party then crossed the Black Sea to Sevastopol in the Crimea, where the harbour was full of Allied warships. There Poole met Vice-Admiral Sir Somerset Gough-Calthorpe on his flagship,

> He is an active little man and no fool. He is rather at sea on Russian matters, as he gets the whole of his information from the 'bourgeois' class and consequently his ideas are tinged to suit their views. He appears to me to have formed an exaggerated idea of the Bolshevik importance and possibilities in Sevastopol. However, he has sound ideas as to the necessity for Allied intervention.[2]

Poole still clearly believed in Allied intervention in Russia, even though Germany had now surrendered. This had ended the nightmare possibility of Germany gaining control of Russia's resources, circumventing the Allied

---

1 Poole, Diary, note inside front cover.
2 Poole, Diary, 8 December 1918.

South Russia

blockade and escaping defeat. Intervention now, however, begged the question of whether any Russian force could be found prepared to fight the Bolsheviks. Poole had already seen, as Commander-in-Chief of Allied Forces in North Russia, that there was little appetite do so even before he prepared to form an assessment of the capabilities of the White forces in South Russia.

Calthorpe arranged for HMS *Northesk* to take the party to the port of Novorossisk, where their arrival was totally unexpected. The following day, Poole and his party proceeded by train 135 kilometres inland to the headquarters of General Denikin at Ekaterinodar (now called Krasnodar), which they reached on 11 December 1918. They were welcomed there with much feasting and the General being made a chieftain of the Kuban Cossacks. The day after his arrival there was a Cossack supper, which began at 9 p.m. and continued to 3 a.m., at which the General was tossed in the air from a blanket as a mark of appreciation.

Notwithstanding the warmth of the party's welcome, the lack of realism among the Whites was soon apparent once serious talks began: 'Denikin produced his demands. He drew a very pretty picture on the map (which doesn't really accord with actual facts!) and asks that we cover his mobilisation by landing eighteen divisions and four cavalry divisions over Russia from the Baltic to here'.[3] This was a repetition of the Russian tactic of making impossible demands, to which the General had grown accustomed since attending the Inter Allied Conference hosted by Nicholas II. It carried the implicit message that the Whites hoped the Allies would be their saviour in defeating the Bolsheviks.

Worse still was an unrealism about how the country had changed since the Revolution: 'In afternoon I had long talks on politics with Sazanov and Rodzianko – both rather disappointing. They are such extraordinarily stupid people as regards the change of situation. The latter, though very verbose, is much more up to date than the former, who lives in the atmosphere and ideas of the old regime'.[4]

In his capacity of Russian Foreign Minister, until his dismissal by Czar Nicholas II, Sergey Sazanov had been regarded as a leading European statesman and he had been the initial choice of the Provisional Government as

---

3   Poole, Diary, 14 December 1918.
4   Poole, Diary, 18 December 1918.

ambassador to Britain. Rodzianko, for his part, had tried in vain to persuade the Czar to accept a peaceful change from autocratic to constitutional rule.

By this time reports of General Poole's arrival had spread throughout the territory held by the White forces. Delegations from the different factions were sent to meet him. Poole himself sent a messenger to Peter Krasnov, the Ataman of the Don Cossacks, offering to meet him. The reply epitomised the problem faced by the Allies in any attempt to support the Whites. 'A messenger came down from Krasnov with a long secret letter for me, putting forth fully the whole position in the Don and asking for a lot of help from us in troops and material, but also saying he feels it impossible for him to serve under Denikin.'[5] At the heart of this were the differing objectives of Denikin and Krasnov. Denikin wished to restore Russia as a whole to a non-Bolshevik government, while Krasnov wanted to establish an independent state or independent states in the Caucasus.

Nevertheless, a meeting was arranged and Poole set out by train from Ekaterinodar at midnight on 25 December accompanied by Keyes and by General Dragomirov, representing Denikin. The meeting took place the next day at Kustchevka Station on the main line from Rostov-on-Don to Baku.

> Comfortable journey and arrived at Kustchevka 8 a.m. It is just the frontier between the Don and the Kuban. Krasnov and his party arrived about 9.30 a.m. and we soon got to business. We began by a terrible row, which nearly wrecked the whole show. Dragomirov went over officially to meet and greet Krasnov and said we proposed to have the meeting in our carriage and that they should lunch with us. Krasnov said he had decided that we should meet in his carriage and lunch with him. After a few heated words Dragomirov withdrew saying that the matter had better be referred to me. Then Krasnov came in great excitement to pay his official call on me and at once opened up this matter. I supported Dragomirov's view. Krasnov got very excited. I then proposed a compromise – not that I cared one way or the other – but I felt it inadvisable to let him have a victory in the first tussle for mastership. I said we could visit in his carriage and he could lunch with us or vice-versa and I left the decision to him.

---

5   Poole, Diary, 20 December 1918.

He refused absolutely and then I followed suit. He then made a final bow and he left the carriage.

This looked as if the compromise was nipped in the bud. However, as it was obviously a trial of strength, there was nothing for it but to keep a stiff upper lip and take no notice. I sent out an olive branch in the shape of Keyes to see Krasnov – but with no success. We then made up our minds to start back in about an hour and meanwhile went out and did a walk on the platform! Our attitude perplexed Krasnov, who then began to come round. He sent a message to me that if I would come and make a formal call on him, he would agree to my proposals. I went and we made up the quarrel and began the discussion.

He was full of wiles and wriggled badly, but he was caught and knew it. I brought him up to the point once or twice but he always slipped away and would not agree to Denikin's nomination. At last he said the Don Cossacks were not in need of anything from the Allies. I replied that in that case it was only a waste of time to go on talking and I got up to say goodbye. This brought him to his bearings and he became reasonable. He proposed as a compromise to recognise Denikin as Commander-in-Chief, to hand over to him twenty thousand Don Cossacks and the whole of the Southern Army, and for the rest of the Cossacks that he should remain in command but would execute Denikin's orders if they were conveyed to him as a request and not as a command.

Dragomirov, as Denikin's representative, agreed to this one. We accepted and after that were the best of friends. We had the usual big lunch with the usual speeches. Krasnov's was a masterpiece: a sort of explanation of his dealings with the Hun and extravagant in his praise of England. It was a sort of rebaptism for him, casting off his pro-Hun tendencies and developing strong pro-British ones. However, we have scored a great diplomatic triumph and really helped along Russia. Krasnov departed about 6 p.m. and we at about 9 p.m.[6]

Back in Ekaterinodar the General had 'an interesting talk with

---

6   Poole, Diary, 26 December 1918.

Erdeli, who seems to have quite sensible views'.[7] This had unwelcome consequences. General I.G. Erdeli went off to Tiflis and Baku. His presence in Transcaucasia was unwelcome, as the British wanted to keep this area of economic importance under their influence and the Whites to concentrate on fighting the Bolsheviks. On Friday 17 January Poole received notice of recall, 'A batch of cables in – one saying they would like me back as soon as possible'.

On his return from Russia, as it became clear that the Allies had lost interest in Russia, Poole had no further military role to play. The Allies had won the war, ending the strategic imperative of preventing the Germans gaining control of the Russian economy. Given the huge debts incurred in fighting the war, and the terrible losses incurred, they now had no appetite for further intervention. Poole's contribution was, however, recognised by a knighthood. He was given the substantive rank of colonel and, on his retirement from the army in February 1920, was also given the honorary rank of major general.

---

7   Poole, Diary, 1 January 1919.

21

Cornwall

Major General Sir Frederick Poole was only fifty in 1919 when he returned to Cornwall after a war in which he had played a remarkable role. He was in good health, and full of optimism and energy. He tried his hand at politics and business, pursued his love of sailing and hunting foxes, led a busy social life, served as a justice of the peace, and played an active role in the community. With further inheritances, following the death of his father-in-law in 1922 and mother-in-law in 1924, the family was comfortably off with an income of some £3000 p.a.

He had little difficulty in adjusting to peacetime life, playing lip service to the conventions of that age whilst thoroughly enjoying himself. He got a chance to enter politics as a Conservative candidate after his father-in-law, Sir Charles Hanson, resigned as MP for Bodmin because of ill health in 1921. Poole stood on a platform of retrenchment, as he saw no alternative to cutting public expenditure if the huge borrowings incurred in financing the war were to be repaid. This message, however, did not resonate in a county with high unemployment and low wages after the brief post-war boom collapsed. His Liberal opponent, Isaac Foot, the father of a notable political dynasty, proved a formidable campaigner, as a local man well attuned to the nonconformist streak in Cornwall. Although he campaigned vigorously, Poole lost three times: in the by election in 1922 and the general elections of 1922 and 1923.

After giving up his political ambitions, General Poole revisited the battlefields where he had fought on the Western Front. He also re-established contact with friends from Russia now in exile. In 1925 he became joint Master of the Fowey Harriers after the retirement of his brother-in-law. In 1926 he took delivery of the *Diana*, a forty-three-foot-long sailing cruiser he had commissioned. It was built in Falmouth with separate quarters for a crew of two as well as a lady's cabin for Alice. On its maiden cruise the *Diana* brought back George Chirinsky, once his ADC and now a friend, from France. In 1928 Poole moved from Cotswold House in Fowey to Torfrey, a much larger house with stables and grounds overlooking the River Fowey at Golant.

In 1923 he became chairman of the Mocimboa (Mazimbwa) Sisal Development Syndicate. It was backed by the expertise that had made sisal planting successful in the former German colony of Tanganyika before it was killed off by the war. This opportunity was identified by his long-term friend and former junior officer, Percy Notcutt, who set up and ran the plantations financed by capital raised through Poole's connections. The total investment had grown to £125,000 by 1928.

After the General's return from inspecting the plantations in 1928, there was an optimistic report in the national press:

> Major General Sir Frederick Poole, with whom I dined this week, tells me that the future of the big sisal estate … is extremely rosy. With sisal making close on £40 per ton, the 3500 acres under cultivation and the 2000 now sown should yield something very soon to the four clever soldiers who organised the enterprise and have raised no less than £125,000 capital in five years entirely on their own account.[1]

All went well until the Great Crash of 1929. Just as success seemed tantalisingly close, sisal prices collapsed and the venture failed. Poole gave up on business ventures, stood down as joint Master of the Fowey Harriers and sold the *Diana*. He remained a well-known figure in the county and in January 1936 was appointed a Deputy Lieutenant of Cornwall. It proved to be a short-lived appointment as in December he caught a cold whilst on horseback, refused to rest until he recovered, went out riding again and the cold turned into pneumonia. This killed him when he was in his sixty-seventh year. He was buried in the churchyard at Golant, near his home at Torfrey. Alice lived on for another sixteen years, dying in 1952.

---

1 *Daily Despatch*, 2 November 1928.

Poole for Parliament

It remains to sum up my grandfather's character and career, in the light of his diaries and letters, and from all that I have discovered about him.

***

Frederick Poole had a conventional upbringing in a clerical family and learned the harsh lessons that were almost inevitably part of a public school education in the second half of the nineteenth century.

His choice of a career was an obvious one for a young man with an adventurous spirit at a time of imperial expansion. He was, however, a model of outward conformity in the early days of his army career. In India he became a freemason in Quetta Lodge in 1896 and, by dint of sitting gracefully through numerous ceremonies, he rose to be a Master Mason in 1899. Then he contrived, without going through the proper channels, to get transferred to South Africa, so that he could fight in the Boer War. This did not go down well with the military establishment. That set the pattern, an example being Poole writing directly to the Inspector General of the Forces in 1912 to apply for a position without first seeking an appropriate recommendation. In any case Poole had no idea how to use recommendations effectively, either choosing an inappropriate person, a non-establishment figure like Lugard in 1906, or simply hoping to beat down any opposition by deploying every contact at his disposal, as when he applied for the post of Chief Officer of the London Fire Brigade in 1909.

It would have been wiser if Poole had devoted part of his energy and talent for writing to produce a book which could have put him back in contention for selection for the Staff College and promotion beyond the rank of major. Whilst his friend Charles Orr was reaping the benefit in his career in the Colonial Office from publishing *The Making of Northern Nigeria*, Poole was thinking about investing in Nigerian tin mines and other dubious money-making schemes.

By 1914 Poole stood out as a misfit, notwithstanding his impressive performance in command of 31 Heavy Battery from 1909. He was commuting from his family home in Lincolnshire to his post in Woolwich, where he occupied rooms befitting a more senior officer, and perching between the two at his father-in-law's palatial London home in Belgravia, epitomising new money made in the dominions. Poole's career might well have remained an undistinguished one had it not been for the outbreak of the First World War in 1914, which led to his rapid promotion.

In 1915 General Franks insisted on his remaining in France and gave him a key role in the heavy artillery at the Battle of Loos. Poole had precisely the qualities that now mattered. He worked well under pressure in hazardous conditions when there was muddle and confusion. He was a quick learner. He could nose out new ideas, put them into practice and explain their relevance clearly and coherently. He played his cards faultlessly until he allowed his interest in trench mortars to develop into an obsession. This resulted in a row with his corps commander in September 1916.

When my grandfather left the Western Front, he was as perplexed as everyone else about how to break the stalemate. It seems that the initial advantage of being quicker on the uptake than his contemporaries had evaporated. His advice to my father when the rise of Hitler threatened another war was, 'Make sure you do not get promoted too early. Wait until the weapons are available that can deliver victory'.

I was astonished to discover my grandfather's dealings with Arthur Henderson, the Labour politician Lloyd George sent out to replace Buchanan as ambassador to Russia. Yet it did him no harm. Henderson left Russia with nothing accomplished and would be dismissed from the War Cabinet, whereas Poole came home with the fresh ideas and resolution that brought him a new mandate in Russia. Lloyd George believed in backing people with imagination and initiative.

Poole's time as Commander-in-Chief in North Russia from May to October 1918 echoes his experience on the Western Front. Initially, he had great success, capturing Archangel with minimal forces, even though the enemy occupied a defensive position of great natural strength and strong reinforcements were on the way. But he failed to see the wider issue, which had been spelt out clearly in his dealings with the Root Commission in Petrograd in the summer of 1917. President Wilson did not wish America to be drawn into Russian politics and his voice mattered, as America was becoming the strongest partner in the alliance. By condoning the military coup against the civilian government at Archangel in September 1918, Poole made a serious mistake that would have led to his disgrace but for the support of Sir Henry Wilson.

Poole was initially successful in South Russia, achieving a considerable personal triumph in his dealings with Krasnov, but he strayed beyond the terms of his mandate and was quite rightly was recalled.

General Sir Frederick Poole

My grandfather had many strengths, especially his courage, initiative and unflappability, whatever the circumstance. He needed, however, a superior who could set boundaries and channel his energies constructively. He could not control the obsessional part of his character, which was made worse by having a streak of vanity brought out by having too much power in Russia. At critical times in his career, he became blind to everyone else's point of view. This left him a little short of the qualities needed to reach the top of his profession.

Frederick Poole had no wish either to tell his own story or read the stories of others, as he had many other interests and ploys to keep him busy and amused. He would, however, have been delighted by the Bishop of Durham describing him as a man who had remained true to the Christian faith and without flinching had done all that was expected of him, when his memorial tablet was unveiled in 1940 at St Mary's church West Rainton, where he had worshipped as a child.

Bibliography

Richard Abraham, *Alexander Kerensky: The First Love of the Revolution* (New York, 1987).
Etienne Antonelli, *Bolshevist Russia: A Philosophical Survey* (London, 1920).
Bernard Ash, *The Lost Dictator* (London, 1968).
Nicholas Astrov and Paul Gronsky, *The War and The Russian Government* (New Haven, 1929).
Alexandre Axelrod, *L'oeuvre économique des Soviets* (Paris, 1919).
Colin Ballard, *Russia in Rule and Misrule* (London, 1920).
Bessie Beatty, *The Red Heart of Russia* (New York, 1918).
Walter Bedell Smith, *Moscow Mission, 1946-1949* (London, 1950).
Henri Béraud, *Ce que j'ai vu à Moscou* (Paris, 1925).
Wilfrid Blunt, *Lady Muriel* (London, 1962).
George Brinkley, *The Volunteer Army and Allied Intervention in South Russia, 1917-21* (Indiana, 1966).
Robert Bruce Lockhart, *Memoirs of a British Agent* (London, 1932).
Robin Bruce Lockhart, *Reilly: Ace of Spies* (London, 1984).
Alekseï Brusilov, *A Soldier's Notebook* (London, 1930).
George Buchanan, *My Mission to Russia* (London, 1923).
Meriel Buchanan, *Ambassador's Daughter* (London, 1958).
Meriel Buchanan, *Petrograd the City of Trouble* (London, 1918).
Yves Buffeteau, *Rouen Le Havre, 1914-1918* (Louviers, 2008).
Charles Callwell, *Experiences of a Dug-Out, 1914-1918* (London, 1920).
Charles Callwell, *Field Marshal Sir Henry Wilson: His Life and Diaries* (London, 1927).
Bohdan de Castellane, *One Crowded Hour* (London, 1934).
Winston Churchill, *The World Crisis, 1916-1918*, ii (London, 1927).
C. K. Cumming and Walter W. Pettit, *Russian American Relations, March 1917 to March 1920* (New York, 1920).

Gustave Demorgny, *Les partis politiques et la Révolution Russe* (Paris, 1919).
Anton Denikin, *The White Army* (London, 1930).
Jules Destrée, *Les fondeurs de neige* (Paris, 1920).
Arno Dosch-Fleurot, *Through War to Revolution* (London, 1931).
James Edmonds, *History of the Great War* (London, 1922-48).
Orlando Figes, *A People's Tragedy* (London, 1997).
F.O.O., *With the Guns* (London, 1917).
David Francis, *Russia from the American Embassy: April 1916 to November 1918* (New York, 1921).
William Gerhardi, *Memoirs of a Polyglot* (London, 1931).
Emma Goldman, *My Disillusionment in Russia* (London, 1920).
Nikolaï Golovin, *The Russian Army in World War* (New Haven, 1931).
Will Gordon, *Roumania Yesterday and Today* (London, 1918).
Stephen Graham, *Russia in Division* (London, 1925).
Tim Greve, *King Haakon VII of Norway* (London, 1983).
Vasiliĭ Gurko, *Russia in 1914-1917* (New York, 1919).
John Hammerton, *A Popular History of The Great War* (London, 1933).
John Hanbury-Williams, *The Emperor Nicholas as I Knew Him* (London, 1922).
Joose Hannula, *Finland's War of Independence* (London, 1939).
Stand Harding, *The Underworld of State* (London, 1925).
Ian Hay, *The Right Stuff: Some Episodes in the Career of a North Briton* (London, 1908).
Keith Hitchins, *Romania, 1866-1947* (Oxford, 1994).
Samuel Hoare, *The Fourth Seal* (London, 1930).
Phelps Hodges, *Britmis* (London, 1931).
James Houghteling, *A Diary of the Russian Revolution* (New York, 1918).
Richard Hovannisian, *The Republic of Armenia: The First Year, 1918-19* (Berkeley, 1971).
Esmé Howard, *The Theatre of Life* (London, 1936).
Michael Hughes, *Inside the Enigma: British Officials in Russia, 1900-1939* (London, 1997).
Michael Ignatieff, *The Russian Album* (London, 1987).
Princess Ileana of Romania, *I Live Again* (London, 1952).
Edmund Ironsïde, *Archangel, 1918-1919* (London, 1953).
Stig Jägerskiöld, *Mannerheim, Marshal of Finland* (London, 1986).
Edwin Jenkins, *Foundry to Foreign Office* (London, 1933).
Philip Jessup, *Elihu Root* (New York, 1938).
Henry Jones, *Over the Balkans and South Russia* (London, 1923).
Edward Keeling, *Adventures in Turkey and Russia* (London, 1924).
Peter Kenez, *Civil War in South Russia, 1919-1920* (Berkeley, 1977).
George Kennan, *The Decision to Intervene* (London, 1958).
Michael Kettle, *The Allies and the Russian Collapse*, i, *March 1917 to March 1918* (London, 1981).

Bibliography

Clifford Kinvig, *Churchill's Crusade: The British Invasion of Russia, 1918-1920* (London, 2006).
Alfred Knox, *With the Russian Army, 1914-17* (London, 1921).
Mathilde Kschessinska, *Dancing in Petersburg* (London, 1960).
Sergei Kournakoff, *Savage Squadrons* (Boston, 1935).
Raoul Labry, *L'industrie russe et la Révolution* (Paris, 1919).
Henri Laporte, *Le premier echec des Rouges* (Paris, 1929).
Lancelot Lawton, *Russian Revolution, 1917-1926* (London, 1927).
Scotland Liddell, *On the Russian Front* (London, 1916).
Francis Lindley, *A Diplomat Off Duty* (London, 1947).
David Lloyd George, *War Memoirs* (London, 1936).
Gustaf Mannerheim, *Memoirs of Marshal Mannerheim* (London, 1953).
Marylie Markovitch (Marylie de Néry), *La Révolution Russe* (Paris, 1917).
George Marye, *Nearing the End in Imperial Russia* (London, 1929).
Charles Maynard, *Murmansk Venture* (London, 1928).
Alexander Michelson, Paul Apostol and Michael Bernatzky, *Russian Public Finance during the War* (New Haven, 1928).
Paul Miliukov, *The Russian Revolution* (Florida, 1978).
Aleksandr Mossolov, *At the Court of the Late Tsar* (London, 1935).
Henry Newbolt, *Official History of the War: Naval Operations* (London, 1931).
Gerald Nicholson, *The Canadian Expeditionary Force, 1914-1919* (Ottawa, 1962).
Boris Nolde, *Russia in the Economic War* (New Haven, 1928).
Aaron Norman, *The Great Air War* (New York, 1968).
Joseph Noulens, *Mon ambassade en Russie Soviétique, 1917-1919* (Paris, 1923).
Dimitri Obolensky, *Bread of Exile* (London, 1999).
Hannah Pakula, *The Last Romantic: A Biography of Queen Marie of Romania* (London, 1998).
Bernard Pares, *My Russian Memoirs* (London, 1931).
Bryan Perrett and Anthony Lord, *The Czar's British Squadron* (London, 1981).
Victor Pétin, *Le drame Roumain, 1916-1918* (Paris, 1932).
John Pollock, *War and Revolution in Russia* (London, 1919).
John Pollock, *The Bolshevik Adventure* (London, 1919).
Peter Polovtsoff, *Glory and Downfall* (London, 1935).
Rhoda Power, *Under Cossack and Bolshevik* (London, 1919).
Hereward Price, *Boche and Bolshevik* (London, 1919).
Philips Price, *War and Revolution in Asiatic Russia* (London, 1918).
Catherine Radziwiłł, *Those I Remember* (Boston, 1914).
Arthur Ransome, *Six Weeks in Red Russia in 1919* (London, 1919).
Frank Rattigan, *Diversions of a Diplomat* (London, 1924).
John Reed, *Ten Days that Shook the World* (London, 1977).
Louis de Robien, *The Diary of a Diplomat in Russia, 1917-1918* (London, 1969).
Mikhail Rodzianko, *The Reign of Rasputin: An Empire's Collapse* (New York, 1927).

Edward Ross, *The Russian Soviet Republic* (London, 1923)
Jacques Sadoul, *Notes sur la Révolution Bolchevique* (Paris, 1919).
John Screen, *Mannerheim: The Finnish Years* (London, 2000).
Victor Serge, *Year One of the Russian Revolution* (London, 1972).
Flora Shaw, *A Tropical Dependency* (London, 1905).
Alexander Shulgin, *L'Ukraine contre Moscou, 1917* (Paris, 1935).
Edgar Sisson, *One Hundred Days* (New Haven, 1931).
Pitirim Sorokin, *Leaves from a Russian Diary* (London, 1925).
John Spargo, *Bolshevism* (New York, 1919).
John Spargo, *The Greatest Failure in All History* (New York, 1920).
Leonid Strakhovsky, *Origins of American Intervention in North Russia, 1918* (Princeton, 1937).
Bertie Stopford, *The Russian Diary of an Englishman* (New York, 1919).
Ernest Swinton, *The Battlefields of 1914-18: Then and Now* (London, 1937).
Christopher Thomson, *Smaranda* (London, 1931).
Leon Trotsky, *History of the Russian Revolution* (London, 1933).
Emile Vandervelde, *Three Aspects of the Russian Revolution* (London, 1918).
Robert Vaucher, *L'Enfer Bolchevik* (Paris, 1919).
L.E. Vining, *The Diary of a British Officer in Russia, 1919-1920* (London, 1924).
Maria Volkonsky, *The Way of Bitterness: Soviet Russia, 1920* (London, 1931).
C. E. Vulliamy, *Letters of the Tsar to the Tsaritsa, 1914-17* (London, 1929).
John Wheeler-Bennett, *Brest-Litovsk: The Forgotten Peace* (London, 1938).
Fedotoff White, *Through War and Revolution in Russia* (London, 1939).
Max Wild, *Secret Service on the Russian Front* (New York, 1932).
R.K. Wood, *The Tourist's Russia* (London, 1912).
Pyotr Wrangel, *Memoirs of General Wrangel* (London, 1929).
Felix Youssoupoff, *Lost Splendour* (London, 1952).

Index

Aberdeen, Scotland, 145
Abinger Common, Surrey, 17
Accurti, Baron, 161
Accurti, Baroness Cassandra, 161, 162, 163, 169, 170 and n., 177, 215, 216; her jewels, 162, 163
Accurti, Tamara, 170, 177, 215, 216
Aeroplanes, 31, 35, 39, 44, 45, 59, 63, 70, 85, 129, 131, 183
Afghanistan, 3, 4
Africa, *see* Nigeria; Somaliland; South Africa; Tanganyika
Åland Islands, 183
Albert Edward, Prince of Wales, 37
Alexander, Grand Duke, 94
Alexander, Major General Ernest, 57n.
Altham, Captain, RN, 200, 202, 215
America, x, 11, 12, 86, 115, 126, 127, 183n., 185, 206, 207, 211, 227; Mississippi, 141n.; New York, 141n.; Washington, 185; *see also* Root Commission
American Civil War, 12
American Embassy, 127, 143
American Military Mission, 158
American Red Cross, 163
Amiral Aube, French cruiser, 201
Anet, Claude, 144
Apeltre, Captain, 'Simmy', 36, 44, 45
Appelbe, Martha Sabina, 12; *see also* Hanson, Martha Sabina
Archangel, **plates 38, 39, 40, p. 33**; 98, 108, 127, 136, 188, 189, 194, 195, 196-204, 205-16, 227; Bereznik, 212, 213; Cathedral, 205; Dvina, river, 128, 202; Ekonomiya, 202; Maimaxa Channel, 202; Modyuski Island, 200, 201, 202; Museum, 205; Nikolski Monastery, 208; Obozerskaya, 212; Solombala Island, 200, 202; Troitsa, 212; Troitsky Street, 205; Yaroslav, 198; *see also* Solovetsky Islands; White Sea
Archangel Command 205-13; A Force, 212; B Force, 212; C Force, 212
Archangel Duma, 211
Archangel Railway, 202, 203; Bakharitsa, 202, 203; Isakagorska, 202
Arctic, 86
Arcturus, ship, 181, 182
Armistice, 11 November 1918, 118
Army, *see* British Army; French Army; Indian Army; Russian Army
Army exercises (1912), 24; (1913), 25
Artillery, **plates 31, 33**, 3, 22-160 passim; *see also* British Army;
Artillery barrage, 79
Artillery Dial Range Corrector, 45
Artois, 69, second battle of, 48, 50; third battle of, 48; Ablain, 69; Carency, 69; *Colline Sanglante* ('Bloody Hill'), 48, 69, 71, 72; Hill 63, feature, 69; Notre-Dame-de-Lorette, 48, 69, 70; Vimy Ridge, 48, 70, 71, 73
Askold, ship (HMS *Glory IV*), 198
Asquith, H.H., 76, 83
Asturian, HMS, 203

Athens, 210
Atlantic Ocean, 12
Attentive, HMS, 200, 201, 202, 203, 215
Aube, see *Amiral Aube*
Austrians, 78, 89, 90, 92, 98, 152
Austro-Hungarian Empire, 12, 90, 101, 128, 190, 193

Baedeker, 97, 151
Bailey, Corporal, 38, 39 and n.
Bakhmeteff, Boris, 127
Baku, 219, 220, 222
Baltic Sea, 86, 97, 182, 219; Gulf of Bothnia, 86, 179
Banks, 157, 171-77; Azoff-Don Commercial Bank, 157; Banque d'Escompte of Petrograd, 157; Commercial Bank of Siberia, 157; International Commercial Bank of Petrograd, 157; Russo-Asiatic Bank, 157
Banting, Captain, **plate 34**, 60, 65, 69, 77, 135, 136, 138n., 147, 169, 187
Baring Brothers, 102
Barron, Brigadier General, 71, 72
Barter, Lieutenant General Sir Charles, 86, 148, 158n.
Battine, Lieutenant Colonel, 141, 142
Beale, Miss, 2
Belgium, 31, 41, 182
Beliayev, General, 96, 96, 104, 107, 108, 11
Bertron, Samuel, 141
Bertron and Storrs, 141n.
Bertron, Griscom and Co., 141n.
Bible, 209
Birch, Brigadier General Noel, 66, 80
Bishop, Lieutenant H.C.W., 157
Black Sea, 126, 132, 157, 199n.; Black Sea Express, 136; Novorossisk, 219; see also Crimea
'Black Maria' howitzer, 33, 34
Blackwood, Captain O'Reilly, 47, 49, 52, 64, 69, 71, 75, 77. 79, 218; his wife, 75

Blair, General Hunter, 27
'Bobby', 167, 180, 184
Bodmin, Cornwall, parliamentary elections, 223, **225**
Boer War, 5, 226
Bolsheviks, **plate 35**, 91n., 111n., 138, 145, 148, 149 and n., 161-70, 171, 173, 182, 188, 190, 192, 193, 197, 198, 199, 200, 202, 203, 205-8, 210, 212. 213, 217, 220, 222
Bonar Law, Andrew, 83
Borden, Sir Robert, 46
Bosphorus, 218
Bouvigny-Boyeffles, château, 69, 70
Bradshaw's railway guide, 151
Brake, Lieutenant Colonel Herbert, 25, 41, 42, 44, 50
Bratiano, 129, 131
Brest-Litovsk, 175; Treaty of, 188, 194
British Army, 126
  First Army, 54, 58, 62, 63, 67, 77, 81, 82
  Second Army, 58, 65, 75
  Fourth Army, 66, 67, 81
  I Corps, 37, 66, 69, 73, 77, 79, 82
  II Corps, 31, 58
  III Corps, 43, 44, 66, 80
  IV Corps, 55, 58, 61, 66, 69, 71, 72, 77, 82
  XI Corps, 77, 81
  Fourth Division, 34
  Fourth Division, Eastern Command, 24
  Seventh Division, 51
  Eighth Division, 81
  Fifteenth Division, 57
  Sixteenth Division, 81
  Forty-Seventh Division, 73
  Artillery:
    III Heavy Brigade, 23, 41, 47, 50, 58, 60, 61, 64, 66, 77
    1 Heavy Artillery Reserve Group, 41, 45, 47, 48, 54, 55, 58, 61

Index

5 Heavy Artillery Reserve Group, 47, 48, 54
31 Heavy Battery, 22, 23, 24, 25, 41, 42, 43, 226
8 Heavy Battery, 61
13 Heavy Battery, 61
19 Heavy Battery, 61
21 Heavy Battery, 50
22 Heavy Battery, 50, 53
108 Heavy Battery, 53
110 Heavy Battery, 34
111 Heavy Battery, 47, 58, 66, 67
112 Heavy Artillery, 47, 58, 66, 67
113 Heavy Artillery, 47, 58, 66
114 Heavy Battery, 29, 30, 31, 33, 35, 36, 39, 40, 41, 42, 43, 44, 60
Royal Field Artillery, 48, 49, 52
63rd Brigade Royal Field Artillery, 58, 60
72nd Brigade Royal Field Artillery, 49-50
108th Brigade, Royal Field Artillery, 52; death of commander, 52-53
117th Brigade Royal Field Artillery, 49, 57, 60
2nd Mountain Battery, 4
Royal Horse Artillery, 48, 51
Other Units:
1st Brigade
10th Infantry Brigade
14th Hussars, 15
15th Battalion, Royal Scots, 213
Camerons, 38
Royal Garrison Artillery, 4, 60
Royal Warwickshire Regiment, 29, 34, 35, 53
See also Indian Army; Somaliland Camel Corps
British Embassy, Petrograd, see Petrograd, British Embassy
British Expeditionary Force, 5n., 29, 31, 49, 61, 62, 76, 78, 80, 84, 86, 99, 195

British Intelligence Mission to Russia, 95
British Military Mission to Russia, 87
Bryant, Louise, 146, 147 and n.
Brooke, Brigadier General, 102, 103
Brusilov, General, 78, 92
Buchanan, Sir George, 86, 95, 99, 103, 108, 118, 121, 130, 135, 136, 138, 140 and n., 142, 144, 146, 159, 167, 173, 174, 212, 214
Buchanan, Meriel, 102
Bucharest, 131
Budapest, 12
Budworth, Brigadier General Charles, 57 and n., 58, 60, 61, 62, 65, 66, 67, 69, 77, 80, 81
Budworth Richard, 57n.
Burma, 3
Burns, John, 121
Bury, George, 115, 121, 122
Byrne, Colonel, 147, 156, 166

Cadet Party, 158, 167
Caldwell, Sir Charles, 89
Camberley, see Staff College
Cambridge, 2n., 5
Canada, 11, 12, 38; Montreal 11; Quebec, 11; see also Borden
Cantacuzène, Princess, 95 and n.
Capper, Major General Sir Thompson, 51 and n.
Carpathians, mountains, 93, 129, 131
Caspian Sea, 152
Cars, **plates 6, 29, 30, 40**, 25, 47, 108, 136; Cadillac, 25; 60/80 Delaunay Belleville, 121; Rolls Royce, 71; Zil, 15n. journey, 90-92
Cassell, Major du, 142
Caucasus, mountains, 122, 128, 136, 153, 157, 164; Caucasus Express, 136, 150, 151; Ekaterinodar, 219, 220, 221; Kislovodsk, 151; Mineralnye Vody, 151; north, 217; Pyatigorsk, 151

Caucasus and Mercury Steamship Company, 153
Cavalry, 5, 48, 51
Cazalet, William, **Plate 34**, 138 & n.
Centroflot, 181, 182
Chaikovsky, *see* Tchaikovsky
Chancellor, Richard, 205
Channel, English, 29, 36, 43, 218; ports, 99
Chaplin, Commander Georgi, 200, 202, 210, 211
Château Mercier, 58, 60
Cheltenham, Gloucestershire, 2, 8, 13, 15
Cheltenham Ladies College, 2, 3
Chelyabinsk, 206
Chernov, 172
Chesma, ship, 198
Chicherin, Georgy, 165, 194
China, 3
Chirinsky, Prince George, 90, 92, 93, 95, 96, 98, 102, 109, 126, 131, 136, 137, 150, 161, 224
Chkheidze, Nikolay, 121
Christmas, 36, 37, 38, 63, 64, 65, 87, 90, 91, 98, 165, 177
Churchill, Winston, 159
Clark, Sir William, 195
Clive, Brigadier General, 102
Coalition Government (1915), 62
Coates, Edward, 59
Coates, Son and Company, 11
Cockburn, Brigadier General, 73, 74, 77
Cochrane, HMS, 188
Colonial Office and Service, 16, 18, 226
Confederacy, America, 12
Connaught, Arthur, Duke of, 185n.
Conservative Party, 22, 83
Constituent Assembly, 172, 194, 197, 206
Corinth Canal, 218
Cornwall, x, 8, 11, 26, 27, 29, 30, 42, 52, 66, 72, 82, 223-25; Bodmin, 223;
Falmouth, 26, 224; Golant, 224; Liskeard, 22; Penarwyn, 9, 11, 12, 14; Penzance, 214; *see also* Fowey
Corona, yacht, **plate 19**, 7
Cossacks, **plate 38**, 114, 145, 146, 147, 149, 164, 167, 168, 205; Don Cossacks, 168, 171, 219; Kuban Cossacks, 219
Counter-batteries, 54, 57-67, 77
Cowan, Commander, RN, 213
Cox, servant, 85, 87, 117, 147, 187, 218
Cox and Company, 97
Crampton, Brigadier General Fiennes, 58, 61, 62 and n.
Creeping barrage, 57 and n.
Crimea, 157; Sevastopol, 157, 218
Cromwell, Oliver, 208
Crossley, Sir Savile, 17, 21 and n.; letter to Frederick Poole, 22
Croydon, George, 35, 36 and n.; his wife, 36
Crum-Ewing, Alec, Alick, 38, 118
Crum-Ewing, Mrs, 38
Cuinchy, France, brewery, 38, 39
Currie, Colonel Arthur, 43, 44, 45
Cuthbert, St 1
Czarevitch, 88, 89
Czarina, 94, 107
Czech-Slovak Legion, 189, 190, 192, 195
Czechs, *see* Czecho-Slovak Legion

Daily Chronicle, 114
Daily Telegraph, 39
Dardanelles, 62, 127, 199n.
Dawson, Ellen, **plate 2**
Dawson, Maud, **plate 2**
Denikin, General Anton, **plate 41**, 128, 217-21
Devon, 23; Plymouth, 35
Diamandi, Count Constantin, 88
Diana, yacht, **plates 11, 16**, 224
Don, area 220
Dosch-Fleurot, Arno, 114

Index

Dove, Florence, 3, 4, 13
Dover, 29, 62
Dover Castle, 29
Dragomirov, General Mikhail, 158, 220, 221
Duma, 172
Dunchurch, Warwickshire, 4
Durham, 1, 2, 5; Bishop of, 228; Cathedral, 1; River Wear, 2; School, 2, 5
Dvina, River (Northern Dvina), 202, 206, 210
Dye, Lieutenant Commander, RN, 173

Edmonds, Sir James, 57n.
Edward VII, King, 21n.
Egerton, Major General Sir Charles, 6
Egypt, 102n.
Elder Dempster Line, 7
Elkington, Lieutenant Colonel, 53 and n.
Elope, Operation, 204
Erdeli, General, 222
Esher, Lord, 122
Eton, 38

Factories, 98, 99, 137, 149; Arbo Auto Works, 155; Mitishi State Auto Works, 155; Putilov, 115
Fawcett, 182
Fearon, the Reverend W., 2n.
Ferdinand, King of Romania, 92, 93, 131, 132
Findlay, Sir Mansfeldt, 145
Finland, 86, 174; Åbo, 182; Helsingfors (Helsinki), 146, 148, 214, Bourse Hotel, 182, Societetshus Hotel, 181; Pori, 179; Tammerfors, 183 and n.; Tornea, 86, 146, 147; Vasa, 179; Viborg, 179
Finlayson, Brigadier General Robert, 77, 79, 106, 112, 134 and n., 169, 180, 195

Finnish Civil War, 179-83, 194, 214; Red Finns, 179-83, 191; White Finns, 179-83, 191
Finnish Railways, 164, 174, 179-84
Finska Steamship Company, 181, 182
First World War, ix, x, 29-222 passim
Flying Corps, 63
Foch, General Ferdinand, 122
Foot, Isaac, 223
Foreign Office, 103, 118, 185, 211, 212
Fowey, 11, 12, 23, 51; Cotswold House, 27, 224; harbour, 34; St Fimbarrus, 19
Fowey, River, 224
Fowey Hall, **plates 8, 9, 10**, 11, 12, 13, 26, 78; building of, 12
France, 5n., 11, 34, 43, 48, 76, 182, 195, 200, 209, 224; Armentières, 43; Arras, 48; Artois, 48; Bailleul, 43; Béthune, 31, 43, 79; Beuvry, 31; Boulogne, 218; Bouvigny, 69; Cuinchy, 38, brewery, 38; Cassel, 81; Douai, 48; Festubert, 35; Frelinghien, 43; Fromelles, 81; Givenchy, 31; La Bassée, 31, 33, 38; La Hue, 34; Le Havre, 30; Lens, 48; Ligny le Petit, 33; Lille, 41; Loos, 47ff, 57; Lorgies, 33; Madrillet, 30; Neuve Chapelle, 31, 41, 42, 43; Paris, 29, 53, 144; 218, Bastille, 144; Pas de Calais, 48; Ploegsteert, 43; St-Eloi, 62; St-Omer, 30; St-Venant, 79, 80; Salomé, 31; Souchez, 72; Verdun, 66, 78; Versailles, 214; Violanes, 34
Francis, David, 127, 142, 143, 174, 207
Franks, Brigadier General George, 41, 42, 46, 47, 49, 58, 61, 65, 75, 81, 227
Franz Josef II, Emperor, 12
Freemasonry, 226
Freitag-Loringhoven, General, 73
French, General Sir John, 23, 29, 36, 62, 78

French Army, 49, 63; artillery methods, 50, 57
  Tenth Army, 48, 66, 69, 77
  IX Corps, 59
  XVII Corps, 71, 727
  20th Artillery, 63
  10th Infantry Division, 63
French cooking, 65, 71, 97
French Equatorial Africa, 8, 30
French factory, 137
French language, 30, 59, 76, 86, 90, 137, 139, 170, 174
French Military Mission, 158
French Revolution, 120

Gallipoli, 199
Games, 3; billiards, 3; bridge, 3, 7, 168n., 207
Garstin, Captain Denys, 214
Gaydon, British officer, 128
Geddes, Sir Eric ('General Campbell'), 194, 195, 196, 197, 200, 207
Geddes, General, 69, 73, 75, 82
George, Grand Duke, 181
George V, King, 83, 101
Germans and Germany, ix, 29, 33, 35, 37, 38, 39, 45, 46, 48, 50, 53, 54, 55, 57, 66, 67, 70, 71, 73 and n., 79, 94, 97, 121, 126, 165, 171, 181, 184, 185, 188-91, 193, 194, 197, 200, 207, 208, 218, 222
GHQ, 65, 66
Gibraltar, 4
Gilbert, Sergeant Major, 30, 33; his wife, 33
Ginsburg, Baron, 113
Glory, HMS, **plate 37**, 189, 195, 196
Gough, Lieutenant General Sir Hubert, 82
Gough-Calthorpe, Vice Admiral Sir Somerset, 218
Graham, Hartley, 5, 7
Grant, President Ulysses S, 95n.

Gravesend, Kent, 27
Gresham Life Assurance Society, 11, 12
Grierson, Lieutenant General Sir James, 24
Grove, Montgomery, 146, 181
Grube, Ernest, banker, 157
Gruzinov, 129
Guchkov, Alexander, 113, 122, 129, 130, 133
Gurko, General Vassily, 88, 89, 104
Gypsies, 110

Haconby, Lincolnshire, **plate 7**, 25
Haig, General Sir Douglas, 24, 62, 76, 78, 84, 122, 195
Haking, Lieutenant General Richard, 81, 82
Hanbury-Williams, Major General Sir John, **plate 28**, 87, 88, 94, 95, 96, 98, 128, 148
Hanson, Alice, **plates 3, 4, 10, 13, 15**, 11, 12; meeting with and engagement to Frederick Poole, 12, 13; and Florence Dove, 13; and Beryl Nicholson, 13-14; and Mary Treffry, 13-14; letter to from Frederick Poole in Nigeria, 15, 16; wedding, 19; *see also* Alice Poole
Hanson, Sir Charles, **plate 6**, 11, 19, 26, 52, 187, 198, 200, 223, 226; business career, 11; London house, 25, 43; Lord Mayor, 85n.
Hanson, Martha Sabina, **plate 6**, 12, 23, 187, 223; *see also* Appelbe
Hanson Brothers, 11
Hay, Ian, *The Right Stuff*, 26
Headlam, Major General John, 31, 65, 71, 80, 102, 103, 108
Heath, G.M., 79
Henderson, Arthur, 135 and n., 136 and n., 138, 139, 140, 141, 142, 144 and n., 214, 227
Hermonius, General, 149, 150, 154, 157

Index

Hill, Captain G., 158n.
Hill, interpreter, 90; killed, 92, 93, 94; his parents, 96, 103, 108
Hill 63, feature, 43, 44
Hitler, Adolf, 227
Hoare, Sir Samuel, 95, 109
Holbrook, 138
Horbling, Lincolnshire, 25
Horne, Lieutenant General Sir Henry, 82
Horse Guards, 23
Horses and ponies, **plates 10, 31**, 30, 34, 35, 47, 129; Surprise, 22, 23; Tin Belly, 7n.
House, Colonel Edward, 141 and n.
Howard, Sir Esmé, 146, 185
Howitzers, 33, 3461
Humphries, butler, 187
Hungary, 129, 193

India, 4, 26, 51, 91, 168n., 226; Ambala, 4; Baluchistan, 4; Bolan Pass, 4; Indian Political Service, 168n.; North-West Frontier, 4, 5, 168n.; Punjab, 4; Quetta, 4
Indian Army, 35, 37, 39, 41, 49
Indian Corps, 35, 37
Lahore Division, 38
Meerut Division, 31, 39, 41, 49
Infantry, 5, 48
Intelligence, 59, 60, 61, 65, 69, 191, 193
Inter-Allied Conference, Petrograd (1916), 83-112, 98, 99
Ironside, Brigadier General Edmund, 214
Italy, 130, 174; Rome, 218; Taranto, 218

Jamaica, 27
Japan, 119
Jaroszynski, 171, 173, 174
Joffre, General Joseph, 66
Josselyn, Lieutenant Colonel, 213
Judson, Brigadier General, 140, 175

Kaledin, General, 90, 168
Kamenka, Boris, banker, 157
Kavanagh, Lieutenant General Sir Charles, 77, 81, 82
Kedroff, 203
Keeling, E.H., 157
Kelly, Major, 64
Kemble, Harry, 26
Kemp, Rear Admiral Thomas, 188, 189, 192, 202, 216
Kerensky, Alexander, 119, 120, 133, 139, 141, 146, 147, 158 and n., 163
Kerensky Offensive, 136
Keyes, Lieutenant Colonel Terence, 166, 168 and n., 171, 172, 173, 176, 220, 221
Khimki, near Moscow, **plate 34**
Kitchener, Field Marshal Herbert, Earl, 86
Knollys, Lord, 21n.
Knox, Colonel Alfred, **plate 28**, 87, 96, 110, 116, 129, 138, 145
Kotlas, 206, 208, 212
Kornilov, General Lavr, 145-49, 158, 164, 165
Krasnodar, 219
Krasnov, General Peter, **plates 42, 43, 44**, 220, 221, 227
Krogius, Lars, 181, 182
Kschessinska, Mathilde, ballerina, 107
Kyetlinski, Admiral 191

La Bassée, battle of 31, 49; map, **33**
La Bassée Canal, 31, 48; Pont Fixe, 38
Labour Party, 119, 135
Lacolle, interpreter, 70
Ladoga, Lake, 179
Lake District, 5
Lavergne, Lieutenant Colonel, **plate 28**, 192
Lawrence, Major, 15
Layton, Walter, **plate 28**, 102
Leahy, Colonel, 50, 53

Leckhampton, Gloucestershire, **plate 2**
Lefort, Colonel, 63, 65
Légion d'Honneur, 64, 66
Leith, 215
Lenin, V.I., 133, 134, 152n., 167, 174, 184, 191, 197, 198
Lessing, Edward, 113, 114, 117, 147n., 156, 165
Liberal Party, 22, 83, 121, 223
Lincolnshire, 25, 34, 40, 226; Fens, 25, 34
Lindley, Francis, 183, 194, 211, 212
Liverpool, 7, 19
Lloyd George, David, 21, 76, 84, 101, 102, 106, 194, 195, 227; Minister of Munitions, 62; Prime Minister, 83; Secretary for State for War, 83, 86
Lockhart, Robert Bruce, 129, 171, 194
Lombe, Major Edward Evans, 21
London, 11, 15, 23, 29, 42, 43, 82, 88, 105, 122, 143, 149, 156, 166, 171, 188, 193, 199, 200, 215, 218; Belgrave Square, 25, 109; Belgravia, 226; Bennett Street, 19; Charing Cross Station, 30, 218; City, 11, 26; Docks, 121; Dover Street, 26; Eaton Square, 85; Euston, 187; Gresham Street, 11; Harrods, 78, 138; Hyde Park, 12; Hyde Park Hotel, 175; King's Cross, 86; Lord Mayor, 187; Mansion House, 187; Piccadilly, 27; St James's, 19; St Pancras, 145; Sesame Club, 4, 26; Savoy, 26; Whitehall, 23; Wilton Crescent, 25
London Fire Brigade, 23, 226
London Gazette, 168, 189
London University, 2
Longstaff, Elizabeth Lawrance, 1 and n.; *see also* Pawlett, Elizabeth; Poole, Elizabeth
Loos, battle of, 47-55, 61, 77, 79; Cité St-Auguste, 54; Bois Hugo, 58; *Colline Sanglante*, 59; Fosse 7, 60; Gohelle Plain, 48, 69; Hill 70, feature, 48, 54, 57n.; Hohenzollern Redoubt, 48; La Bassée Canal, 48; Loos, 57n.; Mazingarbe, 60, 77; Notre-Dame-de-Lorette, 48, 50
Lorraine, Robert, airman, 35 and n.
Lugard, Major E.F., 9, 18
Lugard, Flora, Lady, *A Tropical Dependency*, 14
Lugard, Sir Frederick, **plates 17, 18**, 6, 7, 8, 16, 17, 18, 226; on Frederick Poole, 17, 18; *The Rise of Our East African Empire*, 7n.
Lvov, Prince Georgy, 121, 133, 135, 139, 140, 145

McAlpine, Major, 179
MacIver, Captain K.I., 'Mac', 31 and n., 36, 38 and n., 40, 44, 49
McCullough, Lieutenant Colonel, 66, 69, 73
Maclaren, Commander Malcolm, spy, 191
McGrath, Captain, 196, 202
Macpherson, 187, 216
Manikovsky, General, 96, 108, 111 and n., 119, 138, 150, 154
Mannerheim, General, 184
Maps, 3, 17, 24, 31, 32, 60
Margaret, Crown Princess of Sweden, 185n.
Marie, Queen of Romania, 131, 132
Marshall, Arthur, businessman, 155, 156
Marshall, civil engineer based in Petrograd, 113, 126; his wife, 126
Marshall, consular official at Haparanda, 146
Mathematics, 3
Mattinson, Dorothy, 3n.
Maund, Lieutenant Colonel, 158n.
Maydie, yacht, 26, 34, 51
Maynard, Major General, 191, 195, 201

Index

Medals, 5, 39n., 91n., 93, 96, 112, 132, 135, 169, 213, 214; DSO, 5
Mercer, General Frederic, 66, 67, 72, 76, 81
Mercier, château, 77, 78
Michaelson, General, and Michaelson Committee, 127, 139, 140, 142, 143, 156, 169
Militia, Norfolk, 17
Milner, Alfred, Viscount, 102, 103, 104, 105, 107, 109, 143, 144, 200n.
Mines, 26. 48
Ministry of Munitions, 134, 149 and n., 195
Mirbach, Count Wilhelm, 197
Mocimboa (Mazimbwa) Sisal Development Syndicate, 224
Moldavia, 129, 131
Monro, General Sir Charles, 81
Montgomery, Lieutenant Bernard, 53
Morgand, Pierre, 47
Moscow, **plates 29-33**, 108, 109, 132, 133-44, 148-51, 153, 155, 157, 161, 164, 192, 193, 197, 205; Aerodrome, 137; Cherkisovo, 137; Gyll, 137; Khimki, 138 and n.; Khodynka Field, 136; Kremlin, 138; National Hotel, 136
Muir and Merrilees, 138
Murmansk (Murman, Romanov), 102, 127, 137, 141, 187, 188, 189, 191, 193, 196 and n., 199
Murmansk Railway, 141, 142, 173, 189; Kandalashka, 189; Kem, 189; Petrozavodsk, 189
Murmansk Soviet, 189, 194, 198
Myers, Cornish friends, 23

Nairana, HMS, 200, 201, 213
Natzeremus, 191-94
Naval and Military Club, 25, 27
Navy, Royal, 21; *see also under individual ships*

Neilson, Captain, **plate 34**, 138
Neilson, Helen, née Cazalet, **plate 34**, 138 and n.
Nekrasov, Nikolay, 122, 127, 141
Neuve Chapelle, battle of, 41, 42, 43, 48, 54, 61; Aubers Ridge, 41; Hill 63, feature, 43, 44, 45 and n, 46, 69; Ploegsteert Wood, 43 and **44**
Neva, River, 161, 162
New Zealand, 22
Nicholas I, Czar, 151
Nicholas II, Czar, 86, 87, 88, 94, 95, 98, 101, 103, 104, 105, 106, 107, 119, 120, 163, 164, 181, 196n., 200, 217, 219; meets General Poole, 89
Nicholson, Beryl, **plate 5**, 4, 13, 14, 15, 26, 30, 116, 118; her house, Lane End, 4; and Alice Hanson, 13, 14, 15; death, 116, 118; legacy, 118; *see also* Crum-Ewing
Nicholson, Captain, 4
Niger, river, 7
Nigeria and Northern Nigeria, ix, 6-9, 11, 12, 13, 14 and n., 15, 17, 18, 23, 60, 226; Baro, 7; Benue, River, 7, 8; Forçados, 7; Kaduna, River, 7, 30; Lokoja, 7; map, **6**; Niger, River, 7; Mahdi, 9n.; Munshi, tribe, 8, 9n.; Ogboni tribe, 8; tin mines, 26; Zungeru, **plate 20**, 7, 13
Norfolk, 34
Norfolk Militia, 17, 21
North Sea, 145
Northern Dvina, 128, 202
Northesk, HMS, 219
Norway, 86; Bergen 85, 86; British Legation, 87, 145; Christiana, 86; Oslo, 86, 145, 185, 188
Notcutt, Leslie, 'Percy', British officer, **plates 23, 24**, 41, 44, 45, 49, 64n., 66, 69, 72, 77, 79, 81, 82, 85, 86, 90, 91, 92, 93, 95, 97, 98, 99, 107, 112, 135, 169, 224; his Artillery Dial

Range Corrector, 45; his bomb-proof trench, 44, 46
Noulens, Joseph, 144, 197, 198 and n., 214

Obolensky, Prince, 110
Observations Posts (OPs), 48, 57, 59, 63, 69, 72, 74
Oke, Major, 169
Orr, Captain Charles, 6, 16, 18, 199, 226; his sister, 19; letter to Alice Poole, 199; letter to Frederick Poole on his marriage, 19
Ottoman Empire, 122
Ouroussov, Prince Alexander, 90, 91 and n., 93, 94, 96, 104, 105, 108, 109, 112, 126
Outine, Jacques, 157
Oxford, 2, 5; St Hilda's College 2

Paléologue, Maurice, 130
Parliamentary elections, Bodmin, 223
Pawlett, brother of Elizabeth Poole, 2
Pawlett, Elizabeth Lawrance, 1 and n.; see also Longstaff, Elizabeth; Poole, Elizabeth
Pellarin, General Auguste, 59, 60, 64 and n., 65 and n.
People's Budget (1909), 21
Penarwyn, 9n., 11
Pepper, soldier servant, 40, 41, 47; his wife, 41
Percy, see Notcutt
Persian Gulf, 168n.
Peter the Great, Czar, 97, 155
Petrograd, 83, 84, 92, 94, 95-99, 103, 132, 133-44, 146, 147, 149, 150, 153, 154, 156, 157, 159, 162-65, 172-74, 179, 181, 182, 187, 189, 193, 194, 205, 206, 214, 215, 227; Astoria Hotel, 87, 88, 110, 116, 117, 147; Ballet, 107; British Embassy, 87, 96, 98, 99, 102, 104, 118, 129, 130, 135, 136, 139, 140, 148, 166, 167, 173, 182; Champ de Mars, 87, 125; Cubat, 96, 113; Dagmar Hotel, 95; Donon 139, 143; English Church, 125; Fabergé, 96; Finland Station, 87, 89; Galernaya, 135; Great Morskaya, 96, 113; Hermitage, 102; Hôtel d'Europe, 87, 95, 99, 117, 118; Hôtel de France, 96, 97; Kazan Cathedral, 125; Kronstadt, 121, 122; Marie Palace, 103; Moika, 95, 134; Nevsky Prospect, 114, 115, 116; Nicholas Station, 115; Palais de Justice, 116; Prisons, 122; Privato Frères, 97, 158, 180; St Isaac's Cathedral, 161; St Peter and St Paul Fortress, 173; Saltykov Palace, 87; Singer Building, 114; Smolny, 167; Troitsky Bridge, 87; Tauris Palace, 117; Winter Palace, **plate 35**, 129, 136, 138, 139 and n., 140, 141, 144, 146
Petrograd Soviet, 148, 172
Petsamo, 196
Phipps, 57
Pierson, Captain, 31, 33; his father, 33; his wife, 33
Platonov, Natasha, 161
Platonov, Sacha, 129, 161
Plumer, General Sir Herbert, 66
Pokrovski, 176
Poland, 171, 180
Poliakov, x, 114, 143, 150 and n., 156, 157, 168, 169, 173, 176
Police, 126
Polovtsoff, General, 149
Poole, Alice, Lady, née Hanson (wife), **plates 3, 4, 10, 21**; her family, see Hanson, Sir Charles and Martha Sabina; 11, 12; meeting with and engagement to Frederick Poole, 12, 13; and Florence Dove, 13; and Beryl Nicholson, 13-14; and Mary Treffry,

Index

13-14; letter to from Frederick Poole in Nigeria, 15, 16; wedding, 19; her children *see* Charles and Robert Poole; correspondence with Frederick Poole 3, 14, 15, 16, 18, 23 and passim

Poole, Brigadier General Arthur (brother), 'Babe', **plate 2**, 26, 34, 37, 38, 49, 53

Poole, Colonel Arthur (uncle), 3

Poole, Charles, elder son of Frederick and Alice Poole, **plates 10, 13, 21**, 25, 30, 36, 59, 63, 64 and n., 170n.

Poole, Elizabeth Lawrance (mother), **plate 2**, 1, 2, 8, 75n.; financial recklessness, 2-3; meets Alice Hanson, 14, 15, 75n.

Poole family, 1, 2, 12

Poole, Francis (brother), **plate 2**, 5; his wedding, 5

POOLE, FREDERICK

(Major General Sir Frederick Cuthbert, KBE, CB, CMG, DSO, DL, 1869-1936)

Correspondence, with Alice Hanson, 14, 15, 16, 18; with Alice Poole, 3, 15, 23 and passim

Diary, 34, 39 and passim

Images, **frontispiece, plates 1, 2, 3, 11, 13, 14, 16, 21, 22, 26-35, 37, 38, 41, 42, 43, p. 270**

Personal Life, birth, 1; parents, 1-3; Durham School, 23; chooses army as career, 3; and family, 1-3, 5, 8, 9; and Alice Hanson, 11,12; engagement, 12-14; marriage, 19; children, *see*, Poole, Charles, and Poole, Robert; and Baroness Accurti, 161-63, 169, 170, 177, 215, 216; and Beryl Nicholson, 4, 13, 14, 15, 26, 30, 116, 118; and Florence Dove, 3, 4, 13; later life, 223-26; interests, see Games, Sports; political involvement, 223-25; death 224; summary 226-28

Professional Life, pre-First World War, at Woolwich 4; in Gibraltar, 4; in India, ix 4-5; in Boer War, 5; and Staff College, 5, 17; in Somaliland, 5-6; in Nigeria, 6-9, 13-16; and Sir Frederick Lugard, 6-8, 17-18; Norfolk Militia 21-22; 31 Heavy Battery, 22-25; retires from Army, 27

First World War, in Dover, 29; in France, 30-82; La Bassée, 31-36; Cuinchy, 38; Neuve Chapelle, 41-46; Loos, 47-55; counter-battery work, 57-67; Artois, 69-76; trench mortars, 77-82; in Russia, 83-222 passim; sent to prepare for Inter-Allied Conference, 83ff; at Stavka, 88-89, 84; visit to Ukraine, 89-94; in Petrograd, 95-99; Inter-Allied Conference 101-12; March Revolution, 113-23; Provisional Government, 125-30; visit to Romania, 131, 132; in Petrograd, 133-36; tour of inspection to Moscow, 136-39; in Petrograd, 139-44; and American Mission, 141-44; observer of revolution in Petrograd, 145-150, 157, 159; visit to Caucasus and Moscow, 153-56; visit to Ukraine, 158-60; and the Bolsheviks, 161-170; negotiations to buy Russian banks, 171-77; exit from Russia via Finland, 179-185; sent to North Russia, 185; at Murmansk, 189-98; capture of Archangel, 198-204; military and political events in Archangel, 205-214; involvement in Chaplin's coup, 210-12; recall and return to England; 214-16; Mission to South Russia, 217-22; and Denikin, 218-19; and Krasnov, 220-22

243

Poole, Gertrude (sister), **plate 2**, 2, 3, 8, 25, 66; her house, Haconby Hall, **plate 7**
Poole, Henry (brother), 2, 3n., 57
Poole, Mary (sister), 2, 3, 8, 9, 12, 13; marriage to John de Cressy Treffry, 8-9; *see also* Mary Treffry
Poole, Maud, née Dawson, **plate 2**
Poole, the Reverend R.G. Barlow, 40
Poole, Robert, younger son of Frederick and Alice Poole, **plate 21**, 25, 30, 36, 63, 64 and n., 170n.
Poole, the Reverend Robert (father), 1, 8
Porto, HMS, 192
Prezan, 131
Prescott, Major Sir George, 215, 216
Prince, Captain, 216
Provisional Government, 113, 116, 119, 125-32, 143, 144, 163, 165, 217
Pulteney, Major General Sir William, 43, 44
Putilov, Alexey, banker, 157
Putilov, factory, 115

Ragoza, General, 131
Railways, **plates 20, 36, 41, 42**, 30, 86-88, 89, 99, 111n., 127, 128, 132, 136, 150, 151, 175; visit to Caucasus by train, 150-53; *see also* Archangel Railway; Murmansk Railway; Trans-Siberian Express
Ranchicourt, château, 71, 72
Rane, Captain, 158, 166, 167, 169
Rasputin, 94, 95
Rayner, Captain Oswald, 95
Rawlinson, General Sir Henry, 61, 66, 67, 78
Red Army, 91
Reserve of Officers, ix, 27
Revelstoke, Lord, 102
Revolution (1905), 119
Revolution (March 1917), 113-23, 163, 217

Riggs, Lieutenant, 127, 139, 141
Ringue, Commandant, 213
Riots, 115
Robien, Count Louis de, 172
Robins, Colonel Raymond, 163
Rodzyanko, Alexander, 116, 119, 219, 220
Robertson, Field Marshal Sir William, 84, 85, 86, 112, 123
Romania, 88, 92, 93, 122, 129, 130, 134, 157; Jassy, 92, 132; Ungheni, 132; *see also* Ferdinand; Marie
Romanov, dynasty, 101, 126, 130, 181
Romanov, *see* Murmansk
Roosevelt, President Teddy, 159
Root, Elihu, 127, 139 and n., 142, 143, 181
Root Commission, 139-44
Roubles, 97, 148, 175
Royal Humane Society, 5
Royal Military Academy, Sandhurst, 24
Royston, Hertfordshire, 24
Rowe, Sam, servant, 22, 52
Royal Artillery, 65
Royal Military Academy, 3
Rubáiyát of Omar Khayyám, 7
Rugby, Warwickshire, 4
Russia, ix, 78, 82-222, passim; Bieloostrov, 147n.; Ekaterinberg, 206; Gatchina, 146; Kozlov, 154; Kuban, 220; Mogilev, 94; Samara, 151, 152, 194; Saratov, 154; Siberia, 155; Simbirsk, 152; Syzran, 151; Tambov, 153, 154; Tsarskoe Selo, 98, 103, 104, 110, 111, 128, 140; Viatka, Vyatka, 206, 208; Vladikavkaz, 151; Vladivostok, 127, 128, 136, 139, 141, 190, 206, 207; Vologda, 191, 194, 198, 206, 208; Voronezh, 154, 155; Zhighulév Hills, 152; *see also* Archangel; Black Sea; Carpathians; Crimea; Caucasus; Moscow;

Index

Murmansk; Petrograd; Ukraine; White Sea
Russian Air Force, 94
Russian banks, x, 171-77
Russian Army, 90, 131
   Eighth Army, 90
   XVIII Corps, 90, 91
Russian language, 87, 147n., 216
Russian Navy, 121, 122
Russian Orthodox Church, 208
Russian railways, 122, 136; Black Sea Express, 136; Caucasus Express, 136; *see also* Trans-Siberian Express
Ryabushinsky, Pavel, 15 and n., 155

Saffron Walden, Essex, 24
Saint Petersburg, *see* Petrograd
Salisbury Plain, 25; Fargo Camp, 25
Saxe-Cobourg-Gotha, house of, 101
Sazanov, Sergei, 103, 219
Schirinsky-Schikhmatoff family, 98
'Schleswig Holstein', German attack, 73n., 75, 79
Scott, General, 139
Serbia, 182
Serge, Grand Duke, 86, 89, 99, 102, 103, 104, 105, 107, 109, 128
Servants, 22, 25, 40, 41, 47, 52, 85 and n., 87, 117, 147, 187, 218
Shakespeare, William, 101; *Merry Wives of Windsor*, 101
Sierra Leone, 15
Sisal, 224
Skene, Lieutenant Colonel, 216

Slavs, 199
Slovaks, *see* Czecho-Slovak Legion
Smith, Captain Aubrey, 167
Smith, Ben, 26
Smith, Lieutenant RN, 173
Snow, Major General Thomas, 24
Social Democrats, 119, 120, 121
Social Revolutionaries, 197

Solovetsky Islands, White Sea, 210
Somaliland, ix, 5, 6
Somaliland Camel Corps, 6
Somme, battle of the, 67, 69, 75, 78, 79, 80, 81, 82, 83; Fricourt, 80; Mametz, 80; Montauban, 80; Montigny, 80; Pozières, 80
Soskice, David, 163
South Africa, ix, 5 and n., 102n., 226; Vaal, River, 5
South Russia, 217-22, 227
Southampton, HMS, 195, 196 and n., 197
Southern Cross, 15
Southampton, Hampshire, 29
Soviets, 119; Petrograd Soviet, 119, 121
Spies, 29, 86, 191; *see also* Intelligence
Sports, cycling, 25; boxing, 189; cricket, 3, 13; golf, 25; fishing, 52; hunting, 3, 4 and n., 8, 11, 12, 22, 37, 223; polo, 7 and n.; rowing, 2 and n.; rugby, 2, 3; sailing, 12, 26, 223; shooting, 25
Staff College, Camberley, ix, 5 and n., 226
Startsev, 211 and n.
Stavka, 86, 87, 88, 89, 93, 94, 96, 98, 107, 128, 129, 133, 147, 148, 157, 158 and n., 159, 164, 166; conference at, 89, 90, 94
Stein, von, 111
Stephen, HMS, 203
Stevens, John F., 127
Stopford, Bertie, 118
Sukohna, River, 206
Surprise, horse, 22, 23
Sutton, 'Little', nanny, 1, 19
Sweden, 86, 99, 145; British Legation, 147, 184, 185; Haparanda, 86, 144, 146, 184; Stockholm, 86, 145, 164, 179, 181, 184, 185, 188
Swinton, Sir Ernest, 73n.

Tancred, Brigadier General Thomas, 47, 61, 81

Tanganyika, 224
Tchaikovsky, 205, 206, 208
Telephones, 60, 70, 182
Tereshchenko, Mikhail, 135
Thomas, Albert, 111, 130
Thomson, Christopher, 134
Thornhill, Anthony, 26
Thornhill, Lieutenant Colonel Cudbert, 193, 216
Times, 5n., 95, 117
Tiflis, 222
Tin mines, 226
Tin Belly, polo pony, 7n.
Tipton, Captain R.J., 157
Tirah Expedition, 5, 168n.
Torfrey, Golant, Cornwall, **plates 12, 14**, 224
Transcaucasia, 222
Transylvania, 129
Trans-Siberian Express Railway, 127, 128, 141, 190, 192, 193, 194, 206
Treffry, John de Cressy, 9, 66
Treffry, Mary (Frederick Poole's sister), 2, 3, 8, 9, 12, 13; verse by, 13
Trench mortars, 77-82, 85, 91; trench mortar school at St-Venant, 79, 80
Trotsky, Leon, 134, 148, 173, 174, 188, 191, 197, 198
Tsarskoe Selo, 98, 103, 104, 110, 111, 128, 140
Turkestanoff, Princess, **plates 29, 30**
Turkey, 120, 121, 168n., 218; Constantinople, 218
Typewriting, 59
Typhus, 174

Ukraine, 89, 166; Black Earth, 97; Bukovina, 90; Czernowitz, 90; Donbass, 97; Donetz, 134; Kamenatz-Podolsk, 89; Kiev, 92, 93, 94, 132, 158, 159, 166, 168, 179, 180, Continental Hotel, 89, 92, 93, 94, 136, 159; Kharkov, 134; Odessa, 132; Razdyelnaya, 132; Rostov-on-Don, 153, 220; Sarata-Winsaia, 91; Ungheni, 132
Uniacke, Brigadier General Herbert, 80
Urdu, 4

Valentine, Lieutenant Colonel James, Royal Flying Corps, 129
Vandervelde, Emile, 135
Verkhovsky, Minister of War, 150, 156
Vesselago, 198
Victoria, Queen, 131
Vikzhel, trade union, 163
Vienna, 12
Volga, River, 150, 151, 152, 156; Alexander Bridge, 151; Bow of Samara, 152
Vyschnegradsky, Alexander, banker, 157

Wallace, Sir William, 17
War Cabinet, 139, 199
War Office, 17, 22, 27, 29, 85, 97, 149 and n., 189, 194, 211, 212
Warrender, Sir Victor, 112n., 131, 161, 184
Watt, Major A.F., 24
Wear, River, 2
Weather, 34, 82. 92, 125, 172
Wesley (Wesslin), August, 183 and n., 184
Wesleyans, 11
West Rainton, co. Durham, 1, 228; St Mary's church, 228
Western Front, ix, x, 31-82 passim; map, **32**; 62, 66, 67
White Russians, 217-20, 222
White Sea, 188, 210; Solovetsky Islands, 210; *see also* Archangel
Whittet, Captain, 169
Wilhelm II, Kaiser, 101, 120 and n.
Williams, Harold, 114
Wills, Captain, RN, 212n.

Index

Wilson, Lieutenant General Sir Henry, **plate 25**, ix, 69, 71, 75, 82, 83, 84, 85 and n., 91n., 102-6, 109, 112 and n., 122, 123, 125, 135, 203, 212, 214, 217, 227
Wilson, President Woodrow, 127, 141, 142, 211, 214, 227
Wilton, journalist, 95
Woolwich, 3, 24, 25, 29, 30, 226
'Woolly Bear', shell, 45 and n.

Young, Douglas, 196 and n.
Young, G.M., 142 and n.
Ypres, first battle of, 34n.; second battle of, 43, 49
Yusupov, Prince Felix, 95

Zamoiska, Countess, 179, 180
Zamoiski, Count Adam, 180
Zaionchovsky, General Andrey, 90, 91
Zungeru, Nigeria, **plate 20**, 7, 13